THE NEW CLASH OF CIVILIZATIONS

Also by Minhaz Merchant

Rajiv Gandhi: The End of a Dream (1991)

Aditya Vikram Birla: A Biography (1997)

THE NEW CLASH OF CIVILIZATIONS

How the contest between America, China, India and Islam will shape our century

Selected Writings

MINHAZ MERCHANT

RAINLIGHT
RUPA

Published in RAINLIGHT by
Rupa Publications India Pvt. Ltd 2013
7/16, Ansari Road, Daryaganj
New Delhi 110002

Sales centres:
Allahabad Bengaluru Chennai
Hyderabad Jaipur Kathmandu
Kolkata Mumbai

Copyright © Minhaz Merchant 2013

All rights reserved.
No part of this publication may be reproduced, transmitted,
or stored in a retrieval system, in any form or by any means,
electronic, mechanical, photocopying, recording or otherwise,
without the prior permission of the publisher.

ISBN: 978-81-291-2990-1

First impression 2013

10 9 8 7 6 5 4 3 2 1

The moral right of the author has been asserted.

Printed by Parksons Graphics Pvt. Ltd, Mumbai

This book is sold subject to the condition that it shall not, by way
of trade or otherwise, be lent, resold, hired out, or otherwise circulated,
without the publisher's prior consent, in any form of binding or cover
other than that in which it is published.

To my mother, Fatima,
and my late mother-in-law, Nirmala Arte

Contents

Introduction   xi

SECTION 1: HISTORY

1. The New Clash of Civilizations   3

SECTION 2: NATION

1. India: The Remaking of History   19
2. Political Dynasties Beget Poverty   28
3. Building an $85-Trillion Economy   36
4. The Indian Vote Pyramid   41
5. Secularism: Myth and Reality   47
6. The Cost of Corruption   62
7. The Feudal Congress   69
8. What They Don't Teach at Harvard Business School   77
9. The Politics of Religion   80
10. The Sinecure Industry   87
11. The Right to Know   91
12. The Blight of Misgovernance   95
13. The Spirit Is Willing but the Flesh Is Weak   99
14. How the Black Economy Subverts India's Politics   102
15. Justice for Kashmir's Pandits   105

SECTION 3: WORLD

1. Britain's Apology to Africa — 111
2. Israel: The False Promise of a Disputed Land — 116
3. Make Geo-Economics India's Weapon Of Choice — 123
4. UNSC Reform: A Chimera? — 129

SECTION 4: LEADERS

1. Rahul: The Reluctant Prime Minister — 135
2. Sonia's Endgame — 143
3. Modi: The Moving Target — 149
4. Manmohan Singh's New Reform Agenda — 153
5. Dhirubhai Ambani: Visionary of the Century — 157
6. Om Prakash Jindal: A Leader of Men — 161
7. The Churchill Mythology — 166
8. The Chidambaram Chronicles — 173
9. L.K. Advani: 'Riots Cannot Be Justified Under Any Circumstances' — 176

SECTION 5: SCIENCE & SOCIETY

1. Civilization—In Scientific Terms, Just a Few Seconds Old! — 187
2. The Role of the Scientist in the 'New World' — 192
3. The Intelligent Universe — 196
4. Who Reads Newspapers Anymore? — 200
5. Tendulkar: The Bradman of Our Era? — 206
6. Politics, Economics, Racism — 210
7. How Indian Hockey Was Turfed Out — 213

SECTION 6: VINTAGE

1. It's Time for Us to Build Factories, Not Shrines — 219
2. The West's False Projection of Itself — 225
3. Why V.P. Singh Is Not a Leader — 229
4. The Dual Moral Standards of the West — 234
5. Is There Life in Outer Space? — 238
6. Asia's Time Has Come — 243
7. Voters Raise a Fist in the Face of a Rotten System — 248
8. What Should the Proprietor-Editor Relationship Be? — 251
9. Sycophancy in Public Life — 256
10. Clear the Stables at BCCI — 260
11. America has Neither Money Nor Guns to Control the World — 263
12. The Indian Press and Indira Gandhi — 270
13. At Last, Narasimha Rao Says Something and Decides Something — 274
14. The No Alternative Factor — 280
15. America Was Not Moved by Benazir's Sweet Talk — 286
16. Calcutta, Poverty and Joffe — 292
17. Reflections in a Gimlet Eye — 296
18. The First Refuge of Scoundrels? — 305

Acknowledgements — 308
Bibliography — 311

INTRODUCTION

I began writing when I was nine. It was a novel, written painstakingly by hand, in a Class IV notebook. After a few thousand words I abandoned it. Only my twelve-year-old cousin, now a lawyer in London, and my ten-year-old sister were allowed to read it. They thought it was awful.

Ten years later, aged nineteen, studying for a degree in physics and mathematics, I wrote my first political article. It was about a debate in the Maharashtra assembly which went awry. I sent the piece off to *The Times of India*.

To my astonishment, it was published on the editorial page.

Suitably encouraged, like a Test debutant scoring a boundary off the first ball he faced, I began writing regularly for *The Times of India*, *The Indian Express*, *The Free Press Journal* and other newspapers. Through my teenage years, I wrote copiously on politics, business, science and international affairs.

Forty years and several thousand published columns later, I'm still writing. In between I've founded, edited and published a dozen magazines, launched two media companies, divested one (to the Indian Express group) and written biographies of Rajiv Gandhi and Aditya Birla. Yet the thing I've probably enjoyed the most over these four eventful decades is writing on current affairs. It allows immediacy, enables you to provide a critical analysis on news, helps mould opinion and often leads to stimulating exchanges with readers.

This book emerged from a body of work I have written and published over several years, along with fresh material, most of it written over the past few months. In such an amalgam, common themes have to be threaded together. Older essays have been merged, extensively rewritten and updated to form a seamless narrative.

The book's six principal themes are **history, nation, world, leaders, science & society** and **vintage**. Within these lie the story of India and its evolving role in the world in both a civilizational and contemporary context.

The last section, **vintage**, comprises essays that have stood the test of time and are presented unvarnished. Some of these have back stories—people, subjects, editors. But this isn't a memoir so I'll save them for another day, another book.

But I must make an exception for Nani Palkhivala, the jurist and former Indian ambassador to the United States who was chairman of several Tata companies up to his death in 2002. Mr Palkhivala was my mentor from the first time I met him—I was in my mid-twenties and had sought him for a magazine profile. I had been privileged ever since to be present at the roundtable 'debates' he held at his elegant Mumbai home, over dinner with dignitaries from around the world.

■

Another meeting demonstrates a principle that's largely guided my career. I first met Rajiv at his 7 Race Course Road residence in April 1985 to begin work on my biography of him. He allowed me access to his entire cabinet as well as others outside the cabinet. It was then that I first interviewed Pranab Mukherjee, Madhavrao Scindia, Kamal Nath, Arun Nehru and others.

Prime Minister Manmohan Singh was then a bureaucrat and an academic. No one would have thought he would be finance minister two months after Rajiv's death and prime minister just over a decade later. It was an honour to have Dr Singh—between his stints as finance minister and prime minister, when he was leader of the

Opposition in the Rajya Sabha—as chief guest at the launch of my biography of Aditya Birla in 1998.

But it was an episode in 1985 that taught me the importance of keeping both politicians and businessmen at arm's length to preserve journalistic objectivity. After discussing the biography with Rajiv at his home for a short while, he arranged for me to accompany him on a visit to the Guna constituency in Madhya Pradesh by helicopter. The visit was postponed for a couple of days, putting me in a quandary for I had to return to Mumbai the next day to meet Ratan Tata for a rare interview that he had earlier agreed to. Mr Tata, then under JRD's tutelage, was a stickler for punctuality and there was no way I could skip that meeting.

I apologized to the PMO and left Delhi the next day to keep my appointment with Mr Tata, who appeared on the cover of the inaugural September 1985 issue of one of our group's magazines, *Technocrat*.

I had meanwhile deputized my Delhi Bureau Chief, Atul Dev, to interview Rajiv Gandhi in Delhi in a different context for one of our other magazines. Rajiv was both cooperative and courteous. The interview appeared as a cover story in *Gentleman*'s September 1985 issue—coincidentally the same month as Ratan Tata's cover story in *Technocrat*.

The lesson I learnt was this: always honour your prior commitments, even if it means sacrificing a helicopter ride with the prime minister.

That is a lesson I have practised in my relationships with all our politician-columnists, including—for example—L.K. Advani who wrote a column for *Gentleman* for over ten years. And yet, I have met him just twice in my life—once when he started his column in the 1980s, and the second time when he was the speaker at a live *Face The Press* TV event I moderated at the Mumbai Press Club in March 2011 which appears later in this volume.

In journalism, arm's length, as they say, is the best way.

This book's title theme, placing India alongside the other three civilizational forces—America, China and Islam—that will contest this century, clearly demands a sequel. And one is in the making which will explore this singular theme more fully.

For me, it's been a rewarding and exciting period. I hope readers enjoy the fruits of the labours presented in this book as much as I have enjoyed creating them.

SECTION 1
HISTORY

1

THE NEW CLASH OF CIVILIZATIONS

*'The longer you can look back,
the farther you can look forward.'*
—*Winston Churchill*

As this century unfolds, four competing civilizations will shape it. This new contest of civilizations could determine the balance of power between nations and regions for generations.

Though in decline, Western civilization will continue to influence global policy and culture. China will rise, establishing a powerful Confucian counter-civilizational force with its strong roots in history and a sphere of influence arching from the Pacific to Africa. The third major civilization, again deeply rooted in history, will be driven by India's growing hard and soft power. Strong demographics, a far-flung diaspora and the world's third largest economy will impel India to play a global role unmatched since the thousand golden years between the fifth century BCE and the fifth century CE, when the subcontinent produced two prophets (Buddha and Mahavir Jain), two emperor-statesmen (Ashoka and Chandragupta) and two epics (the Ramayana and the Mahabharata).

The fourth civilizational strain set to compete for space and salience this century is Islam. Though spiritually tethered to Mecca, Islam—unlike its civilizational counterparts—has not had a centre of gravity since the collapse of the Ottoman Empire in 1917 and the abolition of the Caliphate by Turkey in 1924. The West is propelled by American and European values, China by its ethnic homogeneity, India by its ancient religions and philosophy. Each has a clear geographical anchor. But Islamic civilization, whose worldwide influence is strong and growing, is as much at home in East Asia (Indonesia and Malaysia) as it is in Arab West Asia, non-Arab Turkey and Iran, the Central Asiatic republics (Uzbekistan, Kazakhstan), Eastern Europe (Bosnia, Albania), North Africa (Morocco, Libya) and, of course, the subcontinent. Islam transcends nations—both a strength and weakness.

How will the four competing civilizations engage each other as the twenty-first century unravels? Consider first their relative economic power.

According to the IMF, Asia (led by China, Japan and India) will account for 34 per cent of global GDP by 2015. By 2030, Asian GDP will exceed the combined GDP of the United States and Europe. This will not be a shift in the balance of global economic power but a restoration of the status quo. Till 1775, China and India accounted for 50 per cent of global economic output. The colonization of Asia and Africa, the Atlantic slave trade and the invasive settlements of the Americas and Australasia wrenched power from East to West. That process is now being reversed by strong economic growth in the East and relative stagnation in the West.

The slowdown in the Chinese and Indian economies in 2013 does not herald a change in the direction or trajectory of the rise of the East. As *The Economist* observed in July 2013: 'China is in the midst of a precarious shift from investment-led growth to a more balanced, consumption-based model. Its investment surge has prompted plenty of bad debt. But the central government has the fiscal strength both to absorb losses and to stimulate the economy if necessary. That is a luxury few emerging economies have ever had. It makes disaster much less likely. And with rich-world economies still feeble, there is little chance that monetary conditions will suddenly tighten. Even if they did, most emerging economies have better defences than ever before, with flexible exchange rates, large stashes of foreign-exchange reserves and relatively less debt (much of it in domestic current).'

■

Each of the four civilizations that will shape this century has threads going back millennia. Ancient Greece and Rome were the precursors of the US-led West. Chinese and Indian civilizations date back to 3,500 BCE. Islam is the youngest of the four civilizational strains but geographically it too has predecessors in antiquity: Mesopotamia (today's Iraq), Persia and Egypt.

While Christian Europe clashed repeatedly with Islam from the eighth century onwards, the West began its slow ascent in the thirteenth century. Education was the key to this ascension. Oxford, Cambridge, the Sorbonne and Heidelberg—the great universities of the West—were all founded around this time as seats of ecclesiastical learning. They soon evolved into centres of science, arts and the classics. The scientific and industrial revolution that followed the Renaissance in Europe enabled the West to lay the foundation for its modern nation-states.

India and China meanwhile lay dormant, two ancient and weary civilizations in decay. Each was reshaped by contact with the expansionary West and by Islam. But their approach to outsiders was markedly different. China's martial dynasties, confident in their middle kingdom self-image of being the centre of the world, treated upstart seventeenth-century British and Dutch emissaries with disdain and remained largely free of Western influence (except for coastal Hong Kong). India, fragmented and directionless, was plucked, piece by piece, first by Islam and then by the British Empire.

Like a sponge, it absorbed these influences and remade them in its own mould.

Where do Russia and Latin America fit in as world power moves from West to East? Most of Latin America, with growing trade ties to the United States, will remain in the West's sphere of influence. So will Russia, though competitive pressures over the Caucasus will be a continuing source of intra-Europe friction. Russia's sharply declining birth rate and population will weaken it, eroding its long-term capacity to counter the West. Most of Western Europe too will be inundated by ageing and falling populations.

Australasia, though rapidly becoming more ethnically diverse, will continue to operate under the West's geopolitical umbrella even as it seeks more trade with China, East Asia and India. Africa, like Australia, a resource-rich continent, will be contested by both China and India as the West weakens and Islam battles its own schisms.

Thoughout history, civilizations have clashed over territory and faith. The twenty-first century has moderated some of those primal ambitions. But it is in the nature of man to compete for power.

The West is weakening, but will remain a global technological and cultural force for much of this young century; China and India will be restored to their historical pre-eminence in the next two decades; Islam will have to change from within to compete successfully with these other civilizations—it will have to modernize and adapt, whether in Afghanistan, Saudi Arabia, Iraq or Somalia.

Talking to Shekhar Gupta, editor-in-chief of *The Indian Express* in an interview published in October 2013, His Highness the Aga Khan agreed that the clash of civilizations was a clash of ignorance: 'I've used all the methods I thought I had to try and help bridge civilizations rather than have them continue to look at each other in ignorance and discover each other in conflict, and all the rest.

'…if I take what was the definition of an educated child in 1957 (when he became the imam) and ask you, what was the composition of the curriculum at that time, there was nothing on Asia, nothing on Islam, very little on Africa, if anything. The industrialized world was turning around on itself. And today you still see decisions taken between the industrialized world and the Muslim world that would not have been taken if they had known each other back then.'

As a young nation but an ancient civilization, India stands out for its diversity and democracy, the two markers that will determine which civilizational strand shall emerge strongest in an era of contesting but collaborative global values.

■

Niccolo Machiavelli's *The Art of War* and Chanakya's *Arthashastra* have much in common. Together, the two treatises define the dark science of diplomacy. In today's fraught geostrategic environment, they also teach useful lessons in the conduct of foreign policy.

India's two defining international relationships are with the United States and China. The US sees India as a natural counterweight to China, but its realpolitik is Machiavellian. It wants India to play the role of a permanent junior partner, much as Britain has done from the 1950s to the present, while it pursues its own global objectives.

However, if India leverages its economic and demographic strengths with Chanakya's finesse, New Delhi can rapidly emerge as America's most important global partner instead of being a perennially anxious supplicant. According to the International Monetary Fund, US GDP in 2013 was just over $16 trillion. India's GDP (by purchasing power parity) in 2013 was $4.50 trillion. Assuming an average annual growth rate of 7.25 per cent between 2014 and 2045 (a reasonable trendline-based extrapolation), India's GDP will increase nearly eightfold to $32 trillion within just over thirty years. Assuming, further, an average annual growth rate of 2.40 per cent (an equally reasonable trendline extrapolation given a low American savings rate of below 10 per cent and a high budget deficit of over $1 trillion), US GDP will double to $31 trillion during the same period. Thus in thirty years, India's economy, using a mathematical model that factors in several economic and demographic variables, will be larger than America's.

This is not fiction but cold, hard fact. US think tanks have come to the same broad conclusion and so has the Obama administration. Few in South Block, though, recognize its far-reaching implications on the rapidly changing balance of global power.

Chinese strategists, in contrast, fully recognize these implications. Similar extrapolations, assuming average annual Chinese GDP growth at a slower annual trendline growth of 6 per cent, place China's GDP at over $48 trillion in 2045, 50 per cent larger than both the US and India. China is clearly the elephant in the room and already behaves like one. China's principal global objective is to regain its sixteenth-century middle kingdom status as the pre-eminent world power—an era in which the United States did not even exist. From this broad aim flow several others. One, military parity with the US. Two, economic superiority over the US. Three, reintegration with Taiwan. Four, the settlement of Tibet. And five, proving to the world that its alternative non-Anglo-Saxon political model can bring sustained economic prosperity to one-and-a-half billion people.

As the third angle in the isosceles triangle of Great Powers in 2045, India's foreign policy must be at once more sublime and more muscular. India, like China, represents the future, America the present, Europe the past.

■

America's history provides many clues to its current behaviour. It was founded by working-class families escaping religious persecution from newly-Protestant England 425 years ago. These English settlers (Britain as a nation had not yet been formed) massacred indigenous Indians, appropriated their land and shipped in slave labour from Africa to work the fields.

The US won independence in 1776 and as it grew more

powerful, it invaded Mexico and by 1848 had annexed what are today California, Texas, Arizona, Colorado, Nevada, Utah, Wyoming and New Mexico. By the 1890s, it had colonized the Philippines and built a silent empire arching from the Pacific to the Atlantic. After the Second World War, it invaded Korea, Vietnam and Grenada, and propped up dictators and puppet-monarchs in Latin America and the Middle East (including the early Saddam Hussein and the sybaritic Shah of Iran). It made a pact with the sheikhs of the post-Ottoman Middle East to deny Arab citizens voting rights in return for US military protection, ostensibly against Israel but in reality against popular democratic movements in their own countries.

With such a colourful past, it is hardly surprising that the US continues to follow a foreign policy of ruthless self-interest in Asia to secure its geopolitical goals. But both the US and China have an Achilles' heel. The US is a declining power. By 2045, it will not only be relegated to the status of the world's third largest economy (after China and India), but it will also for the first time in its history become a non-white-majority country. African-Americans, Latinos and Asians comprise nearly 30 per cent of America's population today. By 2045, that figure will rise to 51 per cent. The implications of this demographic shift will resonate across social, ethnic, economic and cultural boundaries.

As India's own demographic dividend kicks in, New Delhi's bargaining power with a declining US and a communist China sitting on a tinderbox of suppressed peoples' freedoms, will grow—if South Block gets its strategy right.

This strategy involves deepening India's economic and diplomatic engagement with Africa and Latin America, influencing the course of the post-US Af-Pak world with its scattered terrorist threats, and using old military ties with Russia to create a secure environment in the Indian Ocean to the south and the central Asiatic republics to the north.

In 1700, the British Empire was a distant gleam in the eye of traders from the East India Company who had set up mercantile posts in India's busy port towns. India was a prize catch. Though fragmented after the collapse of the Mughal Empire, it had a population of 165 million and the world's largest economy at the time. China was the world's second most populous nation with 152 million people and was the world's second largest economy after India. Together the two Asian giants produced over 50 per cent of global economic output. The yet-to-be United States was still a smattering of thirteen British colonies.

And Britain? It had a population of 8.6 million and produced a mere 3 per cent of the world's output. Colonization and the industrial revolution changed the world dramatically over the next 150 years. By 1870, the average Briton was six times richer than the average Indian or Chinese.

Beyond the numbers, however, lies the real story. For the first time since the West became the world's dominant geopolitical, military and economic force 200 years ago, the tide has turned decisively. The rise of China and India, the relative decline of the US and the fall of Western Europe will establish a new world order. For India, the next few years present great challenges but even greater opportunities.

The defining relationship of the twenty-first century, US President Barack Obama declared on his visit to India, will be between the US and India. This is a diplomatic overstatement. The defining relationship of this century will be between America and China. For the US, India serves both as a strategic foil against China and as a growing market for the US economy, which can no longer rely on sclerotic Europe. India will have the world's largest middle class by 2025—double today's 270 million. Just as it was in 1700 to European traders and colonizers, India is once again the big prize.

The US is a declining economic power but will remain dominant militarily for several decades. It has the world's largest blue sea naval fleet led by eleven aircraft carriers. In contrast, China's first aircraft carrier is of vintage Ukrainian stock.

But China's rise could be slowed by two imponderables: one, the deep suspicion of its hyperpower among the littoral states of the South China Sea, especially Vietnam. Two, the unsolved dispute with Taiwan. While the present Kuomintang government in Taipei is friendlier to Beijing than previous regimes in Taiwan, the island remains a point of friction between China and the US. Tibet and the restive region of Xinjiang, with its large Muslim population of Uighurs, are other worries for China's Communist government. The largest concern, though, is the possibility of a Chinese Spring erupting as more affluent Chinese seek real freedoms. It is a social time bomb India must note while it nuances its relationship with Beijing.

■

India at first sight seems an unlikely global power. It has an obsessively hostile neighbour to its northwest, a five-decade-old Maoist insurgency, corrupt political governance and, according to the latest Planning Commission of India figures, over 270 million people (22 per cent of the population) who live below the poverty line. India's economy and markets, however, are growing despite political misgovernance. The entrepreneurial energy unleashed by economic liberalization in 1991 has given India's economy self-propelled momentum and a seat at the high table of world affairs. And yet, a timid foreign policy has let slip the advantages a world, starved of growth, can offer India's demographically charged economy.

To play a role in world affairs in line with its size, population and economy, India needs to think and act like a major power. It must fix governance at home, build a strategic foreign policy and leverage its demographic and economic assets. In the emerging world order, the India-US partnership will be as pivotal as the Anglo-US axis was for most of the twentieth century. China will play the role of the old Soviet Union, with economic satellites in Central Asia and Africa, where China is now the world's biggest investor.

As one of the pivots in this new world order, India has three priceless assets and two damaging liabilities. The assets are its expanding economy, market size and plural democracy. The liabilities? Misgovernance and social inequality. Unless good governance overlays India's economic growth, poverty will persist. No nation can be great if nearly half of its people live in penury. Inclusive growth follows from good governance. Without it, India's rise as a great power will falter.

■

As the next few decades unfold, the twenty-first century will not be seen strictly as the century of Asia but as, to coin a new phrase, the BLAJIC century. The acronym stands for Black (i.e., coloured)-majority America, Japan, India and China.

The economic and geopolitical interests of these four countries will increasingly converge. Indian policymakers will have to factor in the changing dynamic of a BLAJIC-led world. New Delhi's relationships with the US, China and Japan must form the core of long-term Indian policymaking. And the portents are good.

Prime Minister Shinzo Abe's second coming has the potential to transform Japan's moribund economy. As Suman Bery, chief economist of Shell International, wrote in *Business Standard:* 'The politics of Asia would be transformed by a vibrant, growing Japan, and India's relations with Japan have been growing steadily warmer.'

The US already has deep military and economic ties with Japan and is China's largest trading partner. Among the three Asian giants, Japan's Indophile prime minister has given his country's ties with India primacy, while India and China are poised to resolve border disputes in order to forge deeper economic links, though China's military doctrine of controlled aggression across Asia, on land and sea, remains a matter of concern to New Delhi.

The BLAJIC century will thus dawn by the 2020s. By the 2040s, coloured-majority America, China, Japan and India will dominate the world economy, trade, commerce and culture as completely as Europe did in the nineteenth century and the US in the twentieth.

There will of course be tensions between the three Asian giants: China, Japan and India will increasingly manoeuvre for economic, trade and military advantage. India's growing diplomatic and economic proximity to Japan is an important card New Delhi should play in nuancing its complex relationship with China.

As author Brahma Chellaney noted perceptively in an essay in *India Today*: 'Given China's mercantilist strategy to assert control over natural resource supplies and their transport routes, the maintenance of a peaceful maritime domain, including unimpeded freedom of navigation, has become critical to the well-being of resource-poor Japan and India. The fast-growing relationship of these natural allies is remarkably free of any strategic dissonance.'

For India, with its youthful population and consumption-led economy, the next few years are critical. Good governance and a working-age 'bulge' will catapult the nation into a new orbit of prosperity and growth.

■

Meanwhile, the West, barely disengaged from conflict in Iraq, Afghanistan and Libya—and uncertain about its strategy in Syria and Iran—faces a resurgent Islam. How, too, will the democratic West deal with the dictators in the Arab world whose families have ruled their countries, protected by Western money and guns, for ninety ruinous post-Ottoman years?

Radical Islam is spreading through Europe, spurring a backlash in Western societies. It is also giving Western leaders, wedded to democracy at home and pliant dictators abroad, a moral escape route in the Middle East on the fraudulent pretext of preserving the region's historical stability. This argument does not survive a moment's scrutiny.

The Ottoman Empire, Ming China and Mughal India were the pre-eminent global powers in 1550. In less than 200 years, each had plunged into terminal decline. The West, till then a warren of pre-nation states plagued by wars between Anglo-Saxons, Jutes, Celts, Visigoths, Gauls and Slavs, forged decisively ahead in the mid-1700s.

Till 1707, Britain did not exist as a country. It was formed when England and Scotland signed the Acts of Union on 1 May 1707. Similarly, modern-day Germany, France, Spain, Portugal and Italy all evolved or devolved, merged or demerged, from agglomerations of sundry kingdoms.

What gave the West the initial edge in global power was science and medicine. They fuelled the Industrial Revolution in the 1770s and raised longevity and productivity. But these weren't the only factors that tipped the scale. The Atlantic slave trade, the most brutal crime in recorded history, provided the newly settled American colonies with bonded African labour for 300 uninterrupted years. It was vital to the West's prosperity. So was technology, a byproduct of the industrial revolution. New maritime technology allowed European nation-states to build the ships that first traded with, and then, carrying soldiers and guns, colonized Asia and Africa.

The Protestant work ethic now kicked in. Colonial officers were loyal to the crown, hard-working and resilient. They drained the colonies of their wealth, made personal fortunes on the side but, bound by their work ethic, also built valuable institutions on the crown's colonial properties: laws, universities, infrastructure, administration. At home, in Europe, democracy spurred economic growth and good governance.

■

What does all this have to do with the unfolding geopolitics of the Arab world and Islam? Following the defeat of its German allies in the First World War in 1918, the Ottoman Empire lost its Muslim lands—in the arc from Egypt to the Balkans—to the US, Britain and France. Only the rump, Turkey, remained. The wave of protests on the streets of Cairo, Sanaa, Amman and Tunis are the reaction of a people whose liberties have been mortgaged to the private interests of their corrupt leaders and their Western paymasters since 1924, when the Ottoman caliphate was officially abolished.

In 1932, the US and Britain established Saudi Arabia—custodian of the holy mosques in Mecca and Medina and a part of the Ottoman Empire since 1818—as an independent Islamic kingdom under the Wahhabi Al Saud dynasty. Over the next thirty years, a pro-West military dictator or sheikh was installed in virtually every Arab country. Between Western Anglo-Saxons and Arab sheikhs, the Arab citizen had no democracy and few liberties but, thanks to oil, reasonable prosperity.

Most Arab dictators were directly funded by the West: Saddam Hussein in Iraq, till he went rogue by invading another Western client-nation, Kuwait, in 1990; the Shah of Iran, the non-Arab Persian sybarite who danced to Washington's tune till the Iranian revolution in 1979; King Hussein (and now his son King Abdullah) of Jordan; and the faceless sheikhs across the United Arab Emirates, Oman, Qatar and Bahrain.

Egypt was the low-hanging fruit for the US. Once the independent-minded President Gamal Abdel Nasser died in 1970, the US co-opted Anwar Sadat (who signed the crucial peace treaty with Israel at Camp David in 1978) and, following his assassination in 1981, Hosni Mubarak. Mubarak quietly guaranteed Israel's security for thirty years along its southern border with Egypt, leaving it free to concentrate its forces on the West Bank abutting Jordan (which followed Egypt in signing a US-brokered peace treaty with Israel) and in the Gaza strip. Mubarak's reward: a huge personal fortune. It took three decades for the Egyptian streets to rebel against a dictator who, with Western patronage, denied his people the democracy that the

West holds dear for itself.

As the democratic tide has ebbed and flowed since the Arab Spring, Islamists have wreaked havoc in Libya, Syria and Egypt. The discovery of vast reservoirs of shale gas promises to make the US independent of Middle-East oil by the 2020s. This could presage the most significant geopolitical change in the Arab world in a century.

For the West, especially the US, the events in Egypt, the Middle East's pivotal nation, are a geopolitical nightmare. President Barack Obama is by instinct a liberal democrat but his country has built its entire foreign policy—over four generations and seventeen US presidents since Woodrow Wilson in 1918—on puppet states in West Asia run by pliant dictators. That era is dying. Egypt represents the end of the beginning.

SECTION 2
NATION

1
INDIA: THE REMAKING OF HISTORY

The three men who created the architecture of modern India had widely differing personalities but were bound by one principle: the idea of a strong, united nation. Mahatma Gandhi in 1947, a year before his death, was at seventy-eight greatly weakened by the numerous fasts he had undertaken in the freedom struggle and the extended periods he had spent in jail.

Jawaharlal Nehru, a relatively sprightly fifty-seven at Independence, was a complex man: liberal, democratic by instinct, scholarly, charismatic—and yet given to the occasional burst of aristocratic petulance.

Sardar Vallabhbhai Patel was Nehru's antithesis: a no-nonsense administrator of farmer-peasant stock. Gandhi shrewdly understood that Nehru and Patel's contrasting personalities were good for the free India they would all nurture. Without Patel, the accession of more than 500 princely states to the Indian union would have been a much harder, even fraught task. Without Nehru, the international acceptance India rapidly gained after Independence too would have been much more difficult to achieve.

Patel knew his limitations. Putting India first, he deferred to

Nehru. Many have thought that, had Patel been India's first prime minister, India's strategic missteps over Jammu & Kashmir (J&K) would not have taken place and the state would not have become the perennial problem it is.

Despite their differences, Nehru and Patel were integral to the concept of a free, liberal and inclusive India. Along with Gandhi, they played a pivotal role in the remaking of Indian history.

■

One of the world's oldest civilizations—along with Sumeria, Egypt and Mesopotamia—India is unique. Mesopotamia is today's Iraq. Sumeria abuts Syria. Egypt lies in the shadow of its great pharaohs. India is not only an ancient civilization, it has given birth to four of the world's nine mainstream religions—Hinduism, Buddhism, Jainism, Sikhism, Christianity, Islam, Judaism, Confucianism and Zoroastrianism. Of these, four originated in South Asia, four in West Asia and one in North Asia.

But being old has its handicaps. India evolved early (Mohenjo-daro, Harappa, the Vedas, Aryabhatta) but decayed early too. Decay breeds inertia. Weakness results. Invasions follow. India's history since 1000 CE has been one of decay, subjugation, inertia and loss of confidence. Only after the freedom movement did India's regeneration begin. This effort is still young and unfolding. A thousand years of war, defeat, disunity and stagnation is difficult to reverse.

Progress is uneven and its manifestations lie before us: political turmoil, social alienation, urban chaos, rural poverty. Regeneration can be painfully slow. India will inevitably regain its civilizational energy—its life force—but another generation, perhaps two, will pay the price extracted by the transition from inertia to vitality.

In his book *The Origins of Political Order*, Francis Fukuyama, one of the world's leading political theorists, says three qualities define a successful democracy: the state, the rule of law and accountable government. A modern liberal democracy combines the three in a stable balance.

'The fact that there are countries capable of achieving this balance,' Fukuyama says, 'constitutes the miracle of modern politics, since it is not obvious that they can be combined. The state, after all, concentrates and uses power to bring compliance with its laws on the part of its citizens and to defend itself against other states and threats. The rule of law and accountable government, on the other hand, limit the state's power, first by forcing it to use its power according to certain public and transparent rules, and then by ensuring that it is subordinate to the will of the people.'

How does the modern Indian state, sixty-seven years after Independence, fare when set against Fukuyama's three tests? Has the sharp decline in economic growth demolished the India story? Or is this just a stumble on the rocky path to India's inevitable rise as a great power despite chronic economic and political misgovernance?

Consider what Niccolo Machiavelli wrote in *The Prince*, his landmark treatise on politics in 1513: 'Two diverse kinds of government are the Turk and the King of France. The whole monarchy of the Turk is governed by one lord; the others are his servants. Dividing his kingdom into sanjaks (provinces), he sends different administrators to them, and he changes and varies them as he likes. But the king of France is placed in the midst of an ancient multitude of lords acknowledged by their subjects and loved by them: they have their privileges, and the king cannot take them away without danger to himself. You will find difficulty in acquiring the state of the Turk, but should it be conquered, great ease in holding it. So inversely, you will find more ease in seizing the state of France, but great difficulty in holding it.'

In short, the sixteenth-century Ottoman state was over-centralized, concentrating power in the hands of one dynastic leader. Within 400 years, the Ottoman empire, which once stretched from southern Europe to Central Asia, had collapsed.

France, meanwhile, less centralized and with plenty of powerful leaders spread in mini-kingdoms across the country, evolved into a democratic nation-state with both a strong rule of law and accountable government.

Codified law is the second pivot on which modern, liberal democracies stand. Friedrich Hayek, the great Austrian economist, traces English Common Law as the fount of legislation that protects the weak from the strong and imposes curbs on the state's power over its subjects. Tracing the relationship between freedom and the rule of law back to Aristotle and to Cicero, Hayek wrote in *The Road to Serfdom,* a classic work on economic philosophy: '[G]overnment [...] is bound by rules fixed and announced beforehand—rules which make it possible to foresee with fair certainty how the authority will use its coercive powers in given circumstances and to plan one's individual affairs on the basis of this knowledge.'

The third pivot is accountable government, one which puts the interests of the people it governs above its own. India, like the Ottomans, is over-centralized. Decisions flow top-down. The reliance on one dynastic leader for major political decisions weakens participative democracy. Judicial, police and administrative reforms have been stalled for decades by governments that have been largely unaccountable to their citizens. Rising public anger against corrupt governance has fed several recent civil society movements but Indians' fabled tolerance, and government tactics Niccolo Machiavelli would have admired, have reduced most to impotency.

■

Seventeenth-century England was the first large country where the three elements Fukuyama proposes came together. It had a strong, unified state without which there would not have been a widely enforceable rule of law and universal property rights. These enabled the House of Commons to impose accountability on the English monarchy. The delicate balance of power between the three principles of a modern nation were thus established: a decentralized but strong state; the rule of law applicable to all; and accountable government. India can look back at its own civilizational history for cues to the future. As Fukuyama says: 'The course of Indian political development demonstrates that there was never the social basis for the development of a tyrannical state that could concentrate power so effectively that it could aspire to reach deeply into society and change its fundamental social institutions. The type of despotic government that arose in China or in Russia, a system that divested the whole society, beginning with its elites, of property and personal rights, has never existed on Indian soil—not under an indigenous Hindu government, not under the Moghuls, and not under the British.'

It is this discrete polity that in the past has been both a strength and weakness—from Mauryan to modern times. But if India, at sixty-seven, is to get its growth story back on track, it must re-establish in a modern context the three basic principles of a decentralized state, the firm but fair rule of law and accountable government.

■

Modern India's evolution can be broken up into four broad phases. The first phase was the brush with Britain. Many of the outcomes of this encounter impoverished India and enriched Britain. But there were collateral benefits: the English language which gave Indians a window to global knowledge, science, technology and modern government; the unification of old kingdoms, regions and provinces which had disintegrated after the fall of the Mughal Empire; the rule of law; and a civil service.

The second phase was the freedom movement. India's English-educated elite led the fight for equality, justice and self-government, but it was the average Indian in whose name the Mahatma won freedom.

The third phase, after Partition, was executing the nation's tryst with destiny. Language, caste and religion had to be reconciled; the economy, denuded by nearly 200 years of colonial occupation, had to be rebuilt; and democracy had to be nurtured.

We are now in the fourth phase of our evolution as a nation. Democracy is firmly established. In the next forty-seven years, according to a study released by the Organisation of Economic Cooperation and Development (OECD) in 2013, India will be the world's largest economy by purchasing power parity (PPP). So in 2060, just over 100 years after Independence, India will have progressed from a de-industrialized colony into the world's premier economic superpower.

But within those next forty-seven years lie several pitfalls. The first is misgovernance. In subsequent pages in this book, I have dealt with the malaise and the medicine—how a new architecture of governance can transform our democratic institutions. Today many of these institutions are hostage to malign governance; they must instead be citizens' guarantors of good governance. India's economic progress has been driven by entrepreneurial energy, not by the government's (often regressive) policies.

Between 1757 and 1947, from the Battle of Plassey, when the British occupation of India historically began, to Independence, India's economy grew at an average annual rate of 0.50 per cent. Between 1947 and 1980, under Jawaharlal Nehru and Indira Gandhi, annual GDP grew at an average of 3.50 per cent. And between 1980 and 2013, the economy grew at an annual average of 6.50 per cent.

As Ashutosh Varshney, Sol Goldman Professor of International Studies and the Social Sciences at Brown University, wrote in *The Indian Express:* 'Indira Gandhi not Nehru is the architect of India's delayed attack on poverty. Under her leadership, India lost 10-15 years of economic progress.'

Nehru inherited an economy in 1947 with virtually no manufacturing capacity, a tiny private sector and a national literacy rate of less than 12 per cent. He was compelled to use 'central planning' and build India's industrial infrastructure through the public sector during the first decades of Independence. It was Indira Gandhi who, after 1966, to consolidate personal political power, slowed Indian GDP growth with poor economic policies at a time when the private sector was about to take off.

Much has been written about the damage Mrs Gandhi caused to India's democracy and institutions, especially during the Emergency. Not enough has been said about the damage she inflicted on India's economy for over fifteen years and how that, as Professor Varshney puts it, 'delayed India's attack on poverty'. In retrospect, therefore, Mrs Gandhi's 1971 slogan 'Garibi Hatao' is cruelly ironic. It is a theme I address frequently in this volume while assessing India's historical economic growth.

■

Historians often compare India and the United States. Both are plural. Both are federal. Both have large minorities. And both are former colonies. Each of these similarities is illusory.

America's plurality is based on the brutal Atlantic slave trade that shipped millions of West Africans to North America as bonded labour between the 1600s and 1800s as well as latter-day immigration. India's plurality is historical, going back millennia, leavened by more recent invasions of the Turk-Mughals.

Again, America's minorities—Hispanics, African-Americans, Asians, indigenous Indians—are minorities in terms of race, not religion, and make up nearly 30 per cent of the population. India's minorities (principally Muslims, Christians and Sikhs) are defined principally by religion. They comprise over 17 per cent of the population, a figure likely to rise to more than 20 per cent by 2050.

Both India and America's federal structures are differently constructed. The United States' electoral colleges, for example, determine elections between two principal political parties unlike India's first-past-the-post parliamentary system, which involves dozens of parties. India is a union of states, America a federation of states. The difference is manifest in the manner we legislate, govern and vote.

Finally, America grew into a nation from a British settlement colony whereas India is an ancient civilization which absorbed every colonial influence, without once losing its original identity as a land of diverse faiths and cultural strands. Yet, India remains a young nation. This has advantages as well as drawbacks. India can only grow, learning from its own and others' mistakes. But it will inevitably go through turbulence while doing so.

The corruption that has weakened our democracy and despoiled our politics over the past few years harks back to 1974 when Jayaprakash Narayan's Sarvodaya (Total Revolution) movement gripped the nation's imagination, led to the infamous Emergency and sowed the seeds for an authoritarianism that even today often emerges as a political reflex action.

As India's economy matures, political reforms are necessary to bridge the gap between First World economic practices and Third World governance. The OECD prediction for India's economy in 2060 will be a chimera if political reforms do not keep step with economic reforms and if good governance does not become the default setting of the country's political ecosystem. With GDP growth slowing to 5 per cent in 2013, the absence of political reforms is a real and present danger to our economy.

■

The subcontinent remains a nation of nations. The Tamils are a nation. The Bengalis are a nation. The Baloch, the Pashtuns, the Marathas and the Punjabis, too, are nations.

Though rearranged linguistically, most of India's twenty-eight states and seven union territories are the size of European and Asian nations. Nation-states are of course a relatively new concept—the United Kingdom was formed in 1707; Germany was part of the larger Prussian Empire—the Deutsches Reich (the German realm) was formed only in 1871.

Many of India's nation-states have a geographical size and population larger than most European countries. Uttar Pradesh (with 200 million people), Maharashtra (112 million), Bihar (104 million), West Bengal (92 million) and Andhra Pradesh (85 million) all have larger populations than Germany, Britain, France, Italy and Spain.

It is a tribute to the Indian civilizational ethos of tolerance that such diverse people—in language, culture, religion and ethnicity—have together forged a lasting idea of Indian nationhood.

India in 1947 was an experiment in nation-building, and as we confront the fourth and final phase in our democratic evolution, it is vital to bring reform to our institutions, clean parliament of criminal elements and make our institutions—the Central Bureau of Investigation (CBI), Comptroller and Auditor General (CAG), Central Vigilance Commission (CVC) and Election Commission (EC)—strong and independent.

A nation is as good as the foundation on which it is built. Our founding fathers laid the plinth. Today's leaders must put up the steel girders. Only then will poverty, malnutrition, corruption and misgovernance be mitigated. And only then will India's tryst with destiny, as promised by Jawaharlal Nehru in 1947, be fulfilled.

2
POLITICAL DYNASTIES BEGET POVERTY

How damaging is dynastic politics to a nation's economy? And is there empirical evidence to show that dynasty begets poverty? Researchers at the Asian Institute of Management (AIM) Policy Centre in Manila set out to test the 'causal' relationship between dynastic politics and poverty in the Philippines. Their findings are significant.

Anecdotal evidence has always suggested that the poorer a country, the more likely it is to have dynastic political leaders. Conversely, in democracies with high per capita income, political dynasties are rare. But the unanswered question has always been one of causality: is poverty the cause and dynasty the effect? Or is it the other way around—is dynasty a principal cause of poverty?

Strong corroborative evidence on the causal relationship between dynasty and poverty in India emerges from the Hunger and Malnutrition (HUNGaMA) survey conducted by the Naandi Foundation as well as a study on Indian political dynasts by author Patrick French. Deconstructing the Naandi Foundation study, it is clear that constituencies with dynast MPs like Rae Bareli have among the highest incidence of severely malnourished children (over 70 per cent of those under the age of five)—a key indicator of poverty.

The AIM Policy Centre similarly found that constituencies in the Philippines with dynastic candidates were 26 per cent poorer than those with non-dynastic candidates. Nearly 68 per cent of legislators in the Philippines parliament are dynasts. In sharp contrast, only 6 per cent of senators in the United States Congress are dynasts. The per capita income of the Philippines (a former US colony) and the US are respectively $2,200 and $48,000.

In India, according to Patrick French, 28 per cent of MPs across party lines in the Lok Sabha are hereditary. Worryingly, 38 per cent of the Congress's Lok Sabha MPs are dynasts (compared to 19 per cent of the BJP's). Worse, 88 per cent of Congress MPs under forty and 100 per cent of Congress MPs under thirty are heirs. The problem will clearly get worse—as a new generation of dynastic politicians assumes its inheritance—before it can get better along with the evolution of Indian democracy. The continuing hold of old national family dynasties like the Gandhis and the rise of new regional dynasties like the Yadavs bodes ill for Indian democracy.

But low per capita income is not the only reason for the high incidence of hereditary politicians in a country. Culture plays an important role, too. The AIM Policy Center researchers say that Asia's sociocultural mores favour political dynasties. In contrast, Anglo-Saxon, Gallic and Iberian countries like Britain, Germany, France and Spain (and their colonial derivatives—the US, Canada, Australia and Argentina) have a culture of egalitarianism.

How do political dynasties fare in older democracies? The first president of the United States, George Washington, took office in 1789. Since then, in 225 years and through forty-four US presidents, only thrice has a single family produced more than one US president: John Adams (1797-1801) and his son John Quincy Adams (1825-1829); William Harrison (who died in office after serving for just a month in 1841) and his grandson Benjamin Harrison (1889-1893); and, of course, most recently the two George Bushes—exceptions who prove the centuries-old rule in American politics: dynasties don't work.

Presidents Theodore and Franklin Roosevelt are often cited as examples of successful US dynasts in the twentieth century—but they were only fifth cousins. Anti-dynasty sentiment in the US is so strong that President John Kennedy's daughter Caroline was denied a bid for a New York Senate seat by the Democrats. (That's like Priyanka Gandhi-Vadra being denied a Congress ticket from Rae Bareli.)

The same principle applies to Britain, France and Germany, western Europe's three largest democracies. There has been no Churchill dynasty, no de Gaulle dynasty, no Adenauer dynasty. In Britain, the last father-son prime ministerial dynasts were William Pitt 'The Elder' and William Pitt 'The Younger', over 200 years ago. Today, a Thatcher heir as future prime minister is unthinkable.

■

In India, culture and poverty collide to create a fertile breeding ground for feudalism. Other South Asian countries with similar cultural histories like Pakistan, Bangladesh, Sri Lanka and Nepal also suffer large economic inequalities—a common feature in dynasty-led countries.

'Almost all poverty indicators spiked in the jurisdiction of dynastic legislators,' says AIM Policy Centre Executive Director Ronald Mendonza, quoting from the Centre's published report. 'Legislators from dynasties tend to be richer.' India is no different. According to a study by the Association for Democratic Reforms (ADR), the number of crorepati MPs in the Lok Sabha more than doubled from 156 MPs to 315 MPs between 2004 and 2009. The more dynastic a constituency, independent analysis shows, the richer its legislators—and the poorer its constituents.

Dynasties in dictatorships pose different questions. Here the causality between poverty and dynasty varies sharply. On the one hand, the sheikhdoms of the Middle East like Saudi Arabia and the UAE are wealthy but ruled by vast family networks of brothers and cousins. On the other, impoverished North Korea has been (mis)ruled by one family for decades: Kim Il-sung was in power from 1945 to 1994, followed by his late son, Kim Jong-il, and now his grandson, Kim Jong-un. North Koreans remain immersed in poverty.

Apologists for dynastic politics argue that India's dynasts are democratically elected and therefore legitimate, unlike dynasts in dictatorships or feudal sheikhdoms. This argument is disingenuous. Like the Philippines, India has a longstanding culture of feudalism. Deep-rooted poverty gives family-backed politicians an electoral advantage. Indian dynasts use this advantage to ruthless effect, severely limiting the democratic choice available to voters.

■

To return to the original question of causality: do political dynasties beget poverty? Or does poverty allow dynastic politicians to exploit economic inequalities electorally, thereby perpetuating dynasty? The empirical evidence of cause-and-effect across Asia points clearly to the former.

Sonia and Rahul Gandhi are aware that dynastic politics in every nation comes with an expiry date. In India, they know that the date is fast approaching and that they must recalibrate their strategy to stay politically relevant. At a public meeting in Delhi honouring freedom fighter Choudhary Ranbir Singh who 'retired' from politics at sixty-four, Sonia remarked that older leaders in the Congress should not cling to office if the party is to capture the energy and integrity of its early years. Sonia is herself sixty-seven and the irony cannot be lost on her.

Rahul is more direct. 'Politics is not a family business,' he told party workers at a rally in Maharashtra. 'I want to put an end to this practice [of dynasty].' Rahul has pledged democracy at every level of the Congress hierarchy—except at the very top. That will no longer do. India cannot be run like a family business in a democratic, globalized world where international politics is increasingly professional and accountable.

When did political dynasty take root in India? Was it when Jawaharlal Nehru appointed his daughter Indira as Congress president in 1959? Or was it when Indira Gandhi, as prime minister, inducted her son Sanjay as a Youth Congress leader in 1972? By that fateful morning of 31 October 1984, when Mrs Gandhi lay lifeless at 1 Safdarjung Road, dynasty was so firmly entrenched in Congress minds that Rajiv Gandhi, in politics for just forty-four months and without ever having held a ministerial portfolio, was the party's default choice to succeed his mother as prime minister.

The Congress has not held a serious election for party president since Sonia took charge in 1998. Barring 2000, when Jitendra Prasada contested against Mrs Gandhi (and soon thereafter went into political oblivion), no Congressman or woman has dared step forward for election. Even Jawaharlal Nehru was Congress president for a total of just four years after 1947. He would have been mortified at the thought of any one individual—especially from his family—holding the post for sixteen successive years as Sonia has done.

■

Constitutionally, in a parliamentary democracy, final political authority lies with the head of the government, not with the head of the party. In the UPA government, it is the other way around. Congress President Sonia Gandhi in effect enjoys the authority of a president in a French presidential form of government—but without accountability. In France, the appointed prime minister (Jean-Marc Ayrault) is constitutionally subordinate to the elected president (Francois Hollande). But India is a Westminster parliamentary democracy where, according to the constitution, the prime minister's 'advice' is final—even to the president of India, not just the president of the party in government.

The most damaging effect of the Congress dynasty is that it has, over the past twenty-five years, legitimized smaller regional dynasties—M. Karunanidhi's DMK, Sharad Pawar's Nationalist Congress Party (NCP), Mulayam Singh Yadav's Samajwadi Party (SP), Lalu Prasad Yadav's Rashtriya Janata Dal (RJD), Parkash Singh Badal's Shiromani Akali Dal (SAD) and Uddhav Thackeray's Shiv Sena (SS). The list is long and lethal. Within the Congress itself, mini-dynasties are now viral: P. Chidambaram's son, Karti, and Pranab Mukherjee's son, Abhijit, number among dozens of filial party acolytes.

But old feudal instincts cannot forever remain immune to change. To protect our democratic institutions from a debilitating culture of feudocracy, which punishes merit and rewards mediocrity, political dynasties across India must go. They have no place in modern democracy.

■

An argument advanced in favour of political dynasties in India is superficially seductive: the sons and daughters of lawyers become lawyers. So do doctors, businessmen and actors. But professionals in medicine and law earn their degrees. Businessmen owe their position to specific financial shareholding. Actors are made and unmade every Friday.

In a desperately poor country like India, however, political dynasties are easy to build. The electorate is divided by caste, religion and region. Votes are bought wholesale. Several dozen MPs in the current Lok Sabha face serious criminal charges (rape, kidnap and murder, to name a few). And yet they get elected—and re-elected. Pappu Yadav, Arun Gawli and Raja Bhaiya have all won parliamentary or assembly elections. Electoral victory, they argue, gives them as much legitimacy as any MP in today's Lok Sabha.

A toxic byproduct of dynastic politics—where real power is concentrated in such few nepotistic hands—is misgovernance and corruption. Poor voters are exploited with inducements of cash, an issue the Election Commission has repeatedly pointed out. Criminals are given tickets to capture votes on the basis of caste and religion to perpetuate a culture of feudal overlordship. Such electoral deception would not succeed with an empowered electorate. It is therefore in the self-interest of dynastic politicians—whether they be the Yadavs or the Gandhis—to pay lip service to development.

But is dynasty all that bad? It surely can't be if we've voted members of the same family into the prime ministership for thirty-eight years (Jawaharlal Nehru: seventeen years, Indira Gandhi: sixteen years, Rajiv Gandhi: five years) and elected to office the same party (the Congress) for fifty-four out of our sixty-seven post-Independence years?

We are voted into power, protest young dynasts from various parties who, following in the Congress's large footsteps, have flourished all across India: the Karunanidhis, the Pawars, the Hoodas, the Abdullahs, the Badals, the Yadavs. They, deliberately, miss the point.

Political parties often don't put up candidates against dynasts from other parties. For example, in a Lok Sabha by-election for the Kannauj parliamentary seat, Dimple Yadav—UP chief minister's Akhilesh Yadav's wife—was elected unopposed. Such inter-party 'cooperation' makes a mockery of parliamentary democracy.

Moreover, political parties give tickets to disproportionate numbers of dynasts from 'safe' seats which are feudal fiefs. The result: parliament is over-represented by dynasts of questionable merit. Their safe constituencies ensure their continued electability but the constituencies themselves remain poor and backward with high levels of child malnourishment.

The purpose of democracy is to widen voter choice—not narrow it. By choosing dynasts over professionals, parties limit the choice voters might have had otherwise and lower the overall level of competence in parliament.

What is the alternative to dynastic politics in a still-evolving feudal society like India's? Consider three:

First, voter education. The Election Commission has already

begun a programme to educate voters on how to resist candidates canvassing on the basis of caste, religion and region. Illiteracy and poverty among voters are the biggest weapons feudal, dynastic and criminal candidates wield.

Second, decriminalization of parliament. With the Supreme Court barring legislators convicted by a trial court for a crime which carries a sentence of more than two years, the onus is on the Election Commission to further tighten norms. A political party giving a ticket to such candidates should be automatically disallowed from contesting the seat in that election. The fierce opposition by political parties to this stricture should not deter the Election Commission.

Third, fixing tenure limits for all political party posts. Most family-run parties don't hold elections except for the junior-most positions. A maximum tenure ceiling of three to five years must be set for all party posts—including, crucially, that of party president. This ceiling will not eliminate nepotism in feudal parties like the Congress, SP, BSP, DMK, NCP, RJD, RLD, NC, SAD, SS and others but it will certainly mitigate it. The Yadavs, Gandhis, Karunanidhis, Abdullahs, Badals and Pawars will be put on notice: dynasty must go.

3
BUILDING AN $85-TRILLION ECONOMY

According to the Wealth Report 2012 study by US banking group Citi, India will be the world's largest economy within thirty-six years. Indian GDP in 2050, measured by purchasing power parity (PPP), will be $85.97 trillion. China, in second place, will have a GDP of $80.02 trillion and the US $39.07 trillion (*see chart on next page*).

With an estimated population of 1.63 billion in 2050, India will thus have a per capita income of just under $53,000—in the range of today's wealthiest countries such as Switzerland and Norway. Sounds too good to be true? Of course it is.

On paper, mathematically, poverty in India should disappear by 2050. The reason it won't is that huge inequalities in income will persist—unless we rapidly implement second-generation economic reforms which deliver real benefits to the bottom of India's socio-economic pyramid.

The first chart in our three-chart collage shows the ranking of the top five countries by GDP in 2050 according to Citi's projections. Indian GDP in 2011 was estimated at just over $4 trillion (PPP). To reach $85.97 trillion in 2050, the Indian economy will have to grow at an average annual rate of 8.75 per cent a year for nearly four decades. Optimistic? Perhaps, but not overly so.

Citi's projections are not linear. Over several decades, a growing economy like India's will ebb and flow. In tough global times it will stumble along at an annual GDP growth of 5-7 per cent. In a more favourable global and local environment, GDP growth could spurt to around 10 per cent a year. Thus, an average annual growth figure of 8.75 per cent, spread over thirty-nine years as projected in 2011 by Citi, is plausible, especially given the Indian economy's average growth rate of just under 8 per cent a year over the first twenty post-liberalization years between 1991 and 2011.

The Dichotomy: GDP vs. Household Income

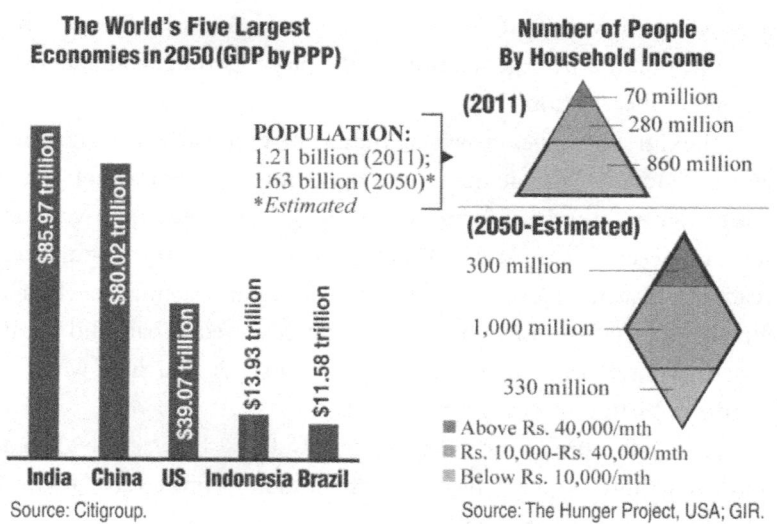

The World's Five Largest Economies in 2050 (GDP by PPP)

- India: $85.97 trillion
- China: $80.02 trillion
- US: $39.07 trillion
- Indonesia: $13.93 trillion
- Brazil: $11.58 trillion

POPULATION: 1.21 billion (2011); 1.63 billion (2050)*
*Estimated

Source: Citigroup.

Number of People By Household Income

(2011)
- 70 million
- 280 million
- 860 million

(2050-Estimated)
- 300 million
- 1,000 million
- 330 million

■ Above Rs. 40,000/mth
■ Rs. 10,000-Rs. 40,000/mth
■ Below Rs. 10,000/mth

Source: The Hunger Project, USA; GIR.

But GDP is only one of many measures of a nation's progress and a people's well-being. The Human Development Index (HDI) is another. As GDP grows, India's HDI ranking (currently an abysmal 136th) will improve but only if good governance replaces the corruption that is endemic in the system today. As Adi Godrej said at the World Economic Forum's India Economic Summit, corruption shaves around 1 per cent off India's annual GDP growth.

Our chart shows that, even after taking Citi's projections into account, 330 million Indians will still live in relative poverty in 2050. Clearly, good governance is necessary to ensure that India's poorest—not just the most privileged—benefit from inclusive growth in the future, by putting in place both political and second-generation economic reforms.

Analysing India's temporary slowdown, Ruchir Sharma, author of *Breakout Nations* wrote presciently in *The Times of India* in August 2013: 'A meaningful turnaround is not likely until the next election. The good news is that a new generation of leaders is on the horizon, many serving as chief ministers in states posting strong growth with low deficits. It will be difficult to push though reform ahead of the election but the new generation could play a strong national role following the election.'

The Citi study relies heavily on India's two dividends: demographic and democratic. The demographic dividend will ensure that India has the largest number of working-age people in the world (over 800 million) between 2015 and 2035 before tapering off as our population reaches a plateau of just over 1.60 billion and starts ageing (as China's already is). Fertility rates of increasingly educated urban and rural Indian women will dip from today's 2.6 to 1.7, which is when a country's birth and death rates equalize.

A large number of working-age Indians between eighteen and sixty, however, will be less than optimally productive if they remain poorly educated and therefore unemployable. To gain from our twenty-year demographic sweet spot between 2015 and 2035, education reform must clearly top the government's agenda. Infosys Chairman N.R. Narayana Murthy was partly right when he said that the standard of IIT students has fallen. It has. Too many are rote-learners, spewed out by coaching classes, and not creative thinkers. Education reform must start with government-run primary schools.

Shockingly, in some villages, primary schools have no teachers, no students and an empty shed that serves as a classroom.

■

The second dividend Citi banks on to project India's rise to the top of the GDP rankings in 2050, especially in comparison with China, is democracy. China's autocratic government, the argument goes, can command 10 per cent GDP growth, build superhighways and create gleaming infrastructure. But beneath the towers of Shanghai and the maglev bullet train tracks of Beijing lurks social tension. As China's per capita income rises, its 1.34 billion people will increasingly yearn for real freedom: a free press, an open Internet and, most crucially, democracy.

If the Chinese government can't deliver these, a Chinese Spring a decade hence cannot be ruled out. That could plunge China into years of uncertainty. Throughout history, as countries grew richer, they grew freer. Will China prove an exception? Unlikely.

By that token, India's democracy is a double-edged sword. Our raucous, open society takes us two steps forward economically and then one step backwards. But if governance reforms—land, electoral, judicial and police—are implemented quickly, the stage will be set for a new phase of economic reforms that will turn our democratic institutions into assets for long-term economic and social growth. We will then move from a culture of high subsidies (leaked to corrupt middlemen) to a culture of high productivity.

Second-generation economic reforms were stuck in UPA-I because of the Left's ideological opposition to them and have been derailed in UPA-II because of muddle-headed opposition from within the fractious UPA coalition itself. It is time to cast off these fetters. We must introduce hybrid agricultural technology to double total crop yields within a decade, modernize infrastructure, make land acquisition fairer to farmers, improve healthcare, pass enabling legislation to unleash the entrepreneurial energy of small and medium enterprises—the backbone of our economy—and implement tough, effective regulation to clean up business practice.

India is set to become the world's third largest economy in the world by purchasing power parity in 2014 largely because Japan's GDP will stagnate at around $4.4 trillion. And if a growing GDP is not to become a cruel irony for India's 445 million still-desperately poor people, this government—or the next one—must begin the second stage of economic liberalization without losing any further time.

Examine the right hand half of our chart. The one on top is pyramid-shaped, split into three sections. It reflects India's current household income structure: a large base of the poor and relatively poor (over 860 million), a narrow intermediate section of the middle class (around 280 million) and a tiny tip of the reasonably well-off (about 70 million).

The chart below it is diamond-shaped and reflects the shape of things to come in 2050 if political and economic reforms have their desired effect. The bottom section comprises around 330 million of the poor and relatively poor (down from 860 million today), the top section comprises the well-off (around 300 million, up from 70 million today) and the intermediate bulge comprises the expanded middle class of nearly one billion (up from 280 million today). That is the future if our government implements second-generation economic reforms. We must lay its foundation today.

4

THE INDIAN VOTE PYRAMID

The 2014 Lok Sabha election could radically alter the nation's political landscape. India's electorate is shaped like a pyramid *(see next page)*. The top 5 per cent comprises approximately 60 million people with monthly incomes exceeding Rs 50,000. The middle 35 per cent of the pyramid consists of around 425 million people—the aspirational middle class.

The large bottom of the pyramid comprises the teeming mass of 725 million Indians. They constitute roughly 60 per cent of India's population which the National Sample Survey Organisation (NSSO) has defined as those who consume less than Rs 66 a day in cities and Rs 35 a day in villages.

The top of the pyramid is largely secular, liberal and English-speaking—traditional Congress supporters. However, an increasingly significant number of voters in this segment consider Hindi or a regional tongue as their principal language. Many are ideologically right of centre—traders, professionals and newly minted entrepreneurs.

The middle of the pyramid is diverse: 425 million middle-class Indians, largely youthful, concerned more with jobs and inflation than political ideology. Their political affiliations are mixed, giving neither the Congress nor the BJP any particular advantage, though institutional corruption has made them increasingly hostile to the incumbent Congress.

It is the bottom 60 per cent of our electoral pyramid that is the most interesting. Steeped in poverty, low levels of literacy and vulnerable to money and muscle power as well as exhortations in the name of caste, religion and region, these 725 million-plus Indians form the core of the Congress's votebase. Muslims are over-represented here. Both the Rajinder Sachar and Ranganath Misra Commissions found that Muslims fall into one of India's poorest socio-economic segments. It is this powerful electoral mix of the poor and the minorities that the Congress thrives on. Of its 28.55 per cent national voteshare in the 2009 Lok Sabha elections, a big chunk came from this bottom of the pyramid.

India has 714 million eligible voters. Around 59.7 per cent (428 million) voted in the 2009 general election. Of these, 119.10 million (approximately 28 per cent) voted for the Congress. Without the poor and the minorities, it would be fair to conclude that the Congress would have won far fewer than 206 Lok Sabha seats in 2009. (As we see later in this chapter, the number of eligible voters will rise to over 800 million in 2014.)

From the wealthy top of the pyramid, where voter turnout is traditionally low (less than 35 per cent), the Congress could have picked up around 4 million out of the 7 million or so who voted in this segment. From the more hostile middle of the pyramid, where voter turnout is higher, the Congress probably picked up just over a quarter of those who voted—40 million out of this segment's base of around 150 million (*see chart*). Thus from these two segments, the Congress would have received around 44 million of its 119 million votes in 2009.

The 428-Million Vote Pyramid

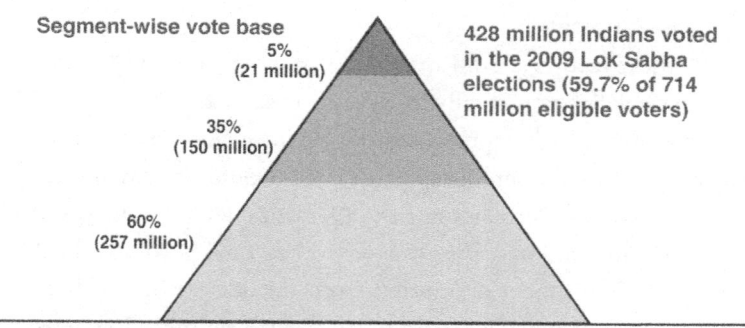

(Total eligible voter base: 714 million; 59.7% or 428 million voted in 2009)

Source: Election Commission of India; NCAER.

The rest—around 75 million votes—would have been drawn from the bottom of the pyramid. This large base comprises 60 per cent (257 million) of those who voted. Thus, the Congress likely won nearly 30 per cent of this segment—significantly higher than its overall voteshare average of 28 per cent. Winning nearly a third of this overweighted segment would have lifted the Congress's national voteshare. Without the extra edge from the bottom of the pyramid, Congress national voteshare could have dropped to around 25 per cent—in line with the proportion of votes it received in the top two segments.

A 25 per cent national voteshare would have translated into around 140 seats as it did in 1998 when the Congress's national voteshare was 25.59 per cent. It won 141 seats. With public opinion hardening against it among voters in the top two segments of our electoral pyramid, the Congress will be even more dependent on the bottom 60 per cent of the voter base in 2014. But that may no longer be enough to return it to office.

Even a small fall in voteshare from 28 per cent to 25 per cent could result in the Congress losing eighty or more seats if the economic downturn continues into 2014. With around 120 seats, and probably fewer than its historical low of 114 in 1999, the Congress's best hope is to 'govern' from outside as it did in 1996-98 when it propped up (and then pulled down) the H.D. Deve Gowda and I.K. Gujral governments.

All these factors should worry a Congress facing the prospect of its lowest Lok Sabha seat tally in sixty-two years. The 2014 Lok Sabha poll will have a higher proportion of younger and less-poor voters than ever before—a demographic that the Congress may not relish.

If neither the Congress nor the BJP win enough seats to form a stable government, increasingly assertive regional parties will cobble together a government supported from outside by one of the two principal parties, which will then pull it down at a time of its choosing. A midterm election could therefore loom in 2017—by when the Congress's large pyramid base of the very poor would have shrunk even further. That is good news for India but electorally bad news for the Congress.

■

The 2014 general election will be a watershed in several other ways as well. No prime minister has won three consecutive Lok Sabha polls since Jawaharlal Nehru's hat-trick in 1952, 1957 and 1962. Indira Gandhi won in 1967 and 1971 but was defeated in the post-Emergency election of 1977. Mrs Gandhi and son Rajiv won in 1980 and 1984 respectively, but Rajiv was routed in 1989. The Vajpayee-led NDA won in 1998 and 1999 but lost decisively in 2004.

The second reason why the 2014 Lok Sabha election will be a landmark is that young people born specifically after July 1991 will for the first time be eligible to vote. In the May 2009 general election, they were still not eighteen years of age.

Why is July 1991 so important? It marks Dr Manmohan Singh's first interim budget, delivered on 24 July, shortly after he was appointed finance minister in the Narasimha Rao government. That budget, followed by the February 1992 budget, laid the foundation for India's economic liberalization.

Those born in or after July 1991—the post-liberalization generation—were still below eighteen during the May 2009 Lok Sabha election. They will vote for the first time in 2014. Those born between 1991 and 1996 (aged between twenty-three and eighteen in 2014) represent an estimated 120 million new voters of the over 800 million voters who will be eligible to vote in 2014.

Why is this demographic slice so vital for the UPA, NDA and regional parties preparing their strategies for 2014? Because these 120 million new voters have grown up in post-liberalization India with little emotional baggage of the past. They want jobs, development and good governance. They despise corruption—both the petty sort they encounter in their daily lives and the mega scams that they read about on the Internet and watch unfolding on their televisions.

For them the Gujarat riots of 2002, the Babri demolition of 1992 and the anti-Sikh pogrom of 1984 are important historical events that need resolution and closure. They do not want these issues to fester like open wounds. They believe India should move on and join the global mainstream in terms of technology, governance and development.

They abhor dynastic politics as much as they deplore ultra-nationalism. Overall they are tolerant but impatient with the misgovernance, corruption and inflation that has blighted their families' lives during the past decade.

They seek change. But when they look around they see national opposition parties like the BJP and large regional parties like the SP, BSP, NCP and DMK practising the same brand of discredited politics as the Congress: nepotistic, corrupt, opportunistic.

■

Narendra Modi was quick to capture the mood of this young demographic. Hence his ceaseless use of the Internet and social media to build a brand not unlike American presidential candidates routinely do.

Blindsided by the Congress's rediscovery of economic reforms and hobbled by its own strategic errors, the BJP's central leadership had little option but to fall in line behind Modi. But can Modi's appeal among younger voters spread to the rest of the electoral demographic? The BJP needs over 25 per cent national voteshare to win 190-200 Lok Sabha seats. It won 182 seats with 25.59 per cent voteshare in 1998 and again the same number, 182 seats, with just 23.75 per cent in 1999 due to a greater number of coalition allies. It won 138 seats with 22.16 per cent voteshare in 2004 and 116 seats with 18.80 per cent voteshare in 2009. It thus needs a swing of around 6.50 per cent from its 2009 voteshare to garner around 200 seats. At that level, it will attract allies like the AIADMK, TDP and others.

In the 2009 Lok Sabha election, following the Mumbai 26/11 terror attack and the Indo-US nuclear deal, the electorate voted for Manmohan Singh's probity and competence. While the prime minister's reputation has since been diminished by serial scams, Rahul Gandhi has acquired little political equity of his own and might not risk a direct prime ministerial contest with Modi.

That, though, is precisely the contest Modi would relish.

5
SECULARISM: MYTH AND REALITY

On a cool spring day over sixty years ago in California, Zulfikar Ali Bhutto, a tall, angular man of twenty-two, was in a garrulous mood. He told my father: 'Ah, Pakistan. See what we will do with my wonderful new country.'

My father, like young Bhutto, a student at the University of California, Berkeley, was unimpressed. 'A country founded on theocracy,' he told Bhutto, 'will never work.' My mother, among the first Indian women-students on the Berkeley campus, agreed. Bhutto walked away in a huff.

Those were heady days after Independence. Bhutto went on to become Pakistan's youngest cabinet minister, at thirty, in 1958. My parents returned to India after four years at Berkeley and got married. My father took charge of the family's petrochemicals business which, thankfully, he was later liberal enough never to coerce me to join.

The difference between Pakistan and India today is the story of how a great religion, Islam, has been distorted by those entrusted to protect its liberal ethos. Pakistan and several countries in the Middle East have used Islam not to liberate but to imprison their people. But it is in 'secular' India that the damage has been most insidious.

Jawaharlal Nehru was a secular man. He would have been horrified at what passes off as secularism in modern India. In its purest, most classical sense, secularism requires treating religion as a private matter. It must not enter the public domain—pray in public or pray in private, but keep your faith at home.

Politicians who have little to offer by way of development—twenty-four-hour electricity, water, housing, sanitation, roads, infrastructure, jobs—will use religion to divert the attention of the common man. It should shame the Congress that the constituency from where Feroze Gandhi—Indira's husband—first entered the Lok Sabha in 1952, Rae Bareli, and from where succeeding generations of Gandhis, including Indira and Sonia, have been elected, is today one of the most backward constituencies in India. Over 70 per cent of children below the age of five in Rae Bareli, for example, are moderately or severely stunted due to malnutrition.

But secularism, not development, has been an article of faith for the Gandhis. The poor and the Muslims—the Muslims in particular—have been entrapped in a fear psychosis that warns them: vote for 'the other' and you will not be safe. The riots in Gujarat in 2002, following the burning of karsevaks in a train in Godhra, have been especially handy in deepening this paranoia.

Muslims from Uttar Pradesh and Bihar, from Maharashtra and Andhra Pradesh, are in effect given this false choice: do you want to be with a 'secular' party like the Congress that can guarantee your physical safety but not one square meal a day? Or do you want to be with a party where you must forever live in fear but will have twenty-four-hour electricity, good housing, roads, jobs and a reasonable standard of living?

Rich electoral dividends have flowed from such fearmongering. In the process, over the decades, regional parties have grasped the fraudulent secular baton from the Congress: the Samajwadi Party may be the most notorious of these but others—like the Telugu Desam Party (TDP) and the Nationalist Congress Party—have all dealt the duplicitous Muslim card.

■

Indira Gandhi introduced the term secularism in the Preamble to the Constitution with the 42nd Constitution Amendment Act, 1976, during the draconian Emergency. Twenty-six years earlier, in 1950, the framers of our Constitution, led by Babasaheb Ambedkar, had not felt it necessary to include the word—despite the then recent horrors of communal riots following Partition.

Ever since, the Congress has used secularism and socialism (another term introduced into the Constitution by Mrs Gandhi during the Emergency) to define itself as the party of the aam aadmi. So how has the aam aadmi fared in over fifty-three years of Congress governments, thirty-six of them under Indira and Rajiv Gandhi and their appointed CEO-Prime Ministers, P.V. Narasimha Rao and Manmohan Singh?

Badly. Poverty remains endemic. Over 14,000 farmers across India committed suicide in 2012. Malnutrition persists. The Naandi Foundation released a report in January 2012—at the hands of Prime Minister Manmohan Singh—on how shockingly widespread child malnutrition is.

Who is to blame? Obviously, the Congress. It has run India for roughly 81 per cent of its post-Independence history. The Opposition, especially in the states, must share some responsibility for this as well. But make no mistake: the primary responsibility for the poverty and malnutrition India still suffers even after sixty-seven of independence lies squarely at the doorstep of the Congress. It has misused the term socialism to enshrine poverty, rather than eradicate it. The poorer the voter, the easier it is to win his vote without bothering about real development issues.

The second Emergency-origin term the Congress has misused is secularism. The term for 'secular' in Hindi is *panthnirpeksh*. In 1977, when Mrs Gandhi's government was voted out soon after the Emergency was revoked, the new Janata Party government introduced a Constitutional Amendment Bill. The word 'secular' was sought to be defined in the Constitution as 'equal respect for all religions'.

The Bill was passed in the 6th Lok Sabha (1977-79), where the Janata Party held a majority. But it was defeated in the Rajya Sabha where the Congress had a majority. Why did the Congress reject the 1977-79 Lok Sabha's definition of secularism—'equal respect for all religions'?

Consider now what UPA Chairperson Sonia Gandhi said during a lecture at the Nexus Institute in the Hague on 9 June 2007: 'India is a secular country. The term means equal respect for all religions.'

How does Sonia's definition of secularism differ from Narendra Modi's? Who is really more secular? Modi? Or Sonia? Or Nitish, Digvijay, Lalu, Paswan, Mulayam, Karunanidhi, Omar Abdullah and Owaisi? Just as some of these leaders have eagerly copied Indira Gandhi's destructive dynastic politics to enrich their future generations while impoverishing India's, regional parties have effortlessly morphed into 'secular' family firms, engaged in exploiting Muslims by cocooning them.

■

My daughter, a designer, often visits areas in Mumbai to source raw materials for her work and to commission artisans. Most of these artisans are Muslims. Most are very poor. Most live in buildings which could collapse at any moment. She asked me: 'Why doesn't the Congress-NCP government in Maharashtra, which wins elections based on votes from poor Muslims, do anything to improve their lives?'

The answer: because poor Muslims who don't have time to think beyond the next meal also don't have time to think of governance and development—and how both have been sacrificed at the altar of secularism.

But then, of course, this isn't secularism. It's communalism masquerading as secularism. What can be more communal than keeping a large part of an entire community of 177 million people in poverty for over six decades?

Theocratic countries like Pakistan have more liberal laws for their Muslim citizens than India has for its Muslims. Turkey, Malaysia and Indonesia have also reformed medieval Islamic canons. Why not India? Because the Congress and its 'secular' regional allies fear the true liberation of the Muslim mind. And that this liberation could set off unintended consequences.

Electoral defeat haunts the Congress and its allies more than issues of governance and development—or even justice. That is why it has moved glacially to deliver justice to the victims of the 1984 Sikh pogrom in which an estimated 5,000 Sikhs—over 3,000 in Delhi alone—were killed by Congress-led hooligan-politicians.

At the same time, po-faced, it uses the 750-plus Muslims killed in Gujarat in 2002 in a riot (not a one-sided pogrom), where over 250 of the dead were Hindus, to extract cynical political advantage with the help of its NGO cottage industry.

Muslim leaders have been willing accomplices in this tragedy. Mullahs issue regressive fatwas against Muslim women and edicts against sensible civil laws. Instead of condemning such fatwas, the government maintains a studied silence, tacitly encouraging extremism and keeping ordinary Muslims stuck in a time warp.

The two real enemies of the Muslim community—communal politicians dressed up as secular politicians to win votes and mullahs deliberately misinterpreting the holy book to retain power over their flock—form a natural alliance. Together they have enriched themselves but impoverished India's Muslims, materially and intellectually, in the name of secularism.

This brings us to the third angle in this infamous triangle: the liberal, secular Hindu. Where does he stand in all this? He is naturally secular in the truest sense of the word: religion is a private matter, he rightly believes. It has no place in politics.

But he is also swayed by the plight of his fellow Indians who happen to be Muslims: impoverished, illiterate, ghettoized, discriminated against. For every Azim Premji and Aamir Khan, there are millions of weavers in UP and spot boys in Mumbai who have no place in corporate India's organized labour force.

Liberal, well-meaning Hindus ask: why? And the answer they come up with is: communal discrimination. Yet the liberal Hindu doesn't dig deeper. The more politicians sequester Muslims into vote silos, the more the middle-class Hindu (not the liberal, well-meaning, Stephanian Hindu) resents them. Discrimination, petty or large, mounts.

The real culprits—communal politicians masquerading as secular politicians—get away scot-free in this narrative. The liberal, secular Hindu's anger against anti-Muslim communalism is therefore misdirected—far away from these real culprits.

The liberal, secular Hindu, meanwhile, points to 'Hindutva' as the real fount of communalism. Is he right? This is how the Supreme Court defined Hindutva, when specifically asked to do so, on 11 December 1995:

'Considering the terms Hinduism or Hindutva per se as depicting hostility, enmity or intolerance towards other religious faiths or professing communalism, proceeds from an improper appreciation and perception of the true meaning of these expressions. These terms (Hinduism or Hindutva) are indicative more of a way of life of the Indian people and are not confined merely to describe persons practising the Hindu religion as a faith.'

For 'secular' parties, 2014 is an election in which they will now have to rely more than ever on raising a fear psychosis against leaders like Narendra Modi who threaten their hold on power—and the financial pipeline that accompanies it but never finds its way into developmental projects, especially for Muslims. After all, they matter only once every five years.

Influential sections of especially the electronic media, suffused with hearts bleeding from the wrong ventricle, are part of this great fraud played on India's poverty-stricken Muslims: communalism with an engaging secular mask. The token Muslim is lionized—from business to literature—but the common Muslim languishes in his sixty-seven-year-old ghetto. It is from such ghettos that raw recruits to the banned Students Islamic Movement of India (SIMI) and the Indian Mujaheedin (IM) are most easily found.

Sixty years ago on that Berkeley campus, my father told Zulfikar Ali Bhutto why Pakistan would fail as a state. Today, my daughter, as she visits Muslim-dominated ghettos for sourcing her raw materials, sees how Muslims in India, too, have failed. The single biggest cause: communalism—but in quite the opposite way the Congress, SP and other 'secular' parties define it.

■

Real secularism, though, has deep Indian roots. A BBC survey revealed that 97 per cent of Indians believe in God—a higher percentage than almost anywhere else in the world. But while their faith is precious to them, the young Indian—Muslim, Hindu, Sikh, Jain—is focused on a better life, not a better mosque or temple. And they have a common secular heritage. As a group of visiting senior Muslim clergy from Ayodhya, with wisdom born of great learning, said once to Swami Shri Swaroopananda Saraswati, the highly respected shankaracharya of Dwaraka: 'Even though our religions are different, we share the blood of the Hindus.' To which the shankaracharya replied gently: 'That makes our Lord Ram your ancestor as well.'

This is not just about genealogy—it reflects India's embedded religious diversity. Six of India's highest constitutional functionaries are, or have recently been, Sikh (prime minister), Christian (UPA chairperson), Muslim (chief election commissioner), Parsi (chief justice of India), Dalit (speaker of the Lok Sabha) and Hindu (president). There is no other country in the world with such breathtaking plurality at the highest level of leadership.

Consider Britain: only Protestant (not Catholic) Christians can be monarch. In Saudi Arabia and Pakistan, minorities (including Muslim Ahmadis) have restricted rights. Unlike burqa-banning Western democracies such as France and Belgium, Indian secularism does not separate church from state. It allows them to swim together in a common, if sometimes, chaotic pool.

Fundamentalists dislike the concept of liberal Islam flourishing in the syncretic soil of India. Indian Muslims, however, remain rooted in a Vedic civilizational ethic that has celebrated our religious plurality for over 3,000 years. Despite Al-Qaeda and the ISI's concerted recruitment efforts, Indian Muslims, except renegades from the Students Islamic Movement of India and the Indian Mujahideen, have consistently spurned the call to jihad. India's innate respect for all religions, which does great credit to its silent Hindu majority, has historically made the country the refuge-of-last-resort for all faiths: Jews, Parsis, Christians, Buddhists.

This secular instinct cannot be elided by politicians. Moderate Muslim clerics like Maulana Mahmood Madani of the Jamiat-Ulama-i-Hind can play a positive role: as the third-generation custodian of the Jamiat, Maulana Madani's word carries weight with influential Deobandis. The maulana and other Muslim clerics must liberate the dialogue between Muslims and Hindus from the counterfeit secularism politicians practice to seek votes.

Significantly, if the Congress loses even half its current Muslim vote due to disaffection over the Ayodhya issue, its overall voteshare could drop dramatically from 28.55 per cent in the 2009 general election to around 25 per cent in 2014. Its Lok Sabha seats would collapse from 206 to under 120. That explains the Congress's careful approach to the Babri Masjid dispute, even as it remains in a state of suspended animation in its final judicial lap. The Congress cannot afford to shed even a sliver of its faithful Muslim vote.

But must this be at the expense of ordinary Muslims who vote for India's largest political party in order to feel protected from Hindutva forces, only to end up in social and economic ghettos—denied jobs, flats and respect by a resentful majority? The cost of keeping the Congress in government is a burden the broader Muslim community should not have to bear.

■

India's 177 million Muslims can be a powerful repudiation of the two-nation theory Pakistan has used to justify a theocratic state— if they recognize where their true interests lie. Those interests lie, first, in modernity. This involves replacing outdated personal laws unsuited to a progressive, secular democracy. Second, modernity is linked directly to education. Madrassas teach maths and science, not just the Quran. But the number of Muslim graduates is far lower than the national average. Muslim literacy is 59 per cent against over 70 per cent nationally.

Modernizing the community means embracing a liberal, forward-thinking ethic without diluting religious tradition. Indian Jews, Christians and Parsis have modernized themselves economically and intellectually without sacrificing their traditions or culture, which originate in the same West Asian geography as Islam. Caught between fundamentalist clerics and vote-obsessed politicians, the average Indian Muslim—hard-working, God-fearing and poor— lives in a time warp. He contributes far less than he could to the national economy and to the intellectual and social resurgence that is reshaping India. His leaders pose as his benefactors but are often his worst enemies.

By appeasing rather than educating 14 per cent of its minority population, Indian politicians have choked a powerful nationalist voice against Pakistan-sponsored terrorism directed at India. As the twenty-first century ebbs and flows, India's global ascent cannot be slowed by a marginalized minority. But imagine how much the ascent could gather pace were that minority turned into an economic and social asset: modern, educated and forward-thinking.

The politics of minority appeasement creates a community cocooned in backwardness—easy prey for minoritarian politicians. Ayodhya is an inflection point. Used wisely, it can reinforce India's civilizational tolerance, which unifies, and reject the counterfeit secularism that divides. The BJP must play its part in this: its effort to raise the issue of building a 'grand Ram temple' at Ayodhya may win it polarized Hindu votes, but it should know that this can only be a short-term electoral tactic, not a long-term strategy.

■

True secularism runs through the bloodstream of India. But that bloodstream has been poisoned by gradual injections of communalism over the last 125 years: first by post-Mutiny British rulers and later by unscrupulous Indian politicians. India has assimilated, mostly with good grace, Islamic, Christian, Persian and Confucian cultures. Every conqueror of India, from 700 CE to the eighteenth century, has remarked on Hinduism's essentially secular philosophy.

Since 'communalism' will be a key issue in the 2014 general election, it is worthwhile to set religion in a historical context rather than in the simplistic framework of an old, irreconcilable rivalry between Hindus and Muslims that both the Congress and the BJP attempt to do.

India's first contact with Islam was in 644 CE when the army of Caliph Umar entered Sindh. It was only sixty-seven years later, in 711 CE, that the Ummayad government of Iraq launched an expedition comprising 12,000 Syrian camels and Iraqi horses against the rajas of Sindh.

Later, Islamic penetrations came through the Khyber Pass. Mahmud of Ghazni was the first, and among the cruelest, of the Turko-Afghan Muslims to invade North India. He was followed by a series of Muslim rulers, including Muhammad Tughlak. The Mughal

Empire was founded by Babur in 1526 and this entire period of intermittent 'Muslim conquest' (from the tenth to the eighteenth centuries) is regarded by proponents of the RSS school of thought as proof of Islam's affray into India. This belief lies at the heart of the sanghparivar's supposed antipathy towards contemporary Muslims.

It is true that the early Turko-Afghan invaders were cruel, even barbaric. They murdered by the thousands, pillaged whole villages and forcibly converted Hindus to Islam en masse. These are unequivocal crimes and history rightly records them as such.

But it is equally true that the later Mughals, especially Emperor Akbar, were secularists: men who honoured Hindus by marrying their women, recruiting their scholars into the highest positions of their court and treating them with dignity and respect. Akbar was the first Muslim ruler to recognize India's great pluralistic past.

That past had been built, brick by secular brick, by great leaders like Ashoka and Chandragupta, by philosophers and scientists such as Ramanujan and Aryabhatta and numerous shankaracharyas whose theological brilliance drove Buddhism from the land of its birth to China and East Asia. When Akbar assumed the throne in 1556, India was already a 4,000-year-old civilization, a country which had given birth to four great religions—Hinduism, Buddhism, Jainism and Sikhism—and granted refuge to a fifth, Zorastrianism.

Emperor Akbar abolished forcible conversions and the hated jizya, a poll tax imposed on non-Muslims. He ruled not as a Muslim but as an Indian emperor. He furthered the idea of a secular India; his thinking was revolutionary for the sixteenth century.

Akbar abandoned orthodox Islam in the 1580s and embraced a mystical Sufism. He borrowed ideas from Hinduism and Jainism, from Sikhs, Parsis and Christians who were regularly invited to Fatehpur Sikri. In the Diwan-i-Khas, learned scholars from every religion would debate the great theological and philosophical issues of the day. Akbar would stand eight feet above on a ramp and throw searching questions at the assemblage, as he paced up and down, sparking arguments and spirited ripostes.

Of course, the Mughal Empire, despite Akbar's erudition and religious moderation, was in the end an imposition from outside. But much of the wealth the Mughal Empire procured from its subjects remained in India. It enriched India though religious denudations—such as the disgraceful destruction of Hindu temples—were frequent. Nevertheless, by the eighteenth century, Islam in India had become integrated into India's deep and hospitable secular milieu.

•

It was the disastrous advent of British rule in the 1750s that spawned and gave rise to modern communalism. After a century of military warfare, the British had conquered various bits of India: from Bengal, Madras and Bombay to Sind, Punjab and the North East. Following the First War of Independence in 1857 (wrongly termed by British historians as the Sepoy Mutiny), Indian sovereignty passed from the East India Company to the British Crown.

One of the first things the British government did as sovereign ruler of India was to plant the poisonous seed of communalism. That seed has germinated over the last 137 years and grown into a panoply of hatred and mistrust, leading to partition, rioting and suffering on a scale matched only by the Jewish experience in the Second World War.

How did the British set about this task? The army was the first target. Indians were strictly divided into regiments of Sikhs, Gurkhas, Pathans, Rajputs and Marathas. Meanwhile, the British 'government' in India removed all import duties on British-made cotton, destroying the infant industry in the subcontinent at a time of famine and widespread starvation-induced deaths in Maharashtra.

Thus, while Britain was systematically eroding India's future industrial and agricultural competitiveness, it was simultaneously injecting calculated doses of communal poison into India's secular bloodstream.

It does not serve the BJP's political ends to stress this aspect of 'foreign rule'. There are no votebanks to be won by attacking an enemy, however ruinous its actions were for India, who is 5,000 miles away. Hindus of a certain mind, mostly poor but comprising even middle-class professionals and businessmen, remain deeply resentful of the Mughal Empire. The realization of how much more economically, socially and psychologically ruinous the British Empire was to India has not sunk in.

As more Indian scholarship of the last 500 years emerges to replace the still largely European body of history and interpretation, that realization will come. For the present, the historical enemy for most Hindus is the Mughal. In a communally-charged atmosphere, the Indian Muslim is therefore a tempting target: he is a next-door neighbour, not thousands of miles across the sea. He competes for jobs, for school admissions and for housing. He is the visible symbol of a hated conqueror. The Protestant British shrewdly concentrated on making money and left conversions to the Catholic Portuguese. They left behind no hostages after 1947. The Mughals, by assimilating into the Indian cultural mainstream, converted millions to Islam. When the empire dissipated, those converted millions remained permanent hostages—in India, Pakistan and Bangladesh.

▪

The Congress, like the British, has played a double game. It has appeased Muslims in quite the worst ways (for example, by not enforcing a uniform civil code) and at the same time kept them economically and socially backward by not encouraging them to emerge out of their medieval mindset. Indian Muslims are among the most backward in the Islamic world. Predominantly-Muslim Malaysia and Indonesia have shown how progressively Islam can be interpreted. Iraq, despite its serious ethnic faultlines, has many reformist social laws, as do Turkey and Egypt. It is only in India, Pakistan and Bangladesh that Muslims remain prisoners of the past.

Politicians are largely to blame for this problem. Few Muslims can forget that some of the worst Hindu-Muslim killings took place in cosmopolitan Mumbai (then Bombay), in 1992-93 because of an internal Congress power struggle between Sudhakar Naik, then Maharashtra chief minister, and Sharad Pawar, then union defence minister. For four days, from 8 to 11 January 1993, as hundreds of Muslims were butchered by Hindu mobs, the city police stood by watching and (in some documented cases) even encouraging the rioters. It is a political disgrace that the government has still not punished the guilty in those riots.

Communalism is obviously not a political invention. But Indian politicians, from both the Congress and the BJP, have nurtured it, as the British did, to serve their own ends. The ordinary people of India have been and are being used, as they have been for centuries, as human fodder. It is time to call a halt to this. India is instinctively a secular society. Poor Muslims and Hindus live cheek-by-jowl in cities and towns around the country in relative peace.

Yet, the festering and real problem is the teeming cauldron of Indian Muslims who live in abject poverty. They are under-represented in the Indian Administrative Service, in business and in the professions: from law and medicine to accountancy, management and engineering. Part of the damage has been done by government appeasement. The other part is self-inflicted: Indian Muslims must stand up and say once and for all that they are Indian first and Muslim only second.

To bring Indian Muslims into the mainstream, the government must also treat them as Indians first, and not only during elections. By giving Muslims a separate civil code, you freeze them in an identity they may not even really want and in a social time warp that can only harm them. American Jews are an enlightening example of progress beyond social restrictions. They are fiercely proud of their religion but they do not let their Jewishness supersede their Americanism.

Take a straw poll of Indian Muslims: Would you prefer to live in India or Pakistan? Nearly 95 per cent would unhesitatingly say India. Pakistan has been socially lacerated by theocracy; India is a more mature country with a deep and long history of religious tolerance and compassion. The strength of India is this secular tradition. While nations struggle with racism and ethnic strife, India has shown that 1,225 million people from dozens of different religions and cultures can live together in relative peace. That is not a small triumph. But it can quickly become a big disaster if we continue to allow politicians to set a communal agenda, however secular its grammar.

As we ready ourselves to elect a new government, the message that should go out is this: the time for communal polities and appeasement of minorities is over. Give your vote to the party that will deliver on its promises of a return to the highest traditions of Indian secularism: equality and justice.

6
THE COST OF CORRUPTION

The gap may appear small. But for a poor country it could be lethal. India's trendline annual GDP growth rate fell from just under 9 per cent in fiscal 2010 to 5 per cent in fiscal 2013. If the deceleration is restricted to a year, or at most two, the economic damage can be contained. If, however, the slump to sub-7 per cent GDP growth extends for a period of time, the consequences for India's economy will be grim.

Consider two scenarios. In the first, growth stays subdued at below 7 per cent. In the second scenario, growth rebounds to 9 per cent within two years, which both the Prime Minister's Economic Advisory Council (PMEAC) and Montek Singh Ahluwalia, deputy chairman of the Planning Commission, say is possible if investment in infrastructure accelerates.

Conditions exist for both scenarios. External factors like Europe's recovery, the price of oil and foreign fund flows can take the annual GDP growth trendline in either direction. But the real solution to growth lies within: decisive execution of stalled economic reforms, a more imaginative monetary policy by the Reserve Bank of India (RBI), headed by Governor Raghuram Rajan, transparent political governance and a return of corporate investment in, especially, domestic infrastructure.

At 7 per cent annual GDP growth, India's economy would climb from $4.46 trillion by purchasing power parity in 2011-12 (taken as the base year for the purpose of this computation) to $6.30 trillion in 2016-17. Per capita income would rise during the same period from $3,700 to $5,100. India will thus still be a low-income country in 2017. The effect on poverty reduction will be relatively small. Poverty levels are currently falling by around 0.9 per cent a year, according to trends in the National Sample Survey Organisation (NSSO). At an annual GDP growth rate of 7 per cent, poverty levels will dip by an estimated 4.5 per cent in 2016-17, consistent with the trend over the last decade. Taking 4.5 per cent of India's population out of the technical definition of poverty—however contentious the NSSO figures may be—means helping 55 million Indians climb into a better future over the next five years.

Now consider the second scenario: 9 per cent annual GDP growth for the next five years. India's GDP (PPP) will rise from $4.40 trillion in the base year 2011-12 to $6.80 trillion in 2016-17. Per capita income (PPP) will climb to just under $6,000—the threshold for a middle-income country.

The 2 Per Cent Difference

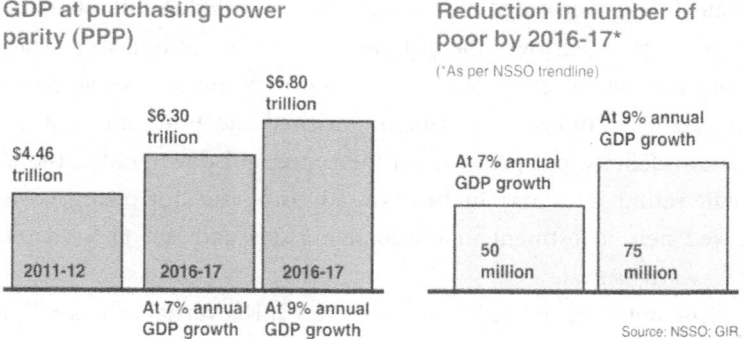

Poverty levels will fall—assuming an annual decline of 1.2 per cent in poverty at this higher GDP growth rate—by around 6 per cent by 2016-17, depending, of course, on how agricultural pricing reforms are carried out in order to distribute income more evenly across rural areas.

This will take nearly 75 million Indians out of deep poverty and give hope to at least as many more in the subsequent five years, if the 9 per cent GDP growth rate holds. Thus, a 2 per cent difference in the annual GDP growth rate over a relatively short period of five years can make a significant difference to the lives of millions of Indians *(see chart)*.

So what are the steps policymakers can take—given external constraints—to regain a 9 per cent GDP growth trendline? Freeing agriculture pricing and loosening monetary policy are important. The Maharashtra government's decision to allow farmers in the state to sell directly to consumers is being keenly watched nationally.

But the real difference will be seen when manufacturing productivity is boosted through new corporate investment in physical assets. This has fallen in the last two years by around four percentage points as Indian industry has been fleeing overseas in the face of policy uncertainty at home.

■

Meanwhile, government expenditure has risen by an unsustainable 15 per cent a year over the last eight years. Corruption in private-public partnership projects and other acts of political misgovernance have reduced foreign investment, widened the trade and current account deficits, put pressure on the rupee and downgraded India's credit rating. This has in turn raised corporate borrowing costs, slowed new investment in productive assets and set off a vicious downwards spiral.

The outcome of such rampant policy misgovernance is a fall of over 2 per cent in the annual GDP trendline growth rate. Over five years, as we have seen, this will take a heavy toll on our poor and our middle class—buffeted as it is by inflation and job losses—and especially on our farmers, who remain victims of an unreformed agricultural sector.

It is a cost India cannot afford. Bad politics makes for bad economics and even a 2 per cent dip in annual GDP growth will have ruinous consequences. It is a price the country should not have to pay. The government has little control over external economic factors but it must ensure more decisive policymaking at home. Coalition compulsions notwithstanding, the Indian government must bite the bullet on reforms.

■

Apart from economic reforms, a raft of administrative, judicial and police reforms are vital to transform India into a modern democracy.

The N.N.Vohra Committee Report laid bare the shocking nexus between politicians and crime syndicates. The report was made public eighteen years ago; the annexures, containing names of specific politicians with links to crime syndicates, remain classified to this day. However, we know that the rot runs deep. Top police officers 'pay' to win promotions to the highest post. Auctioned posts are funded by politicians cutting across party lines and builder-lobbies.

Once ensconced, senior police officers return the 'investment' made on them to their politician-sponsors by turning a blind eye to illegal proxy land deals and other acts of political corruption. Many police officers use their high office not to gather actionable intelligence against terror sleeper cells but to extract 'commissions' from builders who flout FSI regulations and from power brokers who run profitable rackets: the water tanker mafia, kerosene and diesel adulterators, bookies, illicit bar owners and smugglers.

Responding to an RTI query, Maharashtra's Public Information Officer (PIO) revealed that, between January 2009 and January 2011, senior state politicians led by Home Minister R.R. Patil and the chief minister's office 'made 231 recommendations requests to the police department for the posts of additional superintendent, deputy superintendent, inspectors, assistant inspectors and sub-inspectors'. Of these, fifty-four 'requests' were complied with.

India has 15.60 lakh policemen or one policeman for 774 citizens. The average across Europe and the US is one police officer for around 300 citizens. Poor pay, outdated weaponry and appalling living conditions are a blight on Indian law enforcement. When a deputy superintendent of police (DSP) receives a salary of Rs 13,500 and a constable Rs 4,900, corruption is inevitable. Policing is a state subject and all political parties have a vested interest in not ceding control of law enforcement to an independent, professional police force.

The Supreme Court has long been aware of the toxic relationship between politicians and the police. It passed a seminal order in September 2006 to delink the two. The Supreme Court's seven-directive order provides a complete blueprint to transform law enforcement in India.

The first directive mandates the setting up of State Security Commissions (SSCs) to ensure the police is freed from political influence. The SSCs would periodically evaluate policing performance in their state. The second directive requires each director-general of police (DGP) to be appointed for a minimum tenure of two years through a merit-based, transparent process.

The third and fourth directives deal with operational duties of police officers and the separation of the investigative and law and order (beat) functions of the police. The fifth directive—crucially—orders the creation of an independent Police Establishment Board (PEB) to decide transfers, promotions and postings, a much-abused tool in the hands of state politicians.

The sixth directive envisages a Police Complaints Authority (PCA) and the seventh directive a National Security Commission (NSC) for the selection of chiefs of central police organizations.

Taken together, the seven directives of the Supreme Court provide the architecture of an independent, well-paid, accountable police force equipped to deal firmly and fairly with local law enforcement, intelligence-gathering from communities, counterterrorism operations and day-to-day policing. It will sever the umbilical cord that today binds the police with politicians and the underworld. Over the years, the Supreme Court has issued notices to several states which have not complied with its seven directives and are thus in contempt of court. During the past few months, as law enforcement plumbed new depths with Supreme Court-monitored CBI investigations into various scams, there was renewed hope that the states and the Centre wouldfall into line and implement the Supreme Court's directives.

That hope was belied when the UPA government, far from pressing the states (at least where it is in government) to comply with the Supreme Court's seven directives, took the CBI entirely out of the ambit of the RTI. A more regressive approach to policing is hard to imagine. Autonomy for the CBI must now be high on the Supreme Court's agenda even as it seeks to enforce its own order on police reforms.

The Chief Justice of India is a tough and fair arbiter of the public interest. If he concludes that vested political interests are improperly superseding public interest in defying court-directed police reforms, he must use the full force of his judicial authority and initiate contempt proceedings. The bogus concept of 'judicial overreach', floated by apologists of government inaction, certainly would not apply were he to act decisively.

Only by wrenching control of law enforcement away from politicians will we have an effective, modern and accountable police force. The Election Commission's strict code of conduct has dramatically reduced incidents of violence and booth-capturing in recent years. An autonomous, empowered police authority would similarly professionalize the law and order ecosystem in India and give citizens the twenty-first century police force they deserve.

A raft of economic, judicial and administrative reforms will lay the groundwork for good governance, reduce corruption and boost the economy. The benefits of renewed growth, to a large majority of Indians, as our chart on an earlier page shows, is reason enough to pursue these reforms with single-minded purpose.

7

THE FEUDAL CONGRESS

An empowered electorate will increasingly reward political parties that practise good internal governance and punish those that don't. The Congress party's top leadership knows that the tide has turned: growing public anger against corruption could severely damage its electoral prospects. This fear of losing power has sent a stab of fear through the Congress. That fear could yet prove productive if it ignites internal party reforms ahead of the next general election.

The Congress has less time than it thinks to reform itself. India underwent three quickfire general elections between 1996 and 1999. The Congress lost all three.

The architecture of misgovernance has been built over decades of feudal politics. In no modern democracy does a political party depend so heavily as the Congress does on a centralized, opaque leadership. Key political decisions are made by a coterie who owe their positions to loyalty and not merit.

Over the last fifty years, the Gandhi dynasty has ebbed and flowed but never lost its vice-like grip over the Congress. Many Congressmen have challenged it and formed their own parties. Some have succeeded—Sharad Pawar and Mamata Banerjee, for example. Others have failed and sunk into oblivion—or returned. The lesson has been learned by all Congressmen: in feudal, poverty-struck India, it pays to stick with the Gandhis.

Mrs Gandhi won the 1971 general election on the back of the slogan 'Garibi Hatao'. Ever since, poverty has been nurtured to ensure unenlightened voting influenced by caste, region and religion, underwritten by money and muscle power.

Mrs Gandhi realized early on in her prime ministership that minorities were a reliable votebank as well. They, too, were nurtured—but not educated, not enlightened, not empowered. Instead, they were fed paranoia about 'communal forces' taking over if they didn't vote for the 'secular' Congress.

Opposition parties saw how successful Mrs Gandhi's strategy was and they duly copied her. Political dynasties sprung up everywhere. By the 1980s, family-run parties were the norm. Mahatma Gandhi, who had wanted to disband and reconfigure the Congress after Independence, would have been aghast at today's proliferation of Yadavs, Pawars, Hoodas, Badals, Thackerays, Abdullahs and Karunanidhis.

Sonia's father-in-law, Feroze Gandhi, fought corruption throughout his short, eight-year parliamentary career. He died of a heart attack in 1960 at the age of forty-eight when son Rajiv was just sixteen. Born in September 1912, his centenary passed virtually unnoticed. No Congress leader lauded Feroze's enormous contribution in exposing corruption in public life.

Feroze's parliamentary seat of Rae Bareli was 'inherited' by, first, his widow, Indira, and later by his daughter-in-law, Sonia. Feroze believed in open, transparent governance. The Congress, too, stood by that principle. Nehru himself took regular questions from press and public alike. The silence and secrecy that surrounds today's Congress leadership would have been anathema to him.

In a parliamentary democracy, there is only one centre of gravity, never two. In Britain, for example, the buck stops at 10 Downing Street. No caveats, no detours. In the UPA government, the buck does not stop at all: it skips between 7 Race Course Road and 10 Janpath. The ambiguity is deliberate. Speaking in two voices—the government's and the party's—allows the Congress to be flexible with facts. Prime Minister Manmohan Singh bears full constitutional accountability for the government's acts of omission and commission. But, in practice, he does not have absolute authority over those acts. The veto lies with 10 Janpath.

■

Sonia Gandhi, meanwhile, confronts three problems but has solutions to only two. The first problem is the choice of the UPA's prime ministerial candidate in 2014. If the Congress wins more than 150 seats, the answer is Rahul Gandhi. If it doesn't, and it is unlikely it will, the answer becomes more complicated. The focus will turn to finding an interim CEO for the party to replace Dr Manmohan Singh, who will be eighty-two years old in September 2014.

The options though are not electrifying: the reliable but colourless Defence Minister A.K. Antony, the ambitious and mercurial Finance Minister P. Chidambaram, the affable but controversial Home Minister Shushil Kumar Shinde, the speaker of the Lok Sabha, Meira Kumar, and, as a last resort, the family faithful Digvijaya Singh—though his elevation would be considered equivalent to scraping the bottom of a rather empty barrel.

Mrs Gandhi's second problem is rebuilding the party organization in the states from the grassroots which she has left largely to Congress Vice President Rahul and his young team to come to grips with. Her third problem is public perception. The UPA is widely regarded as corrupt. It is held responsible for inflation. It has presided over an economic slowdown. And it has encouraged the worst excesses of crony capitalism.

In 1947, Mahatma Gandhi, freedom achieved, wanted to form new political organizations to contest elections. Sardar Vallabhbhai Patel agreed. Pandit Jawaharlal Nehru did not. Nehru's view prevailed.

Two decades later, in 1969, Indira Gandhi split the Congress to sideline the syndicate of regional satraps led by K. Kamaraj and S. Nijalingappa. The organizational and state-level decline of the Congress began in 1969, though Mrs Gandhi's 1971 election victory and the euphoria over the Bangladesh war disguised it for nearly a decade.

Nehru inherited a colonial administration. After Independence, it continued to serve the government in power. Colonial laws had been written to often protect British injustice, not deliver justice to Indians. Many remain cast in stone 150 years later, delaying and denying justice to ordinary Indians. Yet, Nehru did not impose chief ministers on states. The party's local organization was given a relatively free hand to choose its regional leaders. Indira Gandhi reversed that policy. She imposed state chief ministers, suspended intra-Congress elections, dismissed opposition state governments under Article 356 and undermined the judiciary.

The important lesson for Sonia Gandhi to absorb is to not follow her mother-in-law's autocratic policies but hew instead to Nehru's liberal, transparent leadership. Nehru made many errors: Jammu & Kashmir, China, the United Nations Security Council and even sowing the seeds of dynasty by appointing members of his family to high office—from Indira to his sister Vijaya Lakshmi Pandit. The last thing the battered Congress needs is to emulate Nehru's few missteps and ignore the many excellent examples of governance he set.

In 1998, Sonia took charge of a party fraying at the edges. Sixteen years later, having become the longest-serving president in Congress history, the party's edges have frayed further. In 1999, the Congress won 114 seats in the Lok Sabha, the lowest in its history. To avoid falling below that in 2014, Mrs Gandhi has to solve the leadership problem, strengthen the organization at the grassroots in the states, and restore public confidence.

With its vast army of workers and an overflowing party treasury, the Congress remains a formidable force. It has been underestimated before—in 1980 and again in 2004—when it was supposed to lose the general election but didn't. It can resolve its first two problems—leadership and reorganizing the states—with the right strategies. The third—public perception—may prove more intractable. On that could rest its fate in 2014.

■

The Congress hasn't held a serious internal election for the post of party president for sixteen years. When you neglect democracy within, can you protect democracy without? If Rahul Gandhi is serious about transforming his party into a modern political organization, he must implement three key reforms.

First, ensure internal democracy by holding a free and fair election for party president in which, putting self-interest aside, no member of the Gandhi family offers to stand. Young, professional talent can then rise to the top.

Second, give the prime minister unchallenged authority over all cabinet and policy decisions for the remainder of his term. Power must shift from 10 Janpath to 7 Race Course Road—where it belongs.

Third, end the practice of giving tickets to candidates with criminal backgrounds. Political parties fund their election campaigns with black money from criminal elements and cynically exploit voters on the basis of caste, religion and region.

According to self-attested affidavits submitted by members of parliament to the Election Commission, 162 MPs (nearly 31 per cent of the current Lok Sabha) have criminal chargesheets pending against them. Of these, seventy-two MPs (including fourteen from the Congress) are charged with serious criminal offences: murder, kidnapping, extortion and rape.

The actions of these elected MPs, and those who gave them tickets to stand for parliament, subvert our democracy. Parliament represents the will of the people. The Congress must absorb that democratic axiom and shed its feudal skin.

■

Ponder too the price these feudal parliamentarians exact. Start with accommodation. Most MPs live in or around Lutyens Delhi. Estimated real estate value? Rs 300-700 crore, depending on the size of the bungalow. Ministers—and we have seventy-seven, including ministers of state—obviously get the biggest plots. Many of our 545 Lok Sabha and over 240 Rajya Sabha MPs are multimillionaires and perfectly capable of owning their homes, saving the exchequer a tidy sum.

At Rs 6 lakh a year, MPs' salaries are modest—justifiably so, given the declining number of days parliament functions—but the perks of office compensate. American senators earn a generous annual salary of $1,74,000 but are entitled to relatively modest perks and live in homes that cost a fraction of Indian MPs' bungalows. British MPs receive an annual salary of £65,000. Singapore's largely technocratic legislators command among the world's highest salaries for public servants (S$2,25,000 per year) but again, like their American and British counterparts, enjoy relatively few perks.

In India, the term 'perks of office' has assumed ominous connotations. Becoming an MP is expensive. According to the Election Commission, a winning MP spends an average of Rs 10 crore on a Lok Sabha election and a successful MLA spends Rs 2-3 crore on a state assembly election.

How are these funds raised? First, through cash donations from large, medium and small companies. Second, through bribes from public-private partnership (PPP) projects (airports and national highways among others), large civic works (the Commonwealth Games, for example) and natural resource allocations (2G Spectrum, mines, land). Third, kickbacks from myriad government procurements (including defence ordnance purchases).

All of this points to one conclusion: a broken electoral system. Politicians need far too much money to fight elections. Their parties are forced to fund them with ill-gotten black money. Once elected, MPs pay back their parties' benefactors the only way they can—by engaging in corrupt practices themselves.

It is a vicious cycle. To break it, Prime Minister Manmohan Singh, UPA Chairperson Sonia Gandhi and Congress Vice President Rahul Gandhi have all at different times in recent months suggested state funding of elections. Examine the idea: suppose the state (i.e. the taxpayer) funds 543 MPs in the 2014 Lok Sabha election at a realistic minimum of Rs 1 crore per MP. That would mean more than doubling the current limit the EC imposes on MPs' electoral expenditure (Rs 40 lakh). Even if this were done, and assuming just five candidates on average from EC-registered parties contest every Lok Sabha seat, the state would have to fund over 2,700 candidates, allocating a separate state-funded budget of more than Rs 2,700 crore.

Would it solve the problem? Of course it wouldn't. Corrupt candidates would simply add the state's Rs 1 crore fund to the black money their parties spend on them anyway (an average of Rs 10 crore per winning candidate). The toxic corporate-political nexus—and the post-election quid pro quo—would continue. Honest, independent candidates relying only on state funding still wouldn't stand a chance.

The real solution lies in introducing legislation to give the EC regulatory powers to monitor party expenditure at every level—district, state and central. Today, political parties are exempt from paying tax, immune from financial oversight and allowed to function unregulated except for the brief period before and during an election when the EC's model code of conduct kicks in.

Empowering the EC to audit electoral expenses on a continuous basis, with punitive powers to deregister and derecognize erring political parties, is the best way to cauterize political corruption at its root. MPs (rightly) demand tough regulatory oversight for every profession (including the media) but resist meaningful financial oversight over political parties, including through the Right To Information (RTI) Act. The price Indians pay for that—in terms of unbridled corruption and Lutyens's wastefulness—is a price we should no longer be willing to pay.

As India's oldest party, the Congress has an obligation to set the standard of political conduct, not lower it. To do that it must abandon feudalism and transform itself into a modern, democratic organization—or jeapordize its long-term electability.

8
WHAT THEY DON'T TEACH AT HARVARD BUSINESS SCHOOL

Question: how do you convert Rs 50 lakh into Rs 1,600 crore? You won't get an answer from any of the learned professors at Harvard Business School. But you will if you hire a clever Indian chartered accountant.

Here's how it goes. You run a political party. You accept 'donations' from the public. Your audited balance sheets show that, between 2004-05 and 2010-11, you received Rs 2,008 crore in donations—officially. As a political party you are exempt from all taxes—income tax, service tax, capital gains tax. So you have a fairly healthy corpus of reserves which you are supposed to use—as per Election Commission guidelines—strictly for 'political' purposes.

So what do you do? Why, you go right ahead and give an unsecured loan of Rs 90 crore from your political party's healthy fund reserves, built through public donations, to a defunct newspaper publishing company.

This company, by sheer coincidence, has a debt of Rs 90 crore. The loan from your party extinguishes that debt and makes the defunct newspaper publishing company debt-free and employee-free.

But does the defunct newspaper publishing company have any

value? Well, it owns, among other assets, a large building in the heart of Delhi on land specifically granted to newspaper publishing companies to publish newspapers. The estimated value of the building? Rs 1,600 crore (excluding, of course, other properties scattered across India, worth over Rs 5,000 crore, that the publishing company owns).

So, here we have a defunct newspaper publishing company which does not publish anything, much less a newspaper, with zero debt, zero employees, near-zero sundry expenses—and a building in Delhi valued at Rs 1,600 crore.

Now what? Your clever Indian chartered accountant, not all those learned professors at Harvard Business School, provides the answer: float a new non-profit company to buy up the defunct company's shares for a token Rs 50 lakh.

Kosher? Absolutely.

Laws broken? Perhaps.

But it will take a decade or more to prove they were—if they were—and public memory is conveniently short.

But, your spokesmen say, the political party made 'no commercial gain' from the Rs 90-crore loan transaction. Exactly. The political party in fact made a commercial loss of Rs 90 crore (the unsecured loan). The commercial gain was made by the new non-profit company which now owns a building in Delhi valued at Rs 1,600 crore, having paid just Rs 50 lakh to buy 100 per cent shareholding in the defunct newspaper publishing company.

Interestingly, 76 per cent of the shares of this new asset-rich but non-profit company belong to two senior leaders of the party. Since the defunct newspaper publishing company was owned by dozens of now-deceased shareholders of the grand old party, should not the shares of the new non-profit company belong to the party as a cooperative rather than to a few select individuals? Ah, but this is no ordinary political party. It's a family enterprise.

What next? No newspaper is being published from the building.

All staff have left. The building is empty. The clever Indian chartered accountant regards this as a criminal waste of real estate.

Rent it out, he says, and you do. The income, after all, can always be set off against expenditure designated under the head 'charitable purposes' so that your balance sheet shows no profit. That takes care of the letter, if not the spirit, of the law.

Is renting space in your building illegal? It may not be if your new company has as one of its objectives in its Articles of Association the business of renting real estate. And if it doesn't, it can always be appended later by your clever chartered accountant.

If, on the other hand, you now restart the paper, under media and political duress, all the floors of the building will be needed for operations. Hundreds of retrenched staff will have to be rehired. The current income from rent will vanish into the paper. Expenditure will spiral. Daily newspapers can lose as much as Rs 100 crore a year. Another Rs 90 crore debt write-off may be required in the near future. So restarting a newspaper under duress is a poor option, your chartered accountant tells you.

But what would the Harvard Business School professor, having heard both sides of the story, recommend you do?

Simple. Reverse the entire transaction, he'd say. Return the Rs 90-crore unsecured loan to your political party. Restore ownership of the Rs 1,600-crore building (and other associated properties) to the original defunct newspaper publishing company by transferring back to it the 100 per cent shareholding your new non-profit company bought from it for Rs 50 lakh.

If you do that, this episode will become required reading as a Harvard Business School case study titled: 'How To Place Public Interest Above Private Interest'.

And if you don't? You might well lose the next general election and have to restart the newspaper after all.

9
THE POLITICS OF RELIGION

Uttar Pradesh Chief Minister Akhilesh Yadav's decision to re-examine the cases of jailed Muslims charge-sheeted for terrorism is an example of how 'secular' parties like the Samajwadi Party communalize society for narrow political ends. The poorer Muslims are, the easier it is to bank their votes. Muslim intellectuals and public figures rarely challenge such regressive politics. They must not be afraid to speak up.

Poverty and alienation have created an underclass of young Muslims who are driven to lives of crime, especially in states like Uttar Pradesh where Muslims comprise over 19 per cent of the population. Statistically, the number of Muslims convicted (not simply accused) of terrorism and other crimes is far higher than the community's ratio in the general population. The principal culprit: politicians who promise Muslims job quotas and other sops but keep them mired in poverty. They harm the cause of Muslims while masquerading as their protectors. The result: a community's alienation from the mainstream and a sense of victimhood.

In India, educated Muslims and liberal Hindus fall easy prey to the minority-as-victim narrative. They endorse a fraudulent policy of appeasement—through job quotas and special privileges—which widens, not narrows, communal cleavages. Such well-intentioned policies do more harm than good to the cause of ordinary Muslims frozen in poverty and social backwardness.

Political parties which win significant Muslim votes have little interest in educating Muslims or improving their economic condition. If they did, they would have by now implemented far more of the recommendations of the 2006 Rajinder Sachar and 2007 Ranganath Misra Commission reports. They know that the educated Muslim will ask them uncomfortable questions about development at the time of elections. An educated voter is anathema to most politicians, especially those wedded to the appeasement rather than the advancement of a community. In poverty, the Muslim is a bankable vote. In enlightenment, he is not.

■

Clerics are largely responsible for spreading regressive ideas among the faithful. Like political leaders who often create a sense of paranoia among Muslims in order to win votes, the clergy does the same to keep their flock in medieval darkness. Most Islamic clerics exacerbate the fear that has been instilled in poor, vulnerable Muslims by the cottage industry of neoliberals—who serve their political masters, not the national interest.

The more paranoid and resentful the Muslim, the more tightly shackled he is to regressive ideas. Clerics have little to offer them by way of modern education, fairer personal laws and economic advancement. Playing on the false fears of ordinary Muslims—who, as the Sachar Committee report confirms, are poorer than even Dalits—enables cynical clerics to exercise power over the faithful, a power that they deliberately misuse against their own.

These clerics are the average Muslims' worst enemies, sterilizing them in the Dark Ages. The haggling last year between Shahi Imam Ahmed Bukhari of Jama Masjid and Azam Khan of the SP over ministerial posts for the imam's relatives in the Uttar Pradesh cabinet demonstrates how religion and politics undermine good governance, promote nepotism and damage the interests of ordinary Muslims. The riots in Muzaffarnagar and other parts of Uttar Pradesh over the past year have deeply polarized the electorate—to, ironically, the SP's disadvantage.

Parties like the Congress, the SP, the NCP and the All-India Majlis-e-Ittehadul Muslimeen (AIMIM) promise Muslims succour but give them segregation. Like counterfeit currency, they commit a fraud on an unsuspecting target and Muslim clerics are fully complicit in it.

Are Hindus too soft? Has a thousand years of foreign invasions broken their spirit? Hinduism is the world's most evolved and tolerant religion. It is so open-ended that it is vulnerable to both internal and external abuse.

Over a period of nearly 5,000 years, Hinduism has allowed itself to sanctify an egregious caste system. It has also allowed invaders to subjugate it. When confronted with a choice between war and peace, Hinduism has, more often than not, chosen peace. It has never proselytized abroad. Where Hinduism has spread globally, it has been through priests, pilgrims, traders, travellers and migrants. This is in sharp contrast to at least two of the three Abrahamic faiths, Christianity and Islam, which have invaded, conquered, colonized and converted.

But men of peace are sometimes taken for granted by those who mistake tolerance for weakness. And so it has been with Hinduism. Its civilizational character—tolerance, generosity and uncritical acceptance of other faiths—has allowed political parties to indoctrinate enough liberal Hindus and paranoid Muslims to win elections.

However, this trend is rapidly reversing as Muslims gain education and lose their false sense of paranoia. This process should now be catalysed by responsible governance which encourages Muslims to join India's vibrant mainstream—with all its flaws but outstanding future.

■

Muslim intellectuals, alas, rarely speak up in favour of modernity. Intellectual, creative Muslims—in business, film and the arts—are among the worst offenders. Their silence can be mistaken for complicity—or at best callowness.

On the whole though, poor, ordinary Muslims are more sinned against than sinners. Their insularity is a defensive reflex. Bereft of education, of direction and of icons, they are vulnerable to the politicians and clerics who prey on them.

Indian politicians in particular have done a grievous wrong to the cause of Muslims by treating them as votes rather than a minority in need of education and empowerment. Tokenism now stands thoroughly discredited. Liberal Muslims and Hindus must in one voice expose and condemn those who pose the real threat to a plural, peaceful and prosperous India.

■

Religion is, of course, not India's only faultline. Beyond inter-religion strife lies intra-Hindu conflict: caste. And it has been used as vote fodder for decades as well. Ironically, as quotas for Other Backward Castes (OBCs) were thrust down India's publicly-funded educational system in 2007, the beginning of the 150th anniversary year of the First War of Independence in 1857 passed silently. Caste was central to the mutiny.

In January 1857, a Brahmin sepoy from a British regiment stationed in Dum Dum, five miles north of Calcutta, then capital of Britain's Indian empire, ran into a khalasi, a low-caste sepoy. The khalasi asked the Brahmin for a drink of water from his lota. The Brahmin refused, saying: 'I have scoured my lota, you will defile it with your touch.' Deeply affronted, the low-caste sepoy replied with some vengeful delight: 'You think much of your caste, but wait a little, the sahib-log (Englishmen) will make you bite cartridges soaked in cow and pork fat and then where will your caste be?'

The Brahmin sepoy, reduced to smouldering silence, quickly carried the news to his comrades in the 34th NI British regiment. The rumour spread like wildfire. Both high-caste Hindus and Muslims were aghast. To touch by one's teeth the fat of the cow and the pig violated the most deeply-held religious beliefs of the two communities.

For Brahmins, the cow is sacred and biting gum cartridges greased with the lard of a cow or ox would be sacrilegious. It would also almost instantly cause them to be ostracized. The seeds of the mutiny were sown. Between January and May 1857, anger swelled. Brahmin sepoys began the revolt slowly. Those attached to the 34th NI stationed in Barrackpore refused on 26 February 1857 to receive their percussion caps for the rifle parade the next morning as they suspected that the cartridges were greased with cow and pork fat.

Gradually, the revolt spread. At the 34th NI, where it had all started, the feelings were particularly intense. A sepoy named Mangal Pandey was the leader of the revolt. He called upon his fellow-soldiers to 'join him to defend and die for their religion and caste'.

Pandey, of course, was tried and executed. The 34th NI was disbanded. The British thought they had contained the revolt. They were grievously wrong. The incidents of Barrackpore were repeated at Ambala towards the end of March 1857 and at Lakhanau (Lucknow) in May 1857.

■

The manner in which the British put down the spreading mutiny is a story in itself. British officers and loyal Indian sepoys went on a carnage, burning village after village, spreading terror with their summary mass executions. Over 2 million people were brutally killed in 1857 and 1858. It was the beginning of the end of the British Indian empire for trust between ruler and subject had irrevocably broken down.

The British would be able to extend their occupation of India for another ninety years only with continuous and brute force. The fall of Delhi led to some of the worst atrocities. One eyewitness wrote at the time in a well-chronicled diary: 'Delhi was practically deserted by the inhabitants within a few days of its fall. Large numbers had perished at the hands of the infuriated British soldiers. Enormous treasures were looted and each individual soldier amassed a rich booty. Almost every house and shop in Delhi had been ransacked and plundered after its inmates were killed irrespective of whether they were actual rebels.'

The 1857 War of Independence began with caste. A century and a half later, caste remains as ubiquitous and divisive in India though there has been much social progress, especially in southern India. Excessive reservations of 27 per cent based on OBC quotas have made caste a major social and political issue. The Allahabad High Court's 'ban' on caste-based political rallies in Uttar Pradesh received a mixed response from a polity still mired in casteist rhetoric.

For a truly caste-less society that we must all aim for, reservations on economic criteria are clearly preferable to caste-based reservations. Create an EBC (Economically Backward Candidate) quota—whether they be Brahmins or 'low-caste' khalasis. Those students who deserve educational reservations must do so because they are poor and otherwise denied equal opportunities, not because they belong to a particular caste. With EBC quotas replacing OBC quotas, India will in a generation create opportunities for the poor as well as damp down the tensions that caste differences inevitably create. We cannot banish caste overnight. But we can heal the fissures it causes in a young, sensitive and evolving nation.

•

In post-1990 Mandal India, caste has become an instrument to extract political advantage. In two of India's most caste-sensitive states—Bihar and Uttar Pradesh—the rise of leaders like Mayawati,

Lalu Prasad Yadav, Mulayam Singh Yadav and Ram Vilas Paswan has fractured politics and hampered development for well over two decades after former Prime Minister V.P. Singh changed caste equations forever in 1990.

Dealing with divisions over caste and religion are two of India's most protracted problems. A society that is not free of bias cannot deliver—as it should—equality, justice and prosperity to all its people.

10

THE SINECURE INDUSTRY

The 2012 presidential election threw up two key questions. First, has the respect presidents were once held in declined? Second, should the president be chosen from a strictly non-party background? The answer to each question is yes.

There has been little serious discussion on the two principal qualities the president of the Indian Republic should possess: political neutrality and the toughness to stand up, when required, to the government. Dr Rajendra Prasad, Dr S. Radhakrishnan and Dr Zakir Hussain, India's first three presidents, had both of these qualities in abundance. But since 1969, when Indira Gandhi politicized the presidential election to take control of a split Congress party and install V.V. Giri as president, the Rashtrapati Bhavan's authority and credibility have gradually ebbed.

The symptoms aren't restricted to Rashtrapati Bhavan. A 'favoured' politician, bureaucrat, CBI director or army chief will inevitably get a lucrative post-retirement sinecure. He or she could become an ambassador, a governor or chairperson of an organization like the National Human Rights Commission (NHRC). The ability of the government to grant such grace-and-favour postings after retirement to public servants is unlimited.

Is this important? Why should it matter if an upright retired army general becomes the ambassador to Sweden or if an outstanding retired judge is appointed governor of Tamil Nadu? It matters for several reasons. First, it creates an atmosphere of cronyism in public service. A 'loyal' bureaucrat, general or judge will almost always be rewarded with a prestigious post-retirement sinecure. If, on the other hand, he shows a whiff of independence during his career and puts public interest ahead of vested political interests, he can look forward, after the age of sixty, to a pension but little else besides attending seminars organized by NGOs.

Second, the sinecure system creates a sense of insecurity in public servants. It is designed to do just that. Sinecures are a subtle form of political control. Just as private sector businessmen are kept in check through a tortuous system of clearances over land, environment and other cannily-erected regulations which have replaced the Licence Raj, senior bureaucrats, judges, army officers and revenue officials are dependent on the government for untaxing post-retirement work.

The very existence of prestigious post-retirement posts brimful with the perks of office—free housing, cars, staff, travel and expense accounts—extracts pliant behavior from officers through decades in government service. Upright, independent-minded officers who challenge this cronyism within the system are quickly identified as troublemakers and either sidelined over promotions or pushed into a corner so that early voluntary retirement is often their only option. The vast majority of honest and efficient officers soldier on, unable to change the system. Like crony capitalism, crony officialdom barters favours to advance private interests, not the public interest.

■

The rot has spread from the bureaucracy and politics to the defence services, where corruption is now endemic. Most of the accused in the 2G Spectrum, Commonwealth Games and Coalgate scams are serving or former bureaucrats, army officers and politicians.

The nexus is rooted in the practice of privilege. Public servants know that a rewarding official post-retirement assignment awaits them if they are part of this nexus. It is a self-perpetuating system, much like an atomic clock, never missing a beat. It receives guaranteed protection from those at the very top of this corrupt political food chain.

■

Is there an alternative? The clear remedy is to pass legislation to disallow former public servants from holding high constitutional, statutory or consular office after retirement. That would rule out the appointment of former judges, IAS officers and armed forces chiefs in sinecure posts, and reduce the scope for cronyism during their service years. There are many academics, eminent professionals and other distinguished private citizens—wholly divorced from politics—who can be appointed to such posts.

The time of retired senior judges can be put to more productive use heading special arbitration courts to bring down the number of pending litigation cases (currently over 32 million). Similarly, retired senior army personnel can serve national interest far better by heading training centres for anti-insurgency and counterterrorism operations. Former bureaucrats can help set up task forces to implement long overdue administrative reforms rather than hanker after ambassadorships, governorships, chairmanships of statutory government bodies and other sinecure postings.

We inherited a colonial administrative grid from the British designed to perpetuate a master-serf relationship. Reforming this corroded system is where the minds of political leaders, distinguished retired army generals, government secretaries and senior judges should be focused. Not on quid pro quo sinecures which can compromise the independence of public servants during their years in office. A 'committed' judiciary, army, bureaucracy and polity is not in the interest of anyone except those who thrive on granting and receiving privilege.

Reform must begin from the top. It is time to stop using Rashtrapati Bhavan as India's most expensive retirement home for loyalist politicians and restore it as the country's moral centre of gravity by installing an occupant with an independent mind. Whether the present incumbent, Pranab Mukherjee, posseses one will be put to severe test in the coming months.

11
THE RIGHT TO KNOW

The move to place political parties under the Right To Information Act has drawn sharp protests from every major political party. The principal argument: political parties are not public authorities.

Under Section 2(h) of the RTI Act, 2005, a public authority is defined as any 'non-governmental organization substantially financed, directly or indirectly, by funds provided by the appropriate government'. The Congress and the BJP, for instance, received Rs 2,008 crore and Rs 994 crore respectively between 2004-05 and 2010-11 from mostly undisclosed sources.

Placing political parties under the RTI Act will open politics to public scrutiny, regulate political party funding and clean up our electoral ecosystem. Transparency will also discourage transactions such as the Congress's reported Rs 90-crore loan to a non-profit company, Young Indian, owned by Congress President Sonia Gandhi and Vice President Rahul Gandhi.

The prospect of submitting themselves to public scrutiny through RTI has united political parties across the ideological spectrum. The political class has much to lose by operating in a transparent ecosystem. The public, though, has everything to gain.

Because politics is seen as a 'rentier' profession, with huge rewards post-election, the demand for seats vastly outstrips supply. There are 543 directly elected Lok Sabha MPs, 250 collegium-elected Rajya Sabha MPs and over 4,000 MLAs. Winning a seat in Parliament or the assemblies is seen as a ticket to wealth, not public service. The result is that three kinds of people are given tickets by most political parties: those who can pay for it; those who belong to political dynasties; and those who can draw votes based on religion or caste.

The Election Commission concedes that its Rs 40 lakh expenditure limit for Lok Sabha candidates (Rs 25 lakh for the Vidhan Sabha) is routinely violated. The average expenditure per Lok Sabha seat for a candidate belonging to a mainstream party is estimated at between Rs 10 crore and Rs 20 crore. The public admission by BJP leader Gopinath Munde that he spent Rs 9 crore on his 2009 Lok Sabha election may have got him into trouble with the Election Commission but it surprised no one.

Parties fund some of their candidates. In most cases, candidates 'sponsor' their own candidatures. Both party and candidate have two sources of funding: corporate donations and money skimmed off scams. With around 3,000 serious candidates contesting 543 Lok Sabha seats, the cash that courses through every Lok Sabha election is over Rs 30,000 crore.

Black money from illegal gratification in PPP projects, social welfare schemes, land allotments and natural resource allocations, bolsters candidates' spending power. The EC's tough monitoring has been unable to stem the relentless flow of unaccounted cash into elections.

The scourge of black money in elections can be reduced by introducing a system of detailed audit of all registered political parties. The Comptroller and Auditor General has 48,000 employees. It can, jointly with the EC, execute a rigorous quarterly audit of political party funding and expenditure. This audit should be made public.

Failure to get an EC-CAG audit certificate every quarter would disqualify the party from putting up a candidate for that seat in the next assembly or Lok Sabha election. The deterrent may not eliminate corrupt funding of candidates but it will reduce it significantly.

■

To infuse merit into our legislatures, it is critical to make it harder for criminals to become MPs or MLAs. To strengthen the Supreme Court-imposed legal bar, add another filter: a three-member adjudicating committee comprising the chief election commissioner (CEC), the chief vigilance commissioner (CVC) and a Supreme Court judge to vet party candidates to ensure fairness (by sifting politically motivated chargesheets) and firmness (a party wilfully giving tickets to an ineligible candidate would be disqualified from contesting that seat even with another candidate). The fear of deterrent punishment will mitigate the epidemic of criminals in our parliament and assemblies.

The reform jigsaw needs one more element to enforce political accountability: an independent Central Bureau of Investigation. The government today controls the CBI's funds, transfers and promotions. Permission to prosecute lies with the department of personnel in the PMO and the home ministry.

Would an autonomous CBI be a law unto itself, as some fear? Not necessarily. It could be held accountable to a judicial oversight board comprising, for example, the chief justice of India, the CVC and the CEC. Any abuse of authority can be checked by such a robust mechanism.

The Supreme Court's seven-point directive on police autonomy, discussed in detail in an earlier chapter, can meanwhile be applied to the CBI. Of these seven directives, the fifth and sixth could apply immediately to an independent CBI: the creation of an autonomous Police Establishment Board to decide transfers, promotions and postings, and the establishment of a Police Complaints Authority. At present, the government's tepid moves, at the prodding of the Supreme Court, to give the CBI a semblance of autonomy are largely cosmetic.

Corruption will be a decisive issue in the 2014 general election. Corruption leads to misgovernance. Misgovernance exacerbates poverty and malnutrition because resources meant for the poor are siphoned off by political middlemen and local officials.

Congress spokespersons have in the past spoken of the 'tyranny of the unelected and unelectable'. The real tyranny, as events unfolding before us have shown, is the tyranny of the elected—and of those related to the elected. Politics in India is now a family business.

Politicians regard themselves above the people. They are wrong. Their job is to serve. The ministers and spokespersons who defend members of their feudal dynasties should understand whom they are accountable to—the aam aadmi who pays the bills of these feudal dynasties and their courtiers.

As Indian democracy evolves, poverty declines and literacy rises, the feudal order will fade. A democracy of, by and for the people must serve three purposes. It must reflect the peoples' will, encourage their participation in democratic governance and deliver benefits to them. That is the change we must wring from today's feudal governance.

Congress President Sonia Gandhi knows that the corruption charges levelled, for example, against her son-in-law Robert Vadra are a proxy attack on her and the Gandhi family. The Gandhi dynasty has retained its hold over the Congress so far because it controls huge financial resources.

Without resources, the party cannot fund its candidates. Its vote bank of the rural poor and minorities together provided the bulk of its 28.55 per cent national voteshare in the 2009 Lok Sabha election. If it does not nurture that votebank, the party will lose power and soon fall prey to centrifugal forces, splintering into little bits.

12
THE BLIGHT OF MISGOVERNANCE

Global business abhors uncertainty. The ministerial-level corruption in UPA-2 has slowed FDI and FII inflows. To take India's growth story forward in the twenty-third year of economic reforms, political reforms must catch up. Misgovernance won't do in a globalized, interconnected world.

Two kinds of political corruption blight India: episodical and ongoing. Episodical corruption—from the 2G Spectrum to Coalgate—has denuded the public exchequer. Ongoing corruption is more insidious and, therefore, more damaging. For example, over 10 per cent of India's installed power capacity of nearly 2,00,000 MW is stolen every year with government connivance. At least 35 per cent and possibly up to 50 per cent of funds allocated to MGNREGA are siphoned off by district level officials—an estimated loss of around Rs 20,000 crore per year. Illegal mining, water theft and land allotment frauds skim several thousand more crores of public funds.

All this public theft needs a nexus: politicians, businessmen and bureaucrats form the core and an army of district officials, contractors and middlemen form the base. Judicial oversight has replaced ministerial oversight in matters that lie firmly in the domain of the executive. The Supreme Court cannot—as it has been compelled to—play the role of the PMO.

The government must implement three urgent institutional reforms: One, enact legislation to give the Lokpal at the Centre and Lokayuktas in the states suo moto powers to prosecute ministers, MPs, MLAs and IAS officers. The proposed Lokpal bill is an eyewash. The bill gives the Lokpal advisory powers. He cannot prosecute a minister or MP accused of corruption without government approval. The alternative civil society Lokpal bill, which gives the Lokpal independent authority to prosecute ministers and other public servants, is the only way to attack corruption at its root.

Two, pass a special act of parliament to vest the Central Bureau of Investigation with statutory autonomy, like the Election Commission, freeing it from government control but with strong parliamentary and judicial oversight. This will allow the CBI to investigate and prosecute without fear, favour or fetter. The government's tepid moves to uncage the 'parrot', as the apex court described the CBI, have been merely cosmetic.

Three, end through constitutional amendment the practice of 'political' governors and speakers. The moment a governor or speaker is appointed, he or she should forfeit for life the right to serve in any other public office and also cease immediately and permanently to be a member of a political party. The Bhardwaj-Buta Singh model of governorship must be buried for good.

New anti-corruption legislation must allow for prosecution of ministers, bureaucrats and other public officials by an independent CBI and Lokpal. Land, mining and other natural resources—from spectrum to gas—must be taken out of discretionary government hands (state and central) by law not words. Bihar has effectively combated corruption by introducing special courts under the Bihar Special Courts Act. Under this act, such courts, headed by a sessions judge with high court approval, have the power to confiscate property and cash of government officials accused in corruption cases.

The role of the Election Commission is critical: the roots of political corruption lie in the black money used to fight elections. Candidates with criminal backgrounds buy themselves tickets while parties subvert voters with money and divisions of caste, religion and region.

To improve the quality of our democracy, the EC must impose term limitations for all office bearers in EC-registered political parties. No individual should be permitted to hold office for more than ten years. Internal elections to all party posts including for party president must be held every year. If the ten-year time limitation rule is violated, derecognition of the party would automatically follow. This will weaken the feudal structures of our dynastic political parties and strengthen India's democratic institutions. The restoration of global business confidence in India will be a natural corollary.

In the tenth and decisive year of his prime ministership, Dr Manmohan Singh is already India's longest serving prime minister after Jawaharlal Nehru (seventeen years) and Indira Gandhi (sixteen years). But history does not judge leaders by longevity. It judges them on performance. A see-no-evil, hear-no-evil technocratic PMO makes it vulnerable to malfeasance. That vulnerability lies at the heart of all the recent scams that have come to light, including 2G Spectrum and Coalgate.

Companies and politicians who have abused the system in the 2G Spectrum, Commonwealth Games and other frauds must now receive exemplary, not token, punishment. Without a credible deterrent, a new cast of characters will repeat a new set of crimes. It is equally vital for the government to break the nexus between politics and big business and to engage more frequently with the media. The relationship between the first and the fourth estate must be constructive but adversarial—and distant. Familiarity breeds complicity.

In a well-governed society, the relationship between the

government and the citizen is clearly defined. The people are sovereign. Through elections, they delegate the task of governing India to the cabinet. The lexicon of political discourse must concurrently change: ministers do not come to power, they take office; governments do not rule, they serve; the Congress is not the ruling party; it is the party in government. Language reflects mindset.

The prime minister must act on political reforms with the same seriousness he showed twenty-two years ago over economic reforms. As Edmund Burke, the eighteenth-century British-Irish statesman famous for impeaching Warren Hastings, warned: 'The only thing necessary for the triumph of evil is for good men to do nothing.'

As he nears the end of his decadal prime ministerial tenure—and of possibly his political career—Dr Manmohan Singh sadly appears to have neither the time nor the nous to heed Burke's warning.

13

THE SPIRIT IS WILLING BUT THE FLESH IS WEAK

If you tossed a coin to decide who is more corrupt—the average Indian politician or the average Indian bureaucrat—the coin wouldn't know which side to fall on. As Kaushik Basu, the former chief economic advisor to the Ministry of Finance (MoF) and now senior vice president and chief economist of the World Bank, wrote in *The Times of India*, reform of India's bureaucracy must now top the nation's agenda.

The IAS—which, for its do-nothing inertia, could easily stand for Indian Asphyxiation Service—has remained an elite bureaucratic system tied up in red tape. Today, apart from the red tape, it is also awash in corruption. The 2G Spectrum, Tatra trucks, coal mining, Adarsh and CWG scams were abetted by civil servants on behalf of politicians. None of these would have been possible without the connivance of the bureaucracy.

All efforts to reform the IAS have failed. The second Administrative Reforms Commission (ARC), headed by former Law Minister Veerappa Moily before he stepped down in December 2009, has not been implemented. Even the colonial-era nomenclature of its officers—district collector, for example—is a relic of the parasitical

British practice of collecting huge taxes from the peasantry, comprising nearly 50 per cent of their agricultural income.

The second ARC's report is an outstanding document with over fifteen closely argued, well-written chapters on reforming the bureaucracy. If implemented, it would transform the IAS and the quality of public services in India. That is a key challenge for the prime minister in the last few months of his ten-year tenure.

The British set up India's bureaucracy to control a vast nation with as few administrators as possible: no more than 1,000 officers of the Indian Civil Service (ICS) ran the lives of 300 million Indians. 'The ICS,' former British Prime Minister David Lloyd George declared, 'is the steel frame on which the whole structure of government and of administration in India rests.'

The ICS was peopled by bright young men from Britain's emerging middle class. They ran India efficiently but made tidy fortunes on the side. The seeds of bureaucratic corruption, sown by English hands 150 years ago, are in full viral bloom in India today. The number of politicians currently in jail or out on bail is matched only by the number of bureaucrats facing corruption charges.

Final responsibility—and power—for tax collection lay with ICS officers, driving Jawaharlal Nehru to remark caustically: 'The ICS, with which we are unfortunately still afflicted in this country, is neither Indian, nor civil, nor a service.' But India's first prime minister did very little himself to reform the ICS after Independence, apart from renaming it.

■

Over the years, the Ministry of Defence has come to be dominated by IAS generalists who, having served in Family Planning in Aurangabad or Animal Husbandry in Meerut, find themselves vetting complex defence deals of high-tech fighter jets and battle tanks worth several billion dollars. They fall easy prey to the rapacious arms lobby which has made the MoD a happy hunting ground. The nexus between

MoD bureaucrats, arms lobbyists and retired armed forces officers lies at the root of corruption in India's defence purchases.

There are, of course, outstanding, honest bureaucrats who work selflessly across sectors. Many are young, operate in India's most dangerous Naxal-infested areas and play a crucial role in bringing economically backward communities into the mainstream. But the steel frame of the civil service has become so rusted by years of rubbing up against the political class and middlemen representing vested business interests that the work of these few good men and women is often compromised.

The 'infrastructure' of corruption that rewards, instead of punishing, dishonesty has pushed India down to number ninety-five in Transparency International's ranking. In the spring of 1964, shortly before his death, Nehru was asked in private by his closest colleagues what he regarded as his greatest failure as India's first prime minister. Nehru replied: 'I could not change the administration. It is still a colonial administration and one of the main causes of India's inability to solve the problem of poverty.'

Prime Minister Manmohan Singh, himself a career bureaucrat—though not IAS—knew exactly what needed to be done to reform the bureaucracy. But as in other matters of governance, while his spirit was willing, the flesh was weak.

14
HOW THE BLACK ECONOMY SUBVERTS INDIA'S POLITICS

How much does it cost to run a political party? If you go by the audited balance sheet of the Congress for 2011-12 (the latest available), the answer is Rs 525.97 crore. This is a party with several million workers, offices in every one of our thirty-five states and union territories (UTs) and which fights an average of seven assembly elections each year. The audited balance sheet of India's second largest party, the BJP, is equally modest. Its annual expenditure for 2011-12: Rs 261.74 crore.

Who funds the gap? The parallel black economy. Estimates vary but the black (cash) economy constitutes roughly a third of India's nominal GDP of Rs 110 lakh crore. That amounts to over Rs 35 lakh crore. Of this, around Rs 35,000 crore courses through the political ecosystem every year. The bulk goes to political parties, MPs, MLAs and myriad office-bearers to run their political organizations, fight elections and buy votes. This is quite apart from the money siphoned off in the PDS, MGNREGA, Bharat Nirman, Public-Private Partnership projects and civic works and through outright scams like 2G Spectrum, Coalgate and the Commonwealth Games. Political parties are tax-exempt. They pay absolutely no tax—no income tax, no service tax, no professional tax, no TDS.

Approximately 3.50 crore Indians do pay income tax. The salaried middle class is the most diligent taxpayer. TDS is extracted from employers every quarter. The proposed move to GST will tax people at the point of consumption, not income. The richer you are, the more you consume—and the more you are taxed. It is a fairer system than one in which the very rich end up paying an average of 10-12 per cent of their gross income as tax and limited companies pay an average of just 13-15 per cent because of generous exemptions in corporation and personal tax, and excise and customs duties, and 'tax foregone'. (In contrast, the defence budget, at 2 per cent of GDP, is less than half of tax foregone on account of exemptions—in corporation and personal taxes, and excise and customs duties.)

A lot of the black money which evades tax washes up at the doorstep of political parties. The resultant quid pro quo between politicians, business and middlemen lies at the root of land, mining and natural resource scams in India. With better political governance, India's economy has the potential to grow at over 9 per cent a year. Misgovernance costs the economy at least 2-3 per cent in annual GDP growth on account of corrupt practices, poor infrastructure and retrograde taxation laws.

The long-term remedy for a malignant political ecosystem which rewards scamsters and punishes honest taxpayers is voter education. We need to rapidly achieve a critical threshold of an educated and enlightened electorate. As a result, political parties will find it increasingly difficult to exploit an empowered electorate on the spurious grounds of religion, caste and region. Election funding meanwhile must be made open and transparent. The Tata and Aditya Birla groups have dedicated trusts to donate funds officially to political parties, a model other corporate houses should follow.

■

In a reflection of how warped our electoral and political systems have become, the cumulative wealth of India's ten richest people is 6 per cent ($114.50 billion) of India's GDP. In comparision, the cumulative wealth of America's ten richest people is a mere 2 per cent ($311.30 billion) of America's GDP. For a poor country where poverty lines are defined at $0.46 a day, there could be no greater indictment of how the black economy has subverted political governance.

■

As declared 'public authorities', political parties must face at least the same level of scrutiny as, for example, listed entities governed by SEBI's strict regulatory code. Political parties must put up on their websites the latest audited balance sheets. Crucially, these balance sheets must reveal a list of all donors. It is important to know which business house or individual has donated how much to which party. Possible conflicts of interest would then unravel.

As an electoral reform, state funding is a red herring because it won't solve the problem of black money spent during elections. No audit can prevent illegal cash from going into the deep coffers of political parties. As long as India's black economy comprises an estimated one-third of the real economy, political parties—like businessmen—will exploit this structural lacuna. But mandatory public disclosure of the financial statements of political parties will be the first important step in stemming the use of black money in our political system, which sustains and nurtures corrupt electoral practices—from bribing voters in cash or kind to horse-trading of MLA and MPs.

Politicians exploit every voter vulnerability they can—poverty, illiteracy, caste, region and religion—with a combination of muscle power and money. This exploitation has damaged the evolution of our democracy. Voters have to rise above this—and they often do, as we saw recently in five assembly elections. But they would not need to if the attempt to exploit them was not made in the first place.

15
JUSTICE FOR KASHMIR'S PANDITS

Ten years ago, in August 2004, on my way to interview then Jammu & Kashmir Chief Minister Mufti Mohammad Sayeed at his heavily guarded Srinagar residence, the roads were deserted except for grim-faced armymen with assault rifles. Much has changed for the better in the Valley since, despite Pakistan's renewed attempts to foment terrorism. Many shops in Srinagar's Lal Chowk, shuttered a few years ago, are now open till midnight. And yet, serious problems continue to blight the Valley. The first, much debated, is granting greater autonomy to Kashmir within the elastic boundaries of the Indian Constitution. The second, much ignored, is the question of Kashmir's exiled Pandits.

India prides itself on its absolute commitment to protect minorities. In federal India, Muslims, Christians, Dalits and others receive that protection, constitutionally and legally. Sharia, not India's civil code, is the basis for Muslim personal law. Other faiths, including that of Parsis and Jews, have similar rights and guarantees. Today, while Jews have their homeland in Israel and Bosnia's Muslims have been resettled from where they were driven out by the Serbs, nearly three lakh Kashmiri Pandits remain in exile. Hurriyat separatist leaders publicly ask them to return to the Valley and offer them fraternal protection—but in a Valley that they say must be a part of Pakistan.

Kashmir is historically a plural land: Islam became its majority religion only in the thirteenth century. Sufi Islam and the gentle rishi tradition of the Valley's Hindus were complementary. Pandits and Muslims prayed at the same shrines. Later rulers were a mixed brew: Sikhs, Britons and Dogras. The key moment in the region's history came when the British sold Kashmir, which it had annexed from the Sikhs in 1846 after the first Anglo-Sikh war, for Rs 75 lakh to Gulab Singh, the Dogra Raja of Jammu and the great-grandfather of Maharaja Hari Singh who, a century later, would sign the instrument of accession of J&K to India.

By the early-1900s, the Dogra rulers had become unpopular across the region. J&K at the time had a population of 3.20 million—2.5 million Muslims and 0.70 million Hindus. Today, the state's population is around 11 million with Muslims comprising 7.50 million (67 per cent) and Hindus 3.40 million (31 per cent) of the total—a demography that has remained relatively unchanged for over 100 years except for the near-elimination of Hindus from the Valley.

Despite being such a large minority (more than double the Muslim minority of 13.50 per cent in India), 3.40 million Hindus in J&K have a muted political voice. The Congress does not espouse their cause for fear of losing its federal Muslim vote. The BJP is supportive but has limited political influence in the Valley. The National Conference (NC) plays to the gallery, the Peoples Democratic Party (PDP) to the separatists and the separatists to Pakistan.

Opinion polls have shown that less than 3 per cent of J&K's 11 million people want to be a part of Pakistan. The rest are divided between independence and continued union with India. The silent majority of the Valley's Muslims reject Islamist radicalism and support the return of the Pandits. The dialogue between India and Pakistan on trade across the LoC and confidence-building measures

(CBMs) in the Valley are positive signs of a new spirit of reconciliation among Kashmir's stakeholders.

Good governance, infrastructural development, non-intrusive policing and greater political autonomy can help integrate Kashmir constitutionally and emotionally into the Indian union. In this enabled environment, a way to end the exile of the Valley's peace-loving Pandits must be found.

SECTION 3
WORLD

1
BRITAIN'S APOLOGY TO AFRICA

One of the great hidden secrets of British colonialism is the slave trade. It was a 250-year-long trade that disgraced Britain and brutalized an entire continent. British historians routinely gloss over it and Africa, hit twice by European rapacity (first by the slave trade, then by the colonial carve-up of the continent in the nineteenth century once 'slaving' had officially ended), has not yet developed the historical scholarship to deal with and expose the full horrors of slave trafficking.

One of the pioneers of the largely British-run African slave trade (55 per cent of 'slavers' were British) was Sir John Hawkins, who captured and kidnapped Africans off the west coast of Sierra Leone. Most of the slaves endured a nightmarish journey from their home country to either the West Indies or North America where they were auctioned to British colonial settlers.

Lord Hugh Thomas, one of the world's most accomplished historians on the Atlantic slave trade, describes the hellish journey inland even before the slaves were packed on to the slave ships: 'The slaves were usually secured by placing the right leg of one and the left leg of another onto the same pair of fetters. If the fetters were connected by a string, these men could walk, though slowly.

Every four slaves might also be fastened together by the necks, with a strong rope of twisted thongs and, at night, additional fetters would be put on their hands. Sometimes, a chain would be passed round their necks. Those slaves who protested were imprisoned in a thick billet of wood about three feet long and, a smooth notch being made upon one side of it, the ankle of the slave was bolted to the smooth part by means of a strong staple, one ring of which was passed on each side of the ankle. All these fetters and bolts were made from African iron.'

In 2006, Andrew Hawkins, a descendant of Sir John Hawkins—the slaving pioneer—travelled to Gambia, a West African country from where thousands of Africans had been kidnapped and sold into slavery. He went, self-bound in chains, along with other chained white Englishmen and made a symbolic apology on behalf of his family to the people of Gambia. He was received by the vice president of Gambia, Isaton Njie Saidy, and 25,000 other ordinary Gambians.

Here, in Hawkins's words, is what happened next: 'I apologized on behalf of my family. I apologized for the adults and children taken. Then there was a long pause and we really didn't know what to expect—it was very nerve-wracking. They could have said, "We don't accept your apology, go away," and we were ready for that—it would have been understandable. But the vice president came forward and accepted the apology very graciously. She offered her forgiveness and then came forward and took the chains off. That was entirely impromptu and very moving.'

Hawkins's apology was part of a series of symbolic gestures of penance organized by a group called The Lifeline Expedition which aims at achieving reconciliation between Europeans and Africans. As Hawkins admitted, that won't be easy. 'The action [of the slave traders] caused evil throughout the continent of Africa.'

Hawkins and his volunteers apologized to the vice president of Gambia for the terrible injustice caused by Britain to Africa. But so far, no British prime minister has even hinted at a formal apology. The reason: an official government apology to Africa for the slave trade would open the floodgates for financial reparations and punitive damages for the crimes committed on the African people over a 250-year-long period. And those punitive damages would be substantial.

The small compensation British courts have forced the UK government to give to the victims of the Mau Mau uprising in Kenya in the 1950s, based on classified documentary evidence recently made public in Britain, is the thin edge of the wedge.

Consider: Africa was denuded of its most able-bodied male workforce for ten generations. The loss to the continent's minerals-rich economy was staggering. While the rest of the world was industrializing in the eighteenth and nineteenth centuries, Africa was Europe's slave pit. Nearly 20 million young Africans were captured and sold into lifelong captivity in North and South America and the West Indies.

At a notional, inflation-adjusted cost of $100,000 per person in terms of net lost lifelong wages in his own country, the punitive damages on Britain as the principal slaving country would amount to $2 trillion. Such reparations could change the face of modern Africa. But they would bankrupt Britain.

■

Slave trading, based on commerce, was justified by racism. White racism has a curious history. Before 1600 CE, it did not exist. Nor did nationalism. In 1600 CE, there were few 'nations'. The United States was a colony of new European settlements. Britain comprised two Celtic-Saxon islands made up of the constantly-warring states of England, Wales, Scotland and Ireland. The four formed a constitutional union (the United Kingdom) only in 1707. France, Spain, Holland, Portugal and Prussia were all a patchwork of pre-industrial fiefdoms with movable borders and little central authority.

Europeans trading with Indian or Chinese rulers in the 1600s were respectful, even obsequious. They came to flatter and profit, not insult and alienate. Things changed dramatically with the onset of the African slave trade. Britain, France, Spain and Portugal were the principal offenders.

Slaving made nouveau riche Europeans contemptuous of the poverty-stricken and helpless Africans they sold into lifelong bonded labour in the Americas and the Caribbean. Emboldened, European trader-adventurers now set about colonizing Asia, and later, Africa. The newly wealthy traders used guns and bribes to conquer vast tracts in the Indian subcontinent which had become politically fragmented in the wake of the dissipating Mughal Empire.

White racism thus has its roots in slavery and colonialism followed by invasive European settlements in countries like Australia and South Africa. Racism was a self-serving tool. It was both a bludgeon and a justification.

White slave traders and colonialists exploited Asian and African weaknesses (poor military technology and political disunity) to capture territory. From all this sprang many of the great injustices of the twentieth century—apartheid in South Africa, constitutionally-mandated black segregation in the United States and the official 'white Australia' immigration policy.

Some argue that even India has its skeletons—the caste system, for instance—and thus has no moral authority to condemn racism. This is disingenuous. Indian dalits have suffered enormously but not by constitutional mandate. They are protected by the Indian Constitution. In Australia, South Africa and the US, pernicious anti-coloured policies were official state law till a few decades ago.

The two ancient civilizations of India and China have (besides 1962) never fought a war with each other in recorded history. Compare that to the endless savage intra-European wars of England, France, Prussia, Spain and Russia over the last 1,000 years.

The principal exchange between India and China during the past 2,500 years was the teaching of Buddhist monks and Hindu priests. Europe's principal interaction during the same period was brutal, invasive warfare.

As Asia grows wealthier, the balance of power, as this book argues, is shifting back from West to East. But racism, slow to spread in the 1700s, will be equally slow to subside in the 2000s. Subside though it will. Europeans came to Asia over 400 over years ago as traders and supplicants. They spotted a vacuum, exploited it, made money, acquired power, abused that power and committed unspeakable crimes on those they conquered. Racial prejudice was a venal by-product of this. Like all by-products, it too will in time disappear.

When China and India once again become the world's pivots over the next few decades, its people must not repeat the mistake of the arriviste West. Humility and respect for others, as these two nations have shown through most of their history, are what separate great civilizations from great powers.

2
ISRAEL: THE FALSE PROMISE OF A DISPUTED LAND

Around 3,900 years ago, a man began a journey that was to lead to the longest and most violent military conflict in modern history.

The man, of course, was Abraham, the founder of Judaism. His journey began in the small, bustling town of Ur, in today's Iraq (then Mesopotamia), and ended in Hebron, in today's Israel. It is Abraham's legacy of the Promised Land stated in the Old Testament that has created the world's most vexed political problem today.

By all accounts an extraordinary man, Abraham left Ur around 1900 BCE. At the time, nearly 4,000 years ago, Ur was a civilized, developed town under the Ur Nammu, one of the more enlightened Mesopotamian kings.

Abraham migrated westwards to Palestine, the land of the Peleshets from whom the province gets its contemporary name and who were the ancient forebears of today's landless Palestinians. Abraham, while buying land in Hebron, wrote as a preface in the sale deed itself: 'I am a stranger and a sojourner with you.'

This emphasizes the immigrant status of Abraham and clearly bestows the ownership rights of Palestinian land in antiquity to the Peleshets and their descendants, the Palestinians. Hebron itself is a place of great beauty and peace, lying twenty miles south of Jerusalem and 3,000 feet up in the Judaen hills. Abraham and his wife, Sarah, are buried in an ancient sepulchre within the Tombs of the Patriarchs in the Cave of Machpelah.

So how do we tie up Abraham's founding of a great religion, Judaism, nearly 4,000 years ago with international politics today? The answer, of course, is Israel and Palestine, the terrible injustice done to the latter and the strong emotions that as a result attach themselves to the former.

The occupation—by over five million largely European Jews—of Palestine, was one of the stated causes of Osama bin Laden's crusade against the West, the 9/11 terror attacks and the determination of Iran to produce nuclear weapons.

Indeed, the biggest geopolitical threat to Israel remains Iran.

All civilized people have the deepest sympathy for those Jews who lost even a single family member in the holocaust during the Second World War. And yet there is an unacceptable ongoing injustice being perpetrated on the descendants of the Peleshets.

Alas, the Palestinians, who in the original United Nations plan to create a Jewish homeland after the Second World War, had received (rightfully) well over half of today's Israel for themselves, were betrayed by their fellow-Arabs as well as by the West. Obsessed with personal power, the feudocrats of Saudi Arabia, Jordan and Egypt fought three disastrous wars against Israel, each time ceding more territory to the Jewish state, while being aided and abetted by the US.

Today, the US has more Jews (nearly 6 million) than Israel itself (around 5.66 million). Israel receives more aid per capita from the US than any other country. It is virtually a US protectorate. And the Palestinians? They are widely acknowledged as the gentlest, most cultured of all Arabs. Yet today they are refugees in their own homes.

But history teaches us one lesson: to perpetrate a wrong is possible; to sustain it for long is not. A political solution that gives the Palestinians, as originally intended in 1948, over half of today's Israel, including the post-War occupied lands, is the only formula that will quieten the Middle East in the long run and allow the brave, ordinary Jews of Israel to sleep in peace.

■

Is Israel's long-term security as a nation under real threat? This was not a question many asked seriously ten years ago. Today, thoughtful observers of West Asian politics, including friends of Israel, are not only asking the question but coming up with a one-word answer, unthinkable till recently: perhaps.

There are three principal actors in the Israel-Palestine impasse. First, the United States, for its unblinking support of any Israeli action, however excessive, in West Asia. Second, Israel, for its uncompromising position on Gaza and the West Bank. Third, the broader Arab leadership, largely impotent since the creation of Israel in May 1948.

The trade-off is cynical and simple. American military power protects Arab governments from democratic movements in their own countries in return for acceptance of US policy in West Asia. Arab leaders make periodic statements of protest against Israel through the Arab League. But the clear understanding between the US and nearly a dozen Arab countries (including Saudi Arabia, the United Arab Emirates, Qatar, Bahrain, Oman, Kuwait and Jordan) is that America's policy writ in West Asia will not be challenged. Though President Barack Obama has attempted to nuance this policy, it remains an article of faith on Capitol Hill.

Palestine was under Ottoman rule till just before the end of the First World War. Between 1917 and 1948, it was administered under a British mandate. During this period, the population of Jews in Palestine rose sixfold from less than 1,00,000 to over 6,00,000, due mainly to migration of persecuted Jews from Central and Eastern Europe. The massacre of over 6 million Jews by Nazi Germany in the Second World War gave powerful Jewish leaders in Britain and the US a window of opportunity. Public opinion worldwide, outraged by Nazi atrocities during the Holocaust, favoured the immediate establishment of a Jewish state made up largely of European Jews and predicated on biblical prophecies of a Jewish homeland. Had the partition of Palestine into separate Arab and Jewish states under UN resolution 181, adopted on 29 November 1947, been delayed by even a year, the moment would have passed.

Palestine as a separate nation has a solid legal and civilizational foundation. In 1917, Article 7 of the League of Nations mandate stated that a new, separate Palestinian nationality be established. Article 22 of the Covenant of the League of Nations gave international legal status to Palestinian people and territories earlier administered by the Ottoman Empire.

How will the modern Palestinian tragedy play out? Israel, though a nation of determined and talented people whose centuries-long persecution in Europe rightly draws widespread sympathy, has two crucial weaknesses. The first is demographic. Israel has a low birth rate. Net migration, due to the psychological state of siege it lives under, is also now turning negative. Meanwhile, the Palestinian population is exploding. Though confined to narrow strips of land, the number of Palestinians in Israel, Gaza and the West Bank (over 6 million) has already exceeded the total Jewish population of 5.66 million in Israel. If this trend continues, Israel's long-term security will be seriously compromised.

Israel's second weakness is the shift in global, especially European and US, public opinion over its treatment of Palestinians. The international Free Gaza Movement includes European Nobel laureates, American senators and Asian civil society leaders. They are challenging Israel directly and frequently over the Palestine issue.

But Israel's real worries will begin if a separate Palestinian state is established over the next few years based on the two-state solution brokered by the US at the Annapolis Conference in November 2007.

Palestinian demographics and cross-border fungibility could then break down Israel's ring-fenced security, causing even more of its nervous European-origin Jews to migrate back to their homes in Russia, Poland, Germany and elsewhere. The inevitability of long-term reverse migration is what really haunts the Israeli political leadership. The result of reverse migration could be a creeping, back-door takeover by a neighbouring Palestinian state of much of the territory it has lost. It is this very real fear of retribution that drives Israel's policy on Palestine.

■

After winning the 1967 and 1973 Arab-Israeli wars and signing the 1979 peace treaty with Egypt (and later Jordan), Israel has lived in relative security. Since 1980, a generation of Israelis has grown up comforted by the two Washington-brokered peace accords. That era may soon be over.

Violent pro-democracy movements across the Arabian Gulf and North Africa and the civil war in Syria have disrupted the region's equilibrium. But the most serious security threat to Israel is non-Arab, Shia-majority Iran with its incipient nuclear weapons capability. Israel's biggest Arab rivals in the region do not, despite growing peoples' anger against autocracy, yet pose a significant threat to the status quo: Syria is riven by its bloody fratricidal conflict; Iraq operates under a fractious government; Saudi Arabia, Bahrain, Oman and Kuwait have had to quell scattered protests; Yemen is too weak, Lebanon too embroiled in Christian-Muslim schisms and Algeria and Tunisia too distant to cause Israel immediate concern.

Meanwhile, powerful vested interests continue to benefit from a status quo in the Middle East. The Sunni and Wahhabi sheikhs have for decades used Arab hostility against Israel as a smokescreen to deny democracy to their own people, and Israel has willingly played bogeyman to keep the sheikhdoms in power: Tel Aviv knows they are the best guarantors of Israel's security. Democratically elected

Arab leaders would be less accommodating of Israel's occupation of Arab lands in Gaza and the West Bank. They would press far more vigorously for an independent Palestinian state.

In America, the Jewish lobby—with enormous wealth and talent at its disposal—ensures that no US president, Republican or Democratic, dares to follow anything but an uncompromisingly pro-Israel line.

Between them, the status quoists control a majority of the world's oil (Saudi Arabia alone pumps over 10 million barrels of oil worth $1 billion every day), military firepower and diplomatic heft. Since 1948, the US has vetoed more than fifty United Nations Security Council (UNSC) resolutions condemning the use of force by Israel on Palestinians and other Arabs. The complicity between Washington and the dozen enormously wealthy Arab families which rule Saudi Arabia, Jordan, Bahrain, Oman, Kuwait, Qatar and the UAE has ensured that Palestinians have remained refugees in their own land.

The Palestinian leadership is divided. Since the death of Yasser Arafat in 2004, Palestinians have lacked a charismatic, centripetal figure. Their cause is just but is trapped in the complex political web woven by Arab dictators, Israel and the US.

■

Israel knows that at some stage it will have to live alongside an independent Palestinian state. This inevitable outcome is part of a tortuous diplomatic peace process stretching from the 1993 Oslo Accords to the 2007 Annapolis Conference. Israel has used this long period to build permanent settlements in the West Bank which it seized during the six-day 1967 war. Despite worldwide condemnation of Israeli encroachments in the West Bank where nearly two million Palestinians lead precarious lives, the steady spread of Jewish settlements continues.

More than 5,00,000 Israelis now live in the West Bank and East Jerusalem. For Israel, the settlements serve two purposes: the creation of a security buffer zone and a future territorial bargaining chip in peace talks. Israel's hawkish prime minister, Benjamin Netanyahu, would like to delay the proposed creation of a Palestinian state under the terms of the Annapolis Conference for as long as he can.

Cascading pro-democracy protests across the Arabian Gulf have sharpened Israel's paranoia. Wahhabi Saudi Arabia and the mercantile Sunni-led Gulf nations of Bahrain, Qatar, Oman, Kuwait and the UAE (all with hostile Shia populations) have paid little more than lip service to the Palestinian cause. This will change when the Arab street's demand for democracy reaches their doorstep.

How soon will this be? Conservative Bahrain, Oman and Kuwait have experienced violent though short-lived anti-government, pro-democracy demonstrations which were unthinkable a few years ago. Feudal monarchies like Saudi Arabia with their vast oil wealth are likely to be the last to succumb to democracy but succumb they eventually will. A worried Israel knows this. So does the extended al-Saud ruling family comprising over 250 cousin-princes.

The wisest strategy for Israel to secure its long-term future is to accept the two-state formula articulated at the Annapolis Conference for an independent Palestinian state next to Israel. Most Israelis dread this. They are used to the unconditional backing of Washington and the tacit support of US-friendly Arab dictators to maintain the status quo.

This tacit support will dissipate in an increasingly democratic Arab world. Progress towards an independent Palestine will be tortuous but events unfolding in the Middle East have made the process irreversible. No one knows this better than the grim-faced men and women who run Israel.

3
MAKE GEO-ECONOMICS INDIA'S WEAPON OF CHOICE

When Alexander the Great, fresh from victory over King Darius III of Persia in 330 BCE, swept over the Hindu Kush into what is now Afghanistan, he encountered more resistance than he expected. The men who stood in his way were Pashtuns. Alexander wrote to his mother from the mountainous new land that led into India's famed plains: 'I am involved in the land of a leonine people where every foot on the ground is like a wall of steel confronting my soldier. You have brought only one son into the world, but everyone in this land can be called an Alexander.'

The same stock of hardy Pashtuns today forms the core of the brutal, medieval Taliban—with whom the majority of Afghans have nothing in common. And yet the Taliban hold the key to, in former Home Minister P. Chidambaram's words, 'the most difficult neighbourhood in the world'.

The Durand Line snakes its way up from southern Afghanistan to northwest Pakistan. The Pashtuns have never accepted the Durand Line which cuts their nation into two. Pashtuns make up 42 per cent (12 million) of today's Afghans. The other 58 per cent are mostly Tajiks, Uzbeks, Hazaras and Turkmen who have greater ethnic affinity to Central rather than South Asia. Complicating matters are the 28 million Pashtuns who live in Pakistan, east of the Durand Line, and who comprise nearly 16 per cent of the country's population.

No one quite knows how much mineral wealth lies beneath the war-scorched earth of Afghanistan. Estimates vary between $1 trillion and $3 trillion. For a country with a population of 30 million (less than Kerala's), that works out to $100,000 per Afghan. India is well-equipped to partner the country in mining the aluminium, bauxite and titanium under the forbidding Hindu Kush range to transform the fortunes of a landlocked and benighted nation. Unlike Pakistan which fathered the Taliban, India enjoys enormous goodwill in Afghanistan: it has built highways, hospitals and schools across the war-torn country.

■

Pakistan has three objectives in Southwest Asia: one, block India's growing economic footprint in Afghanistan; two, ease the US out of Af-Pak and install a Taliban-dominated regime in Kabul; three, replace India with China as principal provider of money and manpower in post-US Afghanistan. As a counter to these objectives, India's political leadership clearly needs to employ a proactive geo-economics strategy in the region alongside continuing to build its conventional military and nuclear deterrent.

India's growing economic power can make peace too profitable for even a demagogic Pakistan to jeapordize. When economies are entwined, war becomes a poor option. The US and Mexico fought bitter border wars in the 1840s. Today, the only conflict on the US-Mexican border is illegal immigration and drug trafficking. At current growth rates, India's GDP in 2020 will be $10 trillion (by purchasing power parity)—twenty times Pakistan's estimated GDP of $0.50 trillion. That's similar to the 18:1 ratio between current US and Mexican GDP ($16 trillion vs $0.87 trillion).

The next twenty-five years will be dominated by four convergent economic power centres. First, the Greater American Economic Area (GAEA) comprising North and South America, led by a multiracial United States. Second, the Greater European Economic Area (GEEA), made up of an ever-enlarging European Union straddling Central and Eastern Europe. Third, the Greater Chinese Economic Area (GCEA), stretching across Confucian North Asia through to the South China Sea. And fourth, the Greater Indian Economic Area (GIEA) with India at the centre of sweeping, intersecting arcs rising up from Africa and West Asia to Central Asia and curving down across the Pacific through East Asia to multicultural Australasia.

By 2050, India will have the world's largest population— 1.63 billion against China's 1.44 billion. To prepare for an era where Indian, US and Chinese interests converge, New Delhi's policy of strategic restraint must give way to a policy of strategic assertion.

Though increasingly radicalized, the Pakistani army will eventually be forced to recognize the diminishing returns of being a Talibanized terrorist state dominated by a rogue military-intelligence cabal. The only productive option before it will be to align its own parlous economy with India's. Geo-economics, not just military or nuclear power, will shape the lands south of the Hindu Kush.

■

Pakistan's governing elite is made up largely of Punjabis, though Pashtuns are well represented in the bureaucracy and the army (70 per cent of which is Punjabi). The unspoken fear that haunts Islamabad is the latent demand for a Greater Pashtunistan, fusing Pakistan's 28 million Pashtuns with 12 million Pashtuns across the Durand Line in Afghanistan. If that demand gathers momentum, and the Balochi and Sindhi nationalist movements grow, it could trisect Pakistan.

This is not in India's long-term strategic interest. A stable, peaceful, undivided Pakistan acts as a buffer zone against the murderous Taliban and its radicalized Pashtun-Balochi fellow-tribesmen. While the Taliban is made up largely of Pashtuns, with a smattering of

Chechens and Arabs, its violent philosophy finds no resonance with the secular Pashtun nationalist movement represented politically by the moderate Awami National Party in Khyber Pakhtunkhwa and historically by Khan Abdul Ghaffar Khan, the Frontier Gandhi.

Pakistan is probably more willing today than at any time since the post-Bangladesh 1970s to accept that its future lies in peace, not conflict, with India. As one observer put it, Pakistan is suffering from 'Kashmir fatigue'. The troubled state was not even an issue in the May 2013 general election in Pakistan. Prime Minister Nawaz Sharif has a finger on the pulse of public opinion and—as befits a businessman-politician—is prepared to put Kashmir on the back burner to get the dialogue with India started again.

However, the depature of the bulk of US and NATO troops from Afghanistan in 2014 has emboldened Pakistan's army to revive terrorist infiltration in J&K. Sharif, a longtime associate of Hafiz Saeed, chief of the JuD, has perfected the art of running with the hares and hunting with the hounds.

What then is the most coherent strategy India should pursue for durable peace with a Pakistan under a prime minister seeking to replace terrorism with trade? As this decade unfolds, the generation of army commanders scarred as young officers by Bangladesh in 1971 will pass. The Pakistani army—including General Zia-ul-Haq's radicalized core—knows it has at most a ten-year window to employ terrorism as an instrument of state policy with Kashmir as the pretext before economic disparities between the two countries shuts that window for good.

■

South Asia houses 23.50 per cent of the world's population. But its 1.65 billion people are among the poorest in the world, with per capita incomes ranging from $1,250 (Nepal) to $5,100 (Sri Lanka). Even adjusted for purchasing power parity, South Asia's median per capita income is around $3,000—one-tenth that of Greece, Europe's most distressed economy.

Apart from poverty, the region shares the same afflictions: widespread corruption, shambolic infrastructure, inadequate healthcare and huge socio-economic inequalities. So how can 23.50 per cent of the world's population, packed together in just 3.20 per cent of the world's land mass, steeped in poverty, sectarianism and fundamentalism, turn things around?

The countries of South Asia have a common civilizational heritage. Four of the world's nine great religions—Hinduism, Buddhism, Jainism and Sikhism—evolved here. Two others—Islam and Christianity—arrived in the subcontinent mere decades after their founding in West Asia and established deep roots in the region. A seventh and eighth—Judaism and Zorastrianism—came here through believers escaping persecution in Palestine and Persia. Only the ninth, Confucianism, stayed away. But its monks travelled frequently from China to India to exchange ideas and debate theology.

In such a plural subcontinent, conflict is inevitable. However, from violence a synergetic society can emerge, bound by a common heritage and common wounds. The scars of Partition, the more recent trauma of state-sponsored terrorism from Pakistan and old memories of Mughal and Protestant conquests give all sides cause to be deeply suspicious of one another.

But now South Asia is at a turning point. Pakistan has belatedly realized that using terror as an instrument of state policy has brought it close to bankruptcy. Prime Minister Nawaz Sharif seeks cooperation not confrontation with India, despite the spike in violations across the Line of Control (LoC) in recent months. The military has a shrinking constituency and goodwill. Islamic fundamentalists are feared but reviled. Thus the three 'As' that defined Pakistan for decades—Allah, Army and America—are no longer omnipotent. From the wreckage, Pakistan can rebuild itself as a prosperous and peaceful nation—but only as part of a prosperous and peaceful South Asia.

Pakistan, in back-channel talks, concedes that the militancy it unleashed on Jammu & Kashmir in 1989 has bled Pakistan, not India. It would, however, be unwise to underestimate the fanaticism that lurks within the Lashkar-e-Taiba (LeT) and other state-sponsored Pakistani terrorist groups, including Hafiz Saeed's JuD into which the LeT has morphed.

Bangladesh has, meanwhile, under the secular leadership of Prime Minister Hasina, pulled itself back from the fundamentalist precipice that former Prime Minister Khaleda Zia had pushed it toward. Sri Lanka, too, freed finally from its devastating conflict with the LTTE, though not from the taint of alleged human rights violations against ethnic Tamils, is ready to move towards a better future for its people.

India is the key to South Asia's emergence as one of the world's most powerful regional blocs. It constitutes 75 per cent of South Asia's total population and 82 per cent of its combined GDP. In this statistic lies the future of India, Pakistan and the rest of South Asia. To counter the nuanced challenge of a rising China taking America's place in Pakistan's post-2014 geopolitical strategy, India will have to overcome political misgovernance at home and assert itself as a responsible—and resolute—regional power.

4
UNSC REFORM: A CHIMERA?

The five permanent members (P5) of the United Nations Security Council (UNSC)—the United States, Britain, France, Russia and China—comprise the victors of the Second World War. They wrote the Charter of the United Nations, giving themselves permanent membership of the Security Council and a powerful veto to establish the post-1945 world order.

This has allowed Britain and France to punch above their geopolitical weight long after the detritus of empire had been swept away. Russia and China used their veto systematically during the Gulf War, the Balkans conflict and the US-led invasion of Iraq. The US employs its veto to protect its interests globally, especially in West Asia, blocking, for example, every significant UN resolution condemning Israeli military action in the region.

If any country merits a permanent UNSC seat, it is probably India. Its international record since 1947 has been impeccable. India has never reneged on an international treaty. It has scrupulously respected all international laws. Britain, Russia and France have officially backed India's candidature to the UNSC. China has given equivocal assent (permanent membership without a veto). Of the five current permanent members, the US alone has been publicly noncommittal. Privately, it backs India's membership but again without a veto.

This in essence means, first, that Washington will back India's permanent membership of the UNSC (without a veto) for an initial period of fifteen years followed by a possible granting of the veto after this initiation phase. It means, second, that in order to secure America's backing for this two-phase plan, India must first mollify Pakistan over Kashmir. Bluntly put, this implies a settlement over Kashmir on terms India might in other circumstances have rejected. Is this a price worth paying in India's long-term national interest? Will permanent membership of the UNSC without a veto (for at least the first fifteen years) give India the diplomatic heft its economy, democracy, plurality and size merit?

In an increasingly raucous and fissured world, permanent membership of an expanded P5 (initially even without a veto) has significant advantages. It will enable India to influence world events in Iran, North Korea, Afghanistan and Syria where today its counsel is not widely sought. Ultimately, of course, it is the size of a nation's economy which delivers global clout as the rise of China has demonstrated.

■

An expansion of UNSC permanent membership, however, remains deadlocked over four competing claimants—India, Japan, Germany and Brazil (dubbed the G4)—each supported and opposed by groups of countries with deep vested interests. Japan has particularly strong backing: it is the only claimant the US officially supports for permanent membership with a veto, placing it on par with the P5.

Former US Secretary of State Condoleeza Rice in a speech delivered at Tokyo's Sophia University in March 2005 couldn't have been clearer about Washington's intent: 'Japan has earned its honourable place among the nations of the world by its own effort and its own character. That's why the United States unambiguously supports a permanent seat for Japan on the United Nations Security Council.'

In sharp contrast, no US official and certainly no US President has given a statement of such clear intent, with no geopolitical strings attached, in favour of India's bid.

Germany, too, has a strong case for membership of an expanded P5. It is the third largest contributor to the UN's regular budget after the US and Japan. It has Russian, French and British backing but significantly not American or Chinese. The fourth member of the putative G4, Brazil, also has the support of Britain, France and Russia but China is ambivalent and the US says it can only back Brazilian membership without a veto.

Clearly then, UNSC reform, despite both serious and cosmetic attempts, remains chimeric. Former UN Secretary General Kofi Annan had proposed in 2005 yet another structure which would in effect create a two-caste UNSC: the old P5 with vetos and a new P6 without vetos plus three new non-permanent members along with the current ten rotating members, making a total of twenty-four countries in this humungous new Security Council. The veto-less P6 would include India, Japan, Brazil, Germany and two others (possibly South Africa and one other representative from Africa).

Mired in conflicting national claims, the Annan plan lies, exactly as the P5 had expected and perhaps hoped, in limbo.

SECTION 4
LEADERS

1
RAHUL: THE RELUCTANT PRIME MINISTER

It was a blistering May afternoon in Delhi. Rajiv Gandhi, still only forty, had been prime minister for less than seven months. We spoke on the patio of his 7 Race Course Road residence about the biography I was writing on him. He was enthusiastic, attentive, engaged.

Exactly six years later, on another hot May afternoon, in the small town of Sriperumbudur, 42 km from Chennai, torn flags of the Indian National Congress lay strewn around the blood-stained rally ground. Twelve hours earlier, Rajiv—at the end of his 1991 Lok Sabha election campaign swing through the south—had been assassinated by an LTTE woman suicide bomber.

I had received the news at 11.30 p.m. and taken the first available early morning flight from Bombay (now Mumbai) to Madras (now Chennai) followed by a bone-rattling ninety-minute drive to reach the scene of devastation in Sriperumbudur just before noon on 22 May. What followed were several months of research and interviews across the country as I raced to complete my manuscript of a life cut tragically short, in *Rajiv Gandhi: The End of a Dream*.

Rajiv was the third member of his family to serve as prime minister between 1947 and 1989. While Rajiv himself was a product of dynasty, he was not enamoured of it. After his younger brother Sanjay's death in June 1980, it took all of Indira Gandhi's famed powers of persuasion to make Rajiv give up his commercial pilot's job and join active politics. Sonia was vehemently opposed to it. Rahul was then barely ten; Priyanka, not yet nine.

In the short decade he spent in politics—1981-1991—Rajiv gave little indication that he was contemplating grooming Sonia, Rahul or Priyanka for a political role. During his father's last and fatal general election campaign in Sriperumbudur in May 1991, Rahul, then nearly twenty-one, was away studying in the United States. Priyanka, nineteen, and Sonia had accompanied Rajiv on several previous election tours during the frenetic campaign. But Rajiv had been apolitical for thirty-six of his forty-six years. Till the end, even when his prime ministership unravelled after Bofors and the Congress plunged to defeat in November 1989, the idea of perpetuating a dynasty—a legacy he had reluctantly accepted—did not enthuse him.

So why does it seem to enthuse Sonia today? And does it enthuse Rahul? What lies behind Sonia's sphinx-like silence? And Priyanka? Is she the one with fire in the belly?

■

Sonia took charge of an imploding Congress in 1997-98 when she realized that her young family needed the party as much as the fractious party needed her family. Her shyness, her shrewdness and, latterly, her secretiveness have evolved over time. Good government, however, means open government. The public's right to know supersedes a public figure's right to privacy—with reasonable restraints. But when in doubt on what constitutes reasonable restraint, democracies err on the side of openness, not opacity.

There are two serious infirmities in Sonia's approach to governance compared to Rajiv's. First, duality of power. Prime Minister Manmohan Singh is the head of the government. He should be the final authority on all policy matters. In her role as Congress

President and UPA chairperson, Sonia, however, has the final say. That is tantamount to a veto over the prime minister and is clearly wrong. Power without accountability compromises governance. It lies at the root of all that ails the UPA government today.

Second, lack of internal party democracy. Rahul has introduced democratic elections for office-bearers within the Youth Congress. He must now hold robust annual elections for party president in which no member of his family stands. After Independence, Jawaharlal Nehru was president of the Congress for only four years (from 1951 to 1954). Nehru deliberately did not offer to stand for election as party president after 1954 because he knew, even in those less dynastic times, that Congressmen would never vote against him.

Having evoked Pandit Nehru's legacy in a past UP assembly electoral campaign, Rahul should follow Pandit Nehru's democratic example and resist the general clamour within the Congress to take over as the party's president when Sonia eventually steps down. He should have the courage to break the feudal link that has seen five members of the Nehru-Gandhi family—beginning with his great-great grandfather Motilal Nehru—serve as Congress president for collectively forty-two years since 1919.

Should Rahul consider himself a future prime minister because of his lineage? Yes, say Rahul's supporters. Besides, in a democracy, they argue, if the Congress chooses Rahul as its prime ministerial candidate and the electorate votes the Congress-led UPA back into office at the next Lok Sabha election, Rahul has every right to be considered prime minister on merit.

The acolytes miss the point. Ours is an evolving democracy. Voters deserve a wider choice than merely between hereditary politicians (Gandhi, Pilot, Deora, Scindia, et. al.). If Rahul has his father's sense of honour, he will continue to decline the prime ministership. By doing so, Rahul will help Indian democracy evolve to the next level.

Ironically, he will find the most resistance to this action from the corrupt sycophants who surround him and often speak for him. They know that the Gandhi family is the glue that binds the Congress. Every Congressman—from MPs to ordinary party workers—has a stake in ensuring that the party's formidable money-making machine keeps ticking. It can only do that when in power. Hence, the party's manic attacks on those political organizations and movements that threaten its hold on power.

Priyanka, meanwhile, has Indira Gandhi's charisma and Sonia's unyielding determination. But she, too, must resist the lure of dynasty. The Gandhi family can serve India better if it works to end the regressive feudalism at every level in our society by setting a personal example.

If the largest political party in the world's largest democracy continues to be run like a family firm—intellectually dwarfed and morally adrift—it diminishes India. It also diminishes itself, which will lead to inevitable electoral defeat and the loss of power it fears most.

■

On 19 June 2013, Rahul Gandhi turned forty-three. That is the same age his father was when his prime ministership was fatally wounded by Bofors. But at forty-three, Rajiv had several accomplishments as well. He had a clear-eyed view of the world. He sought global nuclear disarmament. He implemented Panchayati Raj. He engaged in an entente cordiale with then Pakistani Prime Minister Benazir Bhutto. He spearheaded the information technology revolution.

What then, at forty-three, are Rahul's views on foreign policy? On nuclear weapons security? On Pakistani state terrorism? On Maoism? On economic reforms? On dynasty? Apart from a few issues raised during his speeches, we know little of the AICC vice president's worldview.

While he campaigns for the 2014 general election and rebuilds the Congress at the grassroots in Uttar Pradesh, Bihar, West Bengal and other states governed by non-UPA parties, Rahul must engage a broader national constituency with his thinking on India's key strategic challenges.

Dynastic politics did not burden Rajiv's mind. His children, Rahul and Priyanka, were fourteen and twelve when he became prime minister on 31 October 1984. Sonia was viscerally against politics. Nephew Varun was barely five and sister-in-law Maneka was permanently estranged. Rajiv thus conducted his politics without a thought to Nehru-Gandhi dynastic succession, unlike his mother, Indira, who openly declared Sanjay her heir in the mid-1970s.

Which model will Rahul follow? His father's or his grandmother's? Interestingly, great-grandfather Pandit Jawaharlal Nehru was no admirer of dynastic politics either even though he appointed his daughter Indira as Congress president in 1959 when she was forty-one years old. It seemed an act out of character with Nehru's principled belief in meritocracy. It was only after Pandit Nehru's sudden death in May 1964, and on new Prime Minister Lal Bahadur Shastri's deferential but well-meaning insistence, that Indira joined the cabinet as minister for information and broadcasting. The rest is dynastic history.

Can Rahul reverse that history? Does he want to?

In an imperfect electoral democracy where feudal instincts traduce merit, history-sheeters with money as well as dynasts with bloodlines will often win elections. Neither should overestimate the legitimacy of such electoral endorsement.

Rahul understands these arguments in all their delicate nuances. An intelligent and sensitive man, he concedes he owes his position to his birth. He is not proud of a system that allows such feudal anomalies and wants to bring internal democracy to the Youth Congress by way of transparent elections so that young men and women of merit can enter politics without the shoehorn of a surname.

Rahul is silent about applying the same high standard to the top echelons of the party, including the post of president which his mother Sonia has now held for sixteen consecutive years—a record in the Congress's 129-year history. (Even Jawaharlal Nehru was party president for a total of only eight years, four of them consecutively, from 1951 to 1954.)

This is a situation that should make Rahul feel uncomfortable. Does he have the political will to do something about it? At the moment, perhaps not.

But the gentle decline of the Nehru-Gandhi dynasty has already been underwritten, partly by Rahul himself. He is unmarried so his own progeny are unlikely to ever be India's prime minister. Priyanka and her thirteen-year-old son, Raihan Rajiv Vadra, could keep the dynasty relevant for two decades but by the time Raihan (recently enrolled into the family's alma mater, Doon School) is twenty-five, in 2025, and eligible for electoral office, India will have a more enlightened electorate. It will reject feudocracy and endorse meritocracy. That does not automatically rule dynasts out. But it does not automatically rule them in either.

What about the mini-dynasts who, like amoebae, have proliferated in the states since the 1980s, first tentatively, then increasingly assertively in the dynastic footsteps legitimized by the Nehru-Gandhis? They, too, will eventually wither in the face of an electorate that over the next generation will acquire education and empowerment. Neither surnames nor money will win votes from enlightened voters.

■

Uttar Pradesh could determine Rahul Gandhi's political future. In the 2014 Lok Sabha poll, the Congress will present itself to voters as the party of inclusive growth and secularism. Like all well-laid plans, this too, though, could come unstuck. History is a good reference point. In 1985, the Supreme Court directed Mohammad Ahmed Khan to pay Shah Bano, a penurious sixty-nine-year-old whom he had divorced after forty-three years of marriage, Rs 500 a month as maintenance. The Supreme Court verdict, under Section 125 of the Criminal Procedure Code (CrPC), was widely hailed as a triumph of justice in secular India. Only the outraged Muslim clergy and its obscurantist followers condemned the Supreme Court's 'interference' in Muslim personal law.

What happened next was deeply regressive. In order to appease Muslim electoral sentiment, the Rajiv Gandhi government used its 414-seat majority in the Lok Sabha to nullify the Supreme Court's verdict by passing the Muslim Women (Protection of Rights on Divorce) Act, 1986. The legislation set aside the rights of divorced Muslim women to receive maintenance under Section 125 of the CrPC.

With hindsight, the Shah Bano episode was the single biggest error of judgement Rajiv made in his first two years as prime minister apart from Bofors. Muslims are traditional Congress voters and the legislation against Shah Bano was designed to consolidate that vote. Instead, three years later, the Congress suffered one of the biggest electoral defeats in its history, plunging from 414 Lok Sabha seats to 197 seats in the 1989 general election. The Congress has not won a majority in parliament since.

The lesson? Short-term strategic gain can lead to long-term electoral pain. 'Quota politics' could well help the Congress win back the minority vote it has, over two decades, lost to the SP and the BSP: Muslim votes can still swing a seat in over 120 Lok Sabha constituencies.

The larger battle of 2014 might, however, be lost by the Congress in the same manner the battle of 1989 was lost. Ominously, the two issues that sunk the Congress in 1989 were corruption (Bofors) and minorityism (Shah Bano). The former led to the departure of Rajiv's most trusted friend and minister of state for defence, Arun Singh. The latter cost Rajiv one of his cabinet's most enlightened and genuinely secular ministers, Arif Mohammad Khan, who strongly opposed the government's legislation to overturn the Supreme Court's verdict on Shah Bano.

That, as Rahul revs up his campaign for 2014, will offer him food for thought.

2

SONIA'S ENDGAME

The Rae Bareli seat in Uttar Pradesh has been a Gandhi family bastion since 1952, when Rajiv Gandhi's father, Feroze Gandhi, first stood for election from there. Sonia Gandhi adopted the constituency in 2004 and was re-elected with a huge majority in 2009. It should therefore be one of India's most developed districts. Right? Wrong.

The HUNGaMA (Hunger and Malnutrition) survey, released by the prime minister in 2012, was carried out amongst children under the age of five in 112 rural districts across 3,360 villages in nine states. The results should shame politicians of every major party who represent the poor in these districts. Rae Bareli is a sprawling district spread over 4,608 sq km with a population of 34.04 lakhs. How does it fare? Poorly—even by the abysmal standards of the other 111 districts surveyed. According to the report, coordinated by the Naandi Foundation and reviewed among others by economists, Dr Abhijeet Banerjee and Dr Isher Judge Ahluwalia, 'Rae Bareli with 70.40 per cent, Koraput in Orissa with 68.86 per cent and Dumka in Jharkhand with 63.65 per cent have the highest number of stunted children.'

This picture of poverty, hunger, chronic malnutrition and lack of basic amenities like toilets is common across the districts, in both

Congress and Opposition-ruled states, which were surveyed. If a constituency nurtured by the Gandhi family for over six decades can be so desolate, what does it say about political governance?

Sonia Gandhi plays a role in Indian politics that is unprecedented in our independent history. She is neither prime minister nor president. Yet, as chairperson of the UPA-led coalition government, she is the final arbiter of national policy. Power without accountability of the kind Sonia enjoys flies in the face of democracy. And yet the world's largest electorate tolerates—even endorses—such an arrangement.

Why?

The answer lies in many layers. India is a young, evolving democracy. Its people are undemanding. Feudalism runs deep in our veins. In Tamil Nadu, two families (MGR's and Karunanidhi's) and their associates have ruled the state for decades. In UP, Chief Minister Mayawati inaugurated her own dynasty by announcing her brother as her heir. While the SP, Shiv Sena, NCP, SAD, NC and RJD have their own dynasties in place, no party has embraced sycophancy with the same insouciance as the Congress.

Jawaharlal, Indira, Rajiv, Sonia, Rahul—the family's grip on the party has never slackened except in that seven-year vacuum following Rajiv's assassination, between 1991 and 1998, when Sonia withdrew in shock to leave the party and the government to Sitaram Kesri and Narasimha Rao respectively.

But when Sonia saw power slipping to the Opposition, she sprang into action to reclaim her family's legacy. Kesri was evicted, Rao sidelined, and Sonia took over the party leadership in 1998. In May 2004, she presided over the Congress-led UPA coalition government, renouncing the prime ministership but not power.

Since then, Sonia has consolidated her family's control over the party and created several (subservient and self-serving) mini-dynasties—Murli Deora's son, Milind; Rajesh Pilot's son, Sachin; Madhavrao Scindia's son, Jyotiraditya, and others. The idea is that

Rahul, carefully eased in as party vice president in January 2013, will at the right time have a faithful kitchen cabinet of his own as grandmother Indira did.

The bad news for Sonia is that 2014 will probably be the last time a Gandhi-Nehru is likely to be even a contender for the position of prime minister of India. The reason? India is getting smarter. Once literacy levels (currently 72 per cent) reach the critical threshold of 85 per cent, in around ten years, a strong groundswell of enlightened public opinion will build. That surging, powerful groundswell will demand accountability. It will make good intra-party governance mandatory for electability.

An enlightened India will no longer tolerate a party whose top leaders come from just one family. Such enlightenment will force the future Congress to first become a party of democrats internally before being allowed the privilege of governing a democracy.

■

As the debate, within parliament and outside, over the exact number of India's poor and destitute continues, and Sonia's efforts to legislate 'entitlement', consider a contrasting set of statistics (*see chart on the next page*). The number of MPs who are crorepatis increased from 156 in the 2004 Lok Sabha to 315 in the 2009 Lok Sabha. The story in Vidhan Sabhas is the same: in state after state, the number of crorepati-MLAs has risen by multiples of over 100 per cent. In the specific case of the Manipur assembly, the number of crorepati-MLAs has shot up by 563 per cent over the last five years.

Even as politicians get wealthier, their constituents remain stuck in a vortex of poverty, hunger, malnutrition and primitive infrastructure. The UPA government has tried to tackle the problem with a strategy of ever-rising subsidies. These include MGNREGA, Bharat Nirman and several state-level initiatives. Sonia has made the food security and land acquisition acts pivots of her party's 2014 Lok Sabha campaign.

The Rich and The Hungry

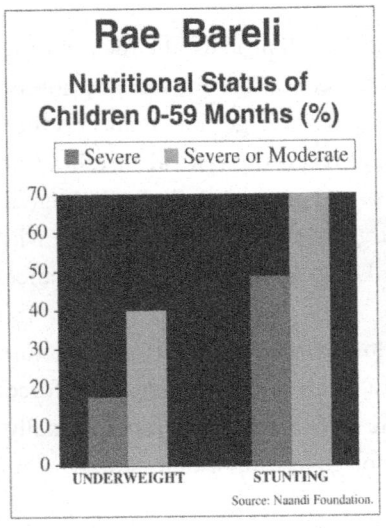

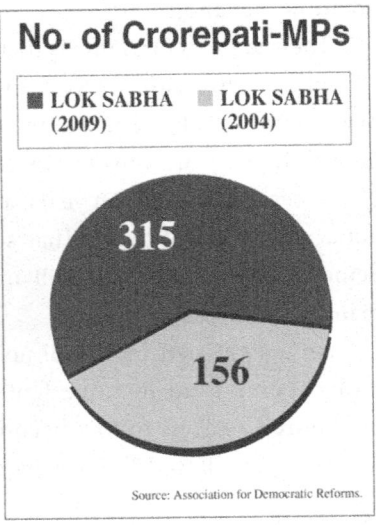

MGNREGA and other welfare schemes, however, remain riddled with corruption. The ecosystem of politicians, bureaucrats, district officials and middlemen siphon off up to 50 per cent of the benefits meant for the poor. Technical loopholes in MGNREGA, for example, allow local officials to pay workers a fraction of the guaranteed wage of Rs 100 a day based on whether they 'qualify' for the scheme—a subjective assessment done locally and vulnerable to abuse.

A study by Shikha Jha of the Asian Development Bank (ADB) and Bharat Ramaswami of the Indian Statistical Institute (ISI) has shown that only 10 per cent of the benefits of the public distribution system (PDS) reach the 'deserving poor'. Around 43 per cent is siphoned off illegally, 28 per cent goes towards administrative costs of the Food Corporation of India (FCI) and the balance 20 per cent is misappropriated by other vested interests. Pouring more money into this leaky system without first fixing it will lead to the worst possible outcome: the poor will remain poor even as politicians become richer.

■

Subsidies are corruption-prone across the distribution chain. The remedy: reduce petro product and fertilizer subsidies. De-control diesel. Use the funds to invest in modernizing agriculture and infrastructure. This will create productive assets to help the poor build prosperous, independent lives.

Debates over anti-poverty programmes miss the larger point: many politicians have a vested interest in the commerce of poverty. That is the principal reason why reforms in the agriculture sector—cutting out middlemen in the food-chain and boosting crop productivity—have been allowed to languish. Food inflation is a malign byproduct of this clear misgovernance. An empowered electorate is not in most politicians' interest: it would reject a government that allowed usurious corruption in anti-poverty programmes.

The debate must move forward from measuring poverty to mitigating it. The Central Vigilance Committee on the PDS, headed by Justice D.P. Wadhwa, delivered this stinging indictment: 'In the PDS it is the Fair Price Shop (FPS) which is the breeding ground of corruption. It is in the knowledge of all, whether he is a politician, bureaucrat or any other public servant. An honest FPS owner cannot survive from the income earned from the PDS. He has to indulge in diversion of food grain in the market. All are involved in this crime of diversion—the FPS owner, transporter, official, bureaucrat or politician.' The Food Security Act (FSA), which the Congress has made the centerpiece of its Lok Sabha poll campaign, is unlikely to plug these leakages.

■

Sonia has developed into one of the Congress's canniest election campaign strategists. She believes that only two factors can save the Congress from a rout in the 2014 Lok Sabha election. The first is the

Food Security Act. The second is the direct benefit transfer (DBT) scheme which, too, has been rolled out on a war footing. Together, Sonia reckons, the food-and-cash handouts will garner significant votes from the rural poor. The criticism that the Food Security Act will entitle the poor to consume more cereals when they are moving away to more nutritious foods has been sidestepped.

This policy of 'entitlement' is paternalistic. It gives the poor what the rich think the poor want, not what the poor really want or need. But will the FSA and DBT give the Congress the votes it needs to escape five years in opposition? The chances are slim.

The contrasting fortunes of MPs in Lutyens's Delhi and the malnourished destitute in districts like Rae Bareli across the country are an indictment of our economic and political governance. That should give Sonia, as she campaigns in impoverished Rae Bareli for the 2014 general election, much to ponder.

3
MODI: THE MOVING TARGET

As she choreographs Rahul's political trajectory, the leader whom UPA Chairperson Sonia Gandhi fears most is Narendra Modi. Why? It can't be the 2002 communal riots alone. More people have been killed in communal riots outside Gujarat—including the 1984 anti-Sikh pogrom—than in Gujarat.

It can't be that Gujarat has been a BJP fortress for nineteen years. The Congress has been out of power in Uttar Pradesh for twenty-five years and in West Bengal for thirty-seven. It can't be governance. Gujarat has been recognized internationally as India's best governed large state. It has had no riots since 2002. There is little apparent nepotism or corruption and certainly no family dynasty. And yet, Modi remains the principal target for vilification. An entire ecosystem has been built to sustain this campaign: journalists, social activists and local dissidents.

A Modi-led BJP could well win 200 Lok Sabha seats on its own due to consolidation of the majority vote. That figure could climb as his 2014 Lok Sabha campaign gathers momentum. The minority vote is not entirely lost to the BJP. Following the Muzaffarnagar riots, several influential Muslim clerics have urged their flock not to fear a 'Modi prime ministership' and warned the Congress that it is rapidly losing the minority community's confidence.

Sonia is an experienced political tactician. She knows that the most realistic possibility for the Congress in 2014 is to win upwards of 110 seats and then offer support from outside to a regional front as it did to Chandra Shekhar for five months in 1990-91 and H.D. Deve Gowda and I.K. Gujral in 1996-98. But to achieve that, she needs to keep the BJP tally down to 140 seats to rule out any possibility of an NDA-3 government.

With Sushma Swaraj or L.K. Advani as the NDA's prime ministerial candidate, that might have been achievable. With Modi, it is not.

Examine the chart below. It shows national voteshare and Lok Sabha seats won by the Congress and the BJP in the last four general elections: 1998, 1999, 2004 and 2009. In both 1998 and 1999, the BJP won power with 182 seats but, due to coalition partner math, clocked voteshare respectively of 25.59 per cent and 23.75 per cent. To get voteshare back up to over 25 per cent and win 180-200 seats, the BJP needs a voteshare swing of around 6-7 per cent from the dismal 18.80 per cent it garnered in 2009 when it won 116 seats.

LOK SABHA ELECTIONS (1998-2009)				
	Congress		BJP	
Year	Voteshare (%)	Seats	Voteshare (%)	Seats
1998	25.82	141	25.59	182
1999	28.30	114	23.75	182
2004	26.53	145	22.16	138
2009	28.55	206	18.80	116

With Sushma or Advani—despite their competence and experience—as the NDA's prime ministerial candidate, the BJP could at best have expected an anti-incumbency swing of 3-4 per cent. That would have taken its voteshare to around 22 per cent (what it received in 2004) and (with fewer allies to help with the voteshare-seat math) around 135-140 seats.

That is the outcome Sonia would have sought: keep the BJP down to 140, curtail the Congress's loss to 110 and then support from outside an unstable government formed by regional parties with 170-plus seats between them—before pulling it down (as in 1991, 1997 and 1998) to force a midterm poll in 2016.

In sharp contrast, Modi's pan-India campaign could plausibly increase the swing in the BJP's voteshare from the normal anti-incumbent 3-4 per cent to the 6-7 per cent needed to take it to over 25 per cent and 200 seats. The Shiv Sena, Shiromani Akali Dal, AIADMK, TDP and others would contribute 60-70 seats, making an NDA-3 viable. Smaller parties would then be needed only as tertiary support.

This is the outcome Sonia has always feared. And that is why Modi continues to be in the Congress's crosshairs as target no. 1 in a slew of CBI investigations.

■

Power is a money-spinner. The balance sheets of political parties reveal the several thousand crore rupees political parties receive from anonymous donors. In power now for nearly ten years, the Congress, according to the two parties' balance sheets, receives twice as much money as the BJP. When out of power, its income will plummet. That in turn will stymie its ability to use money to buy future political allies. When out of power, it will also lose the coercive power of the CBI over Mulayam Singh Yadav and Mayawati to reopen their corruption cases. If it loses badly in 2014, the Congress could be out of power for another ten years—as it was for eight years from 1996-2004. Keeping Modi pinned by cases over the 2002 riots or 'fake encounter' charges is therefore a do-or-die strategy for Sonia.

In poor health herself and with Manmohan Singh ruled out for a third prime ministerial term, Sonia needs Rahul to step up to the plate. Despite the growing crescendo from Congressmen to declare him the party's prime ministerial candidate, Rahul recognizes that he has acquired negative political equity after the Uttar Pradesh assembly elections in 2012 and the Bihar poll in 2010. His campaign rallies for the 2014 general election have been drawing thin crowds—in the thousands—compared to Modi who regularly pulls lakhs to his rallies around the country. If the Congress pitches Rahul directly against Modi as its prime ministerial candidate, the move could backfire. Every major opinion poll has Rahul trailing Modi by a large margin in a head-to-head contest.

The Congress is banking on the dynasty's charisma to carry it through in rural India. That could be an error of judgement. Even if Priyanka campaigns actively for the Congress in 2014, the growing hostility against dynastic politics—manifested in the Congress's losses in eight out of ten assembly constituencies in Amethi and Rae Bareli in the 2012 Uttar Pradesh state elections—could limit her appeal.

Sonia's best hope, as ever, lies with the poor and with Muslims. The poorer the electorate, the more vulnerable it is to charisma, money power, minorityism and false promises. The Congress, in power for fifty-four of free India's sixty-seven years, has been a friend of poverty, not the poor, of Muslim backwardness, not Muslim empowerment.

The Congress will relentlessly target Modi as the 2014 Lok Sabha poll approaches. His success carries too high a price.

4
MANMOHAN SINGH'S NEW REFORM AGENDA

On a warm April evening at Mumbai's Nehru Centre, Dr Manmohan Singh spoke with unusual passion of India's 'enormous economic potential'. The National Democratic Alliance (NDA) government was in office. Dr Singh had completed his five-year term as India's most successful reformist finance minister. He would soon be appointed prime minister in the UPA-I government.

But that evening, as chief guest at the launch of my biography of Aditya Vikram Birla, Manmohan Singh laid out in crisp detail his agenda for India's economic future to an audience comprising the country's corporate elite. It was clear to all of us seated on the dais that Dr Singh was deeply concerned about what he described as 'the unfinished business of reforms'.

As either finance minister or prime minister for fifteen of the twenty-three years since 1991, Dr Singh has wielded more influence over India's economic policy than any other contemporary national leader. Now, with scarcely months left to place his final imprimatur on India's economy, Dr Singh knows he has no time to lose.

The Prime Minister hoped to leave behind three legacies: peace with Pakistan; Indo-US civil nuclear cooperation; and economic reforms. The first two are likely to remain unfulfilled. The third is what he should focus on as his prime ministership enters its final moments.

■

The Indian growth story has frayed and needs a decisive reformist hand to steer it back to a higher trajectory of growth. The prime minister, in the short time left to this government, has four key allies who share his reformist vision: Finance Minister P. Chidambaram, Deputy Chairman of the Planning Commission Montek Singh Ahluwalia, Chairman of the Prime Minister's Economic Advisory Council (PMEAC) C. Rangarajan and RBI Governor Raghuram Rajan.

However, Dr Singh knows that economic reforms need a protective underlay of good governance. Without institutional reforms, economic liberalization will not lead to inclusive growth. Four governance reforms are crucial.

First, make a monthly audit of political party funding and expenditure by the Election Commission mandatory. Unless financial governance within our political parties improves, economic reforms will remain hostage to political caprice.

Second, give the Judicial Standards and Accountability Bill more teeth. A slow judiciary hurts the poor and helps the powerful. The former wait endlessly for justice. The latter, especially politicians and businessmen involved in graft, use the glacial judiciary to delay and eventually derail cases against them. Fast-track courts, special courts for commercial fraud cases, more recourse to arbitration and filling the large number of vacancies of judges in the lower courts are all essential to make the judiciary an effective instrument to protect the public good.

Third, implement the police reforms that were ordered by the Supreme Court in its 2006 judgement. The government is in contempt of the apex court's order which, if and when implemented, will make the police a professional and autonomous force. Accountability and efficiency of law enforcement are key ingredients of good governance. Fourth, execute long-delayed reforms of the civil service. The recommendations of the second Administrative Reforms Commission, headed by former law minister Veerappa Moily before he resigned as chairperson of the ARC in 2009, continue to gather dust. If implemented, they will transform public services in India.

•

Strong, well-governed institutions will help the prime minister focus on the 'unfinished business of economic reforms' he referred to while launching my book. Apart from implementing pending banking and finance legislation, the prime minister should focus on three broad economic measures in the concluding months of his tenure.

One, cut subsidies which are inefficient, leak-prone and do not create productive assets. The remaining subsidies on fuel and nitrogenous fertilizers must go if the government is to keep its budget promise of reducing total subsidies, excluding those on the balance sheets of oil marketing companies (OMCs), to below 2 per cent of GDP in 2013-14.

Two, reduce government expenditure. The central government employs 60 lakh people. Salaries and overheads will consume nearly 25 per cent of the government's total budgeted expenditure in 2013-14. While ministries, paralysed by fear of adverse CAG reports and CBI inquiries, underspend Plan expenditure that builds assets, unproductive non-Plan expenditure continues to balloon.

Three, broaden the tax base. The Goods and Services Tax (GST), an important step forward, has been impeded by colliding state-centre interests. Implementation of GST will significantly increase India's central tax-GDP ratio, which is currently at 10.60 per cent. Every percentage point rise translates into over Rs 1,00,000 crore in additional annual tax revenue.

By, on the one hand, cutting unproductive subsidies and trimming wasteful government expenditure and, on the other, boosting tax revenue, India's fiscal deficit can achieve the 3 per cent target the finance minister has set for 2016-17. For a high-growth economy, this is a reasonable medium-term outcome. The virtuous cascading impact on inflation, the value of the rupee and interest rates will take the economy back into a 7-8 per cent growth trajectory.

As he nears the end of his second and final term as prime minister, Dr Singh will be mindful of three legacies. The first, economic reforms, is in disarray as the economy stumbles to sub-5 per cent growth. The second, India's civil nuclear deal with the United States, is entangled in disputes over liability in the event of an accident involving an American-built nuclear reactor. The third, peace with Pakistan, lies in tatters following Islamabad's renewed terrorism in J&K and infiltration across the line of control.

The opportunity to inflict deterrent punishment on Pakistan has been missed: downsizing its high commission in India to consulate status, suspending most favoured nation (MFN) status and deploying covert intelligence-backed operations in Pakistan-occupied Kashmir (PoK).

Along with stalled economic reforms and halting Indo-US nuclear cooperation, the prime minister's failed policy on Pakistan will disappoint him most. Instead of a legacy, it will be seen as an epitaph.

5

DHIRUBHAI AMBANI: VISIONARY OF THE CENTURY

I still recall vividly the first time I met Dhirubhai Ambani. All of twenty-five years old, I had just moved into new offices at Mumbai's Nariman Point in 1980 to launch the first magazine, *Gentleman*, published by my new media firm, Sterling Newspapers Pvt. Ltd.

One morning, Dhirubhai, whom I had admired from afar following Reliance Industries Ltd's debut IPO in 1977, smiled as we got into the lift together. Reliance had just moved into the same office building on the top floor. We were a floor beneath, on the ninth.

The first thing that struck you about Dhirubhai was the luminosity that gave his face a special cadence. He was then forty-seven and already one of India's leading industrialists. Many battles would lie ahead but his exuberant self-confidence would see him through each one.

We continued to meet in the elevator. One day he invited me to his office towards late afternoon. I walked up one flight of stairs and was ushered into his chamber. It was large but tastefully designed. Dhirubhai sat behind an imposing table, his wide smile both friendly and knowing. The turnover of Reliance Industries Ltd was in 1980 still relatively modest—but I could sense immediately that Dhirubhai represented the future of Indian industry.

Over tea and Gujarati snacks, we spoke of the publications we intended to start. He was encouraging, and so full of energy that some of it used to rub off on others. Dhirubhai had a special way with people. He could read your mind, judge your motives, measure your worth—all in a glance.

Two years later, in 1982, we celebrated the second anniversary of *Gentleman*. By now, Reliance was expanding rapidly. A huge Polyester Filament Yarn (PFA) plant was coming up in Patalganga and the foundation for future growth was being laid—from the Hazira petrochemicals complex and the Jamnagar integrated refinery to telecom and oil and gas exploration in the Krishna-Godavari basin.

Not surprisingly, the readers of our magazine chose him as the 'Man of the Year'. (JRD Tata would be chosen Man of the Year in 1983.) When I informed Dhirubhai of the vote, he was delighted and, with his customary exuberance, invited me up for a cup of tea. He was generous with his time and gave me a long interview which was published as the cover story of our second anniversary issue.

Interspersed with his vision for Reliance were impromptu jokes about life and work, people and their peccadilloes. You never left Dhirubhai's presence without feeling uplifted: he had that special quality that inspired people.

■

As the years rolled by, Reliance grew exponentially as a public company. Dhirubhai pioneered the equity cult. If the history of the Bombay Stock Exchange (BSE) is written, it could easily be broken up into two eras: before Dhirubhai (BD) and after Dhirubhai (AD).

By 1986, our media firm had launched its fifth publication—*Business Computer*—in collaboration with Dutch media giant VNU. The same year, Dhirubhai suffered a stroke that weakend his right hand. Showing his customary grit, he learnt to sign with his left hand.

The next few years were challenging for Reliance. But once

economic reforms took hold in 1991, growth returned. Dhirubhai's health had improved. A major thrust into oil refining, with a state-of-the-art petroleum refinery in Jamnagar, was planned in the mid-1990s. Dhirubhai's elder son, Mukesh, led the team that would in the next few years give Reliance the worldwide reputation for project implementation—within budget and within compressed timelines. The world's largest grassroots refinery was commissioned in a record period of less than three years in 1999-2000 and is today a testament to Indian engineering, and technological and financial capability. A decade later, Reliance's partnership with global leader BP would enhance its deep-sea oil and gas exploration prowess.

■

By the late-1990s, though Dhirubhai's health was stable, he increasingly focused on strategy. He was now sixty-six and had not given an exclusive interview to any newspaper or magazine for a long time. International accolades were meanwhile pouring in. In 1998, he was awarded the Dean's Medal by the Wharton School, University of Pennsylvania.

In late-1999, as the century and millennium came to a close, one of our publications ran a poll to decide the business leader of the century. Dhirubhai topped the poll. We decided to print a special stand-alone magazine to honour Dhirubhai's lifetime of achievement during which he had built India's largest private sector enterprise. But for that we needed an exclusive interview with him.

Dhirubhai himself had long shifted into new offices in Maker Chambers IV. He attended office for a few hours every day but preferred to lead a quietlife. I sent in a request for an exclusive interview. Dhirubhai replied that he hadn't given one in years but that he would make a special exception for us if I sent him a written questionnaire. I did and, true to his word, he replied to every question with the straightforwardness and confidence that had marked his whole life.

It was to be his last major interview. It appeared in our January 2000 issue, honouring Dhirubhai as the 'Business Leader of the Century'.

Just over two years later, in June 2002, Dhirubhai suddenly fell ill. Surrounded by his family, he was taken to Mumbai's Breach Candy hospital. He breathed his last there on 6 July. It was the end of an extraordinary life but the beginning of an enduring legacy.

What was that one quality about Dhirubhai that marked him out as special in a nation of over a billion? He exuded an energy—a force—that transmitted itself to others. The force went beyond mere charisma. He made people believe that he could do the impossible. And he made people believe that they could do the impossible. Such an inspirational life is lived but once in a century.

6

OM PRAKASH JINDAL: A LEADER OF MEN

Some men are born to lead. Om Prakash Jindal unquestionably was. Born on 30 August 1930, in a large family of eleven children—the third of five bothers and six sisters—Om Prakash was not academically inclined. He was, however, deeply interested in technology.

Speaking of his father, Sajjan Jindal says he was a hard taskmaster but fair-minded. He was interested in sports rather than academics. 'My father would look out of the window in his school, watching the passing tractors and cars,' says Sajjan. He would dream about the wonders of technology. They would play a major role in his life.

Om Prakash's father, Netram Jindal, was a landlord and a large-scale farmer. The family lived in Nalwa, a village on the border of Haryana and Rajasthan, 18 km from Hisar. At the age of sixteen, Om Prakash left his village along with a cousin. Destination: Orissa. There, young Om Prakash began trading in wheat and ghee. Orissa had neither, so Om Prakash bought the wheat and ghee in Haryana and sold it in Orissa. Here he learned his first lessons in business: the cut and thrust of trading in a tough new environment.

In 1950, barely out of his teens, Om Prakash joined his elder brother in Calcutta. Tata Steel had a pipe-manufacturing unit called

Indian Steel Tubes. The company used to sell rejected scrap material. Om Prakash and his brother began to buy the scrap material, repair the tubes manually and market them.

The brothers began to make a lot of money. Soon they caught the attention of an Englishman who then headed Indian Steel Tubes. He had heard complaints that the Jindal brothers were selling the pipes as prime pipes. The Englishman called Om Prakash and said that henceforth they would be allowed to take out only six-inch pipes, not full length pipes.

Undeterred, Sajjan says, 'Dad pitched up a tent in Jamshedpur in the factory premises. He put up a machine shop to cut the pipes into small pieces. He literally started his career in the Tatas' backyard.'

The brothers used the cut pipes as sockets for export to Germany. Within a couple a years, however, the Indian Steel Tubes management came to know that the Jindal brothers were doing extremely well and ended their business relationship.

Om Prakash, feisty even as a twenty-two-year-old, decided to set up his own tube mill. He returned to Hissar and designed the factory himself. The Jindal story had begun. 'The tubes became so popular that even today in Punjab, Haryana, Western Uttar Pradesh and Rajasthan,' says Sajjan, 'people are prepared to pay any price for Jindal tubes.' A mere fifty years after Om Prakash set up his first tube pipe mill, the Jindal group now has nearly three times the domestic steel-making capacity of the Tatas in India—20 million tonnes against around 7 million tonnes.

■

Growing up in his village, Om Prakash had been an accomplished sportsman. He wrestled, rode horses and, though of medium height, was extremely strong. The early days on his father's vast farm now stood him in good stead. Living rough and cutting pipes for export to Germany in a difficult, at times hostile, business environment in Jamshedpur, toughened Om Prakash for the challenges that lay ahead. In his interaction with the Tata group in Jamshedpur, he also got a lesson in competition.

The Green Revolution swept India in the 1960s and tubes became an essential component for both agriculture and industry. It enabled Om Prakash to lay the foundation in Haryana for what would become one of the world's largest steel empires.

Om Prakash was a workaholic but still found time to play sports with his employees. Volleyball was a particular favourite. Growing up, the Jindal boys remember their father as a strict disciplinarian—a father they rarely saw because he worked so hard. 'He enjoyed his work,' says Sajjan. 'It was his passion. He was tough and did not pamper us. But he was not short-tempered at all. He was a lovely person.'

As the Jindal empire grew, through the 1970s and early-1980s, Om Prakash, now in his fifties, became increasingly interested in politics. His four sons, Prithviraj, Sajjan, Ratan and Naveen, had begun taking charge of different parts of the group's sprawling businesses.

Industry in Haryana was booming. In neighbouring Punjab, Chief Minister Pratap Singh Kairon had been supportive of the Jindal group. He had helped Om Prakash set up his tube mills in the early-1960s. Having established himself as the leading industrialist in Haryana by the mid-1980s, Om Prakash turned his attention to politics. The catalyst was a disagreement that he had with Haryana Chief Minister Devi Lal and later his son, Bhajan Lal.

Tough as nails, Om Prakash decided to enter electoral politics. Bansi Lal, who had retired from active politics after being sidelined by Rajiv Gandhi, promised him support and the Haryana Vikas Party was formed in 1993. It immediately won the next assembly election and formed the government in Haryana.

∎

Om Prakash, now in his sixties, had already handed over the group's day-to-day business to his four sons. By 2000, he had immersed himself almost totally in politics. The group's flagships, including Jindal Strips, Saw Pipes, JISCO and Jindal Vijaynagar, were split into four sub-groups under the four brothers.

Each brother ran his respective business independently. However, each had a shareholding in the others' business. This arrangement ensured the relationship between the brothers remained free of conflict or rancour.

While he had been a Lok Sabha MP in 1996, Om Prakash soon returned to the Haryana assembly where his real political interest lay. Naveen, his youngest son, would later take his Lok Sabha seat.

After just over a decade in active politics, Om Prakash was appointed Minister for Power in Haryana in February 2005. Though not a minister till then, he had established himself as a force in Haryana politics for years and was clearly a rising star in the state's firmament. He had a vision: to make Haryana India's most prosperous and developed state with a focus on providing water, electricity, health and education to all.

He was upset by the corruption he saw in Haryana's political establishment and knew that clean governance was the key to the state's development. 'He was determined to root out corruption,' says Sajjan. 'He would say that he wanted electricity to flow like water in Haryana. He felt that as a small state Haryana could be a model of development for the rest of the country.'

■

Om Prakash Jindal's vision for Haryana was to remain unfulfilled in his lifetime. Weeks after becoming minister of power, on 31 March 2005, he woke early as was his custom. He had a quick breakfast and, after meeting several people who had come to visit him at his minister's residence, he left for Chandigarh airport. Bansi Lal's younger son, Surinder, accompanied him. The two were headed for Delhi.

They boarded the company helicopter. Om Prakash was seated in the rear; Surinder sat next to the pilot. Halfway to Delhi, the pilot informed Om Prakash: 'Sir, we have lost our engine.'

Unperturbed, Om Prakash asked the pilot: 'Do you know how to handle it?'

The pilot replied: 'Yes, we'll land safely.'

In the end he couldn't. Om Prakash Jindal died as he had lived: bravely, stoically.

He left behind not only one of India's largest business empires with a combined group market value of $15 billion (Rs 95,000 crore) but also the legacy of a leader.

7
THE CHURCHILL MYTHOLOGY

Why did a small northwest European island called Britain spend $50 million (Rs 290 crore) a day to help twenty-seven other countries evict Iraq from Kuwait?

It couldn't have been oil. Britain was then a net exporter of its own North Sea crude. It couldn't have been principle. Britain, in its time, invaded scores of nations far further from its borders than Kuwait is from Iraq's. And it couldn't have been the desire for hegemony in West Asia. Britain knows better than anyone else—from imperial experience—how quickly a global military presence can bankrupt national treasuries.

The reason for Britain's full-throated participation in the Gulf War was more complex and certainly more subtle than America's. The United States has a clear idea of why it is in the Gulf: it wants to establish a unipolar, post-Cold War world order, with Washington as an international gendarme.

To understand fully the motivations for Britain's knee-jerk eagerness to jump into the Gulf fray, it is necessary to read *The Caged Lion*, the second volume of William Manchester's biography of Winston Churchill, the wartime British prime minister. Manchester's 1988 book, widely hailed in the West, has just been issued in soft cover in India and it illuminates the answers to many questions about Britain and its attitude toward war.

The author is a clear-headed (though at times unquestioning) admirer of Churchill. However, while giving free rein to his admiration, Manchester exposes the legendary British prime minister, a man of extraordinary gifts but equally formidable shortcomings, in wholly unconscious ways.

Churchill's father, Lord Randolph Churchill, who was briefly chancellor of the exchequer, loathed his son. His mother, a beautiful American called Jennie, was known to have slept with several powerful men in Britain. Her husband, who suffered from chronic syphilis, could hardly demur.

A syphilitic father who loathes you and a nymphomaniac mother who embarrasses you (one of Mrs Churchill's lovers was the Prince of Wales) are not a perfect recipe for a happy childhood and Winston's was not.

He went to Harrow, finished last in his class, flunked Oxford and Cambridge and was packed off to Sandhurst as a sort of consolation prize. Churchill's lack of a university education nagged him throughout his adult life and he acquired many affectations to disguise it.

Young Churchill left for India in 1895, aged twenty. He spent his time in Bangalore reading Plato, Aristotle, Gibbon, Macaulay and Schopenhauer, honing his skill with words and ideas. They were to serve him well in later years.

■

Churchill was a ruthless manipulator. He inveigled his mother's lover, the Prince of Wales, to get him plum war reporting assignments. By 1899, he was in South Africa, covering the Boer war. He was imprisoned, escaped heroically and became nationally famous at twenty-four. The first phase in Churchill's finely calibrated life had been successfully completed.

He sought and won election to parliament and, by thirty-three, was a cabinet minister. It would, despite his ambition and single-mindedness, take him another thirty-two years to become prime minister.

In between, Churchill occupied every major cabinet post. But his most controversial role came as First Lord of the Admiralty during the First World War. Most people remember the Second World War, not fully realizing how close Churchill had come to losing the First World War for the allies.

As Manchester writes: 'Today military historians agree that the Dardanelles strategy could have ended the war in 1916 with a German defeat. But a timid British admiral, who had been sweeping all before him, turned tail at the first sign of resistance [...] incompetent British generals botched the landings on Gallipoli Peninsula, which flanked the Dardanelles. The British public demanded a scapegoat, and Churchill, as the stratagem's most flamboyant advocate, was dismissed from the Admiralty.'

But Manchester's book also reveals clues to Britain's role in the Gulf War of 1991, exactly seventy-five years after the fiasco of Dardanelles: 'The empire! The mere mention of it aroused patriotic Britons like Churchill, made them brace their backs and lift their eyes. If there was any fixed star in their firmament it was an abiding glory of their realm.' The empire was glorified for years, celebrating the 'magnificence' of imperialism. Britons were taught that when it came to battle, the British always won.

Remember, all this drumbeating, however imbecilic it may sound today, occurred as recently as 1932. In just over fifty years, the British empire, the world's only pre-Second World War superpower, has been reduced to a middle-sized regional European power with a few scattered islandic possessions in various oceans. The decline has been more precipitous than even the fall of the Roman Empire a millennium and a half ago.

As the former British Prime Minister Harold MacMillan said

thirty years ago, Britain had lost an empire but still not found a role. It is this old imperial itch, the harking for a global role, that Britain feels compelled to scratch every now and again: Suez, the Falkands, the Gulf.

The world may no longer come to heel at the snap of a Whitehall finger but the RAF and the Royal Navy doing battle in the Gulf bring back happy memories of war, conquest and dominance.

From imperial conquest sprang imperial grandeur and the grandeur seeped into language. England, Scotland, Wales and Northern Ireland became 'Great Britain', a unique pomposity of nomenclature that endures.

More materially, however, the British empire was struck a death blow in 1914 when the First World War began. Within four years, 3.19 million Englishmen lay dead in 'the slime and gore of trench warfare' in Europe. Many millions more were crippled and maimed. The British imperial economy would never recover from this blow. In a sense, therefore, Germany, despite losing the two World Wars, weakened and eventually destroyed the British empire. That has earned it the unremitting hostility of the British people, a hostility that erupts every now and again against the growing German domination of Europe.

Manchester notes perceptively that only Churchill among Britain's mid-twentieth-century leaders fully understood the long-term danger of the German threat to the British empire. Pacifist Neville Chamberlain certainly did not and contrived the appeasement of the Munich Conference.

Manchester says Churchill understood Hitler's manic character and that they were mirror images of each other. He shrewdly observes: 'Since the embattled defender of Western civilization (Churchill) was the one who was ultimately successful, his vision has prevailed. What would have happened had victory gone to the Nazi leader doesn't bear thinking about.'

This is where Manchester stumbles as biographer and

historian. What exactly was the 'embattled defender of Western civilization' defending? Illegal British rule (and pillage) in over fifty countries around the world? While 'evil' Germany was swallowing Czechoslovakia and Poland, Britain had already gobbled up fifty countries in Asia and Africa and expropriated their wealth.

■

Churchill, to his everlasting discredit, identified himself completely with this policy: fighting Nazi territorial ambitions in Europe while spending most of his adult life pursuing British territorial ambitions in the rest of the world.

Few Indians—and fewer Englishmen—have deciphered the grimmer side of Churchill's character. M.J. Akbar, then still editor of *The Telegraph,* during a speech to a distinguished audience in New York in 1988, compared Churchill to Hitler.

One, Akbar noted, had killed millions of Jews. The other had, less directly but equally certainly, killed two million Indians in Bengal during the famine of 1943, which had been caused by implementing the specific policies of Churchill, then prime minister.

Manchester calls Churchill the 'greatest Englishman since Disraeli'. He was 'brilliant, visionary, generous, heroic'. But, as Manchester points out, he was also 'domineering, ruthless, self-centred, inconsiderate, emotional and megalomaniacal'.

Hypocrisy, however, was Churchill's singular trait. He once told Kingsley Martin in an interview in the *New Statesman:* 'War is horrible, but slavery is worse, and you may be sure the British people would rather go down fighting than live in servitude.'

And yet, at that very moment, the spring of 1929, 475 million people around the world were in effect Britain's slaves, conquered by bigger guns and bigger ships to serve an emperor they owed no allegiance to. It is this obscenity Manchester fails to reconcile with the rest of Churchill's 'heroism'.

America does most of the fighting these days but, across the pond, Britain rallies round to the call to arms as if a time machine had transported the entire nation to a battlefield of the past. But an imperial itch is expensive to scratch at 1991 prices. That is why the British defence secretary, Tom King, went around the world, hat in hand, pleading for 'contributions' to Britain's war effort in the Gulf.

■

Madhushree Mukerjee's book on Churchill and the Great Bengal Famine, *Churchill's Secret War: The British Empire and the Ravaging of India during World War II*, published in 2010, confirms the wartime leader's malign role. Nonetheless for over forty-five years, the Churchill book industry has purred along smoothly, cosetted by Western biographers in thrall to a man described as the most important statesman of the twentieth century. In a 2002 BBC poll, Winston Churchill was voted the Greatest Briton of All Time, ahead of Shakespeare, Darwin and Newton.

Richard Toye's 2010 biography, *Churchill's Empire: The World That Made Him and the World He Made*, sets Churchill's life and politics in a more modern context. Previous biographers of Churchill like William Manchester tiptoed around their subject. The occasional attempt to uncover Churchill's racism, especially his contempt for Mahatma Gandhi, dissolved quickly into platitudes that justified Empire as, on balance, a force for good. Churchill's racism, Toye suggests in a thread that runs through his book, was acceptable in the early-1900s because almost all white people held racist views at the time. This sophistry is the principal reason why Toye's biography, so promising in precept, fails in practice.

Churchill's dysfunctional family forged his attitude to race, imperialism and war. Toye acknowledges Churchill's pathological aversion to India and how he wished partition upon the subcontinent. 'The mere mention of India,' Toye writes, 'brought out a streak of unpleasantness or even irrationality in Churchill. In March 1943, R.A. Butler, the Education Minister, visited him at Chequers. The

Prime Minister launched into a most terrible attack on the baboos, saying that they were gross, dirty and corrupt. He even declared that he wanted the British to leave India, and—this was a more serious remark—that he supported the principle of Pakistan. When Butler argued that the Raj had always stood for Indian unity, Churchill replied, "Well, if our poor troops have to be kept in a sweltering, syphilitic climate for the sake of your precious unity, I'd rather see them have a good civil war.'"

Toye devotes less than three pages to Churchill's malign role in the Great Bengal Famine of 1943-44. Britain's plunder of India is dispensed with equally briskly. He says Churchill's resentment towards India sprung from the money they owed to the country (over a million pounds) for the war effort.

Globally, reviewers have called Toye's new biography revisionist. It is not. It exposes Churchill's warts but, often in the same paragraph, presents a contextual justification for them. The concluding lines of Toye's book reveal where his sympathies lie: 'The decline of Churchill's Empire, much as the man himself regretted it, can be seen in part as a tribute to the power of beliefs that he himself prized dearly.'

It is a disappointing end to a biography that sets out to critically re-examine Churchill but fails the final test, unheroically, like Churchill himself.

8

THE CHIDAMBARAM CHRONICLES

I first interviewed P. Chidambaram when he was finance minister in UPA-1. The forty-minute interview in North Block started badly. We were thirty seconds late. The appointment was for 4 p.m. Knowing Chidambaram's fetish for punctuality, we had arrived at 3.50 p.m.

Then disaster struck. My colleague had to use the ladies room, and North Block is not particularly gender-friendly. By the time my colleague, sprinting to and back from the washroom at the other end of the labyrinthine corridor, returned it was precisely 4 p.m. We entered Chidambaram's chamber thirty seconds later—a cardinal sin in the finance minister's book. He had begun pacing up and down his capacious room, his mood decidedly flinty.

Through much of the interview, however, Chidambaram was pleasant but taciturn, eyes frequently glued to the large plasma TV screen placed to the right of his imposing, clutter-free table. I flashed occasional glances at the TV screen as the interview progressed: it was tuned to a popular business channel, scrolling share prices. Chidambaram's interest in the stock market has since not waned.

Which is not a bad thing. Former finance ministers have been dismissive of the markets—one famously said he was more interested in Khan Market than the stock market. Not Chidambaram. He knows the sensex, vulnerable as it might be to overreaction, is a barometer of the economy.

Stockbrokers are not the dhoti-clad parodies of yore. The Harshad Mehta and Ketan Parekh days are behind us. Most of today's stock brokers are as savvy as their New York, London and Singapore counterparts. They deal in complex derivatives, futures and options, currencies, commodities and, of course, regular stocks. FIIs have imposed financial discipline. SEBI has improved fiduciary standards. Defaults are rare.

■

But back to Chidambaram. As his mood improved during our extended interview, he opened up. By instinct, Chidambaram is a liberalizer—his 'Dream Budget' in 1997 in his first stint as finance minister in the United Front government established his credentials. So what can we expect from Chidambaram 3.0? Alas, not much. His hands are tied. Time is not his friend. He has only one budget, in February, to impose his philosophy on India's economy.

As home minister, a portfolio he accepted reluctantly after 26/11, Chidambaram had a mixed record. His early ambition to set up the National Counter-Terrorism Centre (NCTC) as an intelligence hub-and-spoke remains stillborn. Terror modules of the Indian Mujahideen (IM) and the banned Students Islamic Movement of India (SIMI) are active.

Even if the next general election stretches to its May 2014 limit, the February 2014 budget will be a vote-on-account. So Chidambaram will remain a one-budget minister. Given these limitations, what are Chidambaram's options? First, to fix the mid-year fiscal math. Second, to cut Plan and non-Plan expenditure. Third, raise tax revenues to ensure budget targets are met.

But serious questions remain as annual GDP growth plunges to 5 per cent levels, and the rupee wobbles. Has the bottom fallen out of the Indian story?

No.

Can 8 per cent GDP growth be reclaimed in the near future?

Possibly—if real economic reforms take place. For that, though, we will have to await a government unbeholden to populism.

9

L.K. ADVANI: 'RIOTS CANNOT BE JUSTIFIED UNDER ANY CIRCUMSTANCES'

Face The Press is aimed at holding national leaders to account. L.K. Advani, then chairman of the BJP parliamentary party, debated a wide range of issues with a panel of distinguished editors at the Press Club, Mumbai, on 28 March 2011. Face The Press is an initiative of the Association for Democratic Reforms (ADR), Merchant Media Ltd and the Press Club, Mumbai. The panel of editors at the inaugural event: N. Ram, editor-in-chief, *The Hindu*; Uday Shankar, CEO, Star India; and Kumar Ketkar, chief editor, *Dainik Divya Marathi*.

The interaction was moderated by Minhaz Merchant, group editor-in-chief, Merchant Media Ltd, and Ajit Ranade, co-founder and trustee, Association for Democratic Reforms.

Ajit Ranade began by briefing the distinguished audience on the objective of the initiative: placing an unrelenting focus on accountability and governance, the bedrock of a mature democracy. After Ajit Ranade's opening remarks, L.K. Advani delivered a brief speech followed by a debate with the panel of editors and questions from the audience.

L.K. Advani: I have had the privilege and the good fortune of being an activist in politics since 1951 when Dr Shyama Prasad Mukherjee formed the Bharatiya Jana Sangh. Dr Mukherjee himself was a member of Pandit Nehru's first cabinet. There were two members in that cabinet who were not Congressmen. They were included by Pandit Nehru in his cabinet on the advice of Mahatma Gandhi: Dr Babasaheb Ambedkar and Dr Shyama Prasad Mukherjee.

I have tried, in my own way, to do my best for the country, for the country's politics, for the party and for democracy. In that context, when I received this invitation from Minhaz Merchant, I felt really honoured that he said he would like me to be the first speaker in this series, though I told him that it would have been more appropriate if the prime minister had been called for the inaugural Face The Press.

Minhaz Merchant: Thank you, sir. May I now ask Mr N. Ram, editor-in-chief of *The Hindu*, to commence the panel discussion with Advaniji.

N. Ram: May I ask you a big-picture question, Advaniji? Where would you situate the Indian polity today, looking at the correlation of forces, the major opposition parties, and the government and its allies—and distancing yourself from it to be as objective as possible?

L.K. Advani: Let me confess to you that when the NDA government's tenure was about to come to an end in 2004, I for one did not doubt that Vajpayeeji would get a renewed mandate. We were optimistic, but while we who worked in the government, including Vajpayeeji, were optimistic, in the party generally there was overconfidence.

The effort that you have started here in Face The Press to strengthen democracy, to renew or at least curb the governance deficit and the ethical deficit, that should be the focus of attention. Every country, including an old democracy like the UK, continues to try to improve governance. British Prime Minister David Cameron has been putting forward certain ideas which appeal to me and which I have myself discussed once with the prime minister and with Finance Minister Pranab Mukherjee. I told them: why cannot we also think of something similar about the tenure of a legislature? Why cannot we have a fixed-term legislature? Most democracies in Europe now have a fixed-term legislature.

Minhaz Merchant: May I, on the issue of corruption, bring in Kumar Ketkar. What are your views, not only in the context of individual corruption, but institutionalized corruption, because we have outstanding issues such as autonomy for the CBI, the new Lokpal Bill, police reforms—issues that need an institutional solution.

Kumar Ketkar: I think on the question of corruption Mr Advani has adequately stated his position—how it is ruining our political establishment as well as the political atmosphere. Therefore, I would rather focus on the question of tolerance and intolerance. India's civilizational attribute is tolerance and that is why democracy has survived, but the party which he heads is known for its intolerance. In fact, many people are afraid, many liberal people are afraid of the BJP and they turn away from the BJP. M.F. Husain's paintings have been vandalized in most parts of the country and I do not think the BJP has condemned the vandalization. M.F. Husain himself has been forced to settle outside India and I do not think the BJP has protested against that.

Mrs Sonia Gandhi and Dr Manmohan Singh have apologized to the nation for the 1984 riots in Delhi and even went to Amritsar and apologized for whatever happened during 1984. But I have not seen the BJP apologizing for the riots that took place between 1990 and 1992. Actually, under Advaniji's rath yatra, when the country got communally divided, I do not remember in all my years in journalism, having also seen Partition, the psychological, mental, cultural and religious partition which I experienced after 1990 and which continues partly today. I do not think the BJP has ever apologized that they were responsible for this.

Minhaz Merchant: I think, in all fairness, that is a point

Mr Advani should address head-on and clarify his position.

L.K. Advani: I have no difficulty in responding to this because when I undertook my first rath yatra, which was from Somnath to Ayodhya, I remember that the rath yatra was described by some books as a bloody rath yatra. After the demolition on 6 December 1992 in Ayodhya, there were disturbances in Mumbai itself and I am sure that most of you are aware that I felt so unhappy that day that I wrote an article in *The Indian Express* a fortnight later in which I said it was the saddest day of my life.

So far as my own reaction to the happenings of 1992 are concerned, it has been very consistent. A question was put to me by *The Telegraph* many years ago and the questioner asked me: you write in English, you write in Hindi, you speak in both these languages, which is the word that you like most? The word that I use very often and which I like is 'credibility' and I can say that whatever I have been able to contribute to the country is because of the credibility that I have earned in my life.

Minhaz Merchant: Kumar Ketkar's point was that Mrs Sonia Gandhi, Prime Minister Manmohan Singh and others have apologized for the 1984 Sikh pogrom. On the Godhra riots of 2002 there has been no apology forthcoming from the BJP.

L.K. Advani: It is the official position that riots cannot be justified under any circumstances.

Minhaz Merchant: But is there an apology that has been forthcoming?

L.K. Advani: I have apologized.

Minhaz Merchant: Mr Advani has apologized and as a leader of the BJP, if he has done that, I think we should give him credit for that.

Kumar Ketkar: I do not want to repeat myself, but on M.F. Husain, what is the position of the BJP?

L.K. Advani: On the issue of M.F. Husain, I have not commented. I do not think the party has commented. But there should be tolerance, particularly in the field of art. Vandalism cannot be advocated. It cannot be justified.

Uday Shankar: There are many unanswered questions on the issue of tolerance from the BJP and Advaniji has just said that riots cannot be tolerated under any circumstances, even though there was a very, very bad riot that happened in 2002 in Gujarat under the leadership of the BJP government.

Ajit Ranade: I want to bring back the focus on governance issues and accountability, because accountability and transparency are the bedrock of good governance. Mr Advani has come here as a national leader, so can I ask him a question about criminality? In the current Lok Sabha, more than 128 members of parliament have criminal charges against them and this is based on self-declared affidavits. The party which has the maximum number of such members is the BJP—forty-two. And seventeen out of these forty-two MPs actually have very serious charges against them like rape and murder. Can your party make a commitment that you will not give tickets to candidates who have a single criminal charge pending against them? We have four states and one union territory going to elections. If you can make a statement against criminality in politics, people who are in public life will be held accountable to a higher standard.

L.K. Advani: Very often, violations of Section 144 are also an offence. In India, this has become a pattern of protest—that you violate Section 144 and so this is the criminal charge against me.

Ajit Ranade: But the Indian penal code can be changed by parliament! We can make a distinction between criminal charges. Lawmakers can make such a distinction.

Kumar Ketkar: Even in the 1989 general election, you had said that the main issue before Indian politics and democracy was criminalization of politics and an all-out effort would be made to completely decriminalize politics and democracy in India. As Ajit Ranade was very correctly saying, you can always distinguish between people who are arrested under Section 144 or similar charges and those who are arrested for robbery, murder or rape.

L.K. Advani: You cannot impose it, particularly in a situation when so many serious cases are foisted against you by a hostile government, by a partisan government.

N. Ram: Moving to Pakistan and the dialogue...

L.K. Advani: I am not talking of a dialogue—many in this party disagree that terrorism and dialogue should be delinked. We said zero tolerance towards terrorism means that we will be willing to have a dialogue with Pakistan provided you totally dismantle the infrastructure of terrorism that you have built up.

N. Ram: On the question of engagement with Pakistan, in fact one of the first India cables which *The Hindu* reported through an arrangement with WikiLeaks had the headline that the prime minister is isolated on Pakistan in his inner circle and this information came, according to this source, from M.K. Narayanan. It is well known that Prime Minister Manmohan Singh seems to be under pressure from public opinion. But what is the alternative to engagement with Pakistan, whatever be the problem, considering the fact that Atalji made that famous statement: 'You can't change your neighbours...'

L.K. Advani: What is happening at the moment—India and Pakistan playing a cricket match, inviting Gilani for the match. This is engagement, but engagement does not mean that you start a formal dialogue. It is the formal dialogue about which I say that the minimum requirement is the basic infrastructure for terrorism has to be dismantled.

N. Ram: On the subject of WikiLeaks, Hindutva is seen by the BJP not as a philosophy, but an opportunity. It is not Hindutva philosophy that matters but Hindutva opportunism that matters in politics.

L.K. Advani: Every WikiLeaks cable has three parts. One about the conversation or what are the facts narrated in that cable. Those facts we accept as true, but they are facts which are being conveyed to their own government without the fear of someone being able to read them. Therefore the facts should be accepted as true. The second is interpretation. The third is the advice on that basis given by the US diplomat.

My own view is that the facts should be accepted as true. Interpretation and advice that the diplomat gives is his own, you may agree with it, you may not agree with it. The political counsellor of the US embassy was taken to the residence of Satish Sharma and there he was shown two cases in which there were Rs 50 to 60 crores. Why should we dispute this version, what enmity has that US political counsellor with Satish Sharma that he should be telling lies about this to his own government?

N. Ram: One WikiLeaks cable reveals that Mr Blake—a very senior diplomat who went on to become US Ambassador to Sri Lanka and I think is in a high position in the State Department—said Hindu nationalism, according to Arun Jaitley, was an 'opportunistic' issue, that is the word used. Jaitley conceded that, 'Yes, the meeting took place, all the rest is true, but these are not my words.'

L.K. Advani: I will have to see the exact statement because I saw a statement made by Arun Jaitley that he had never used the word 'opportunistic' and a second statement by the party president (Nitin Gadkari) said that this is an interpretation.

Whatever Arunji said, if he responds to that himself it is better. I do not want to say anything. I will only say, regarding the prime minister's comment on me thinking of the prime ministership as my birthright, that in a democracy nobody has the birthright to be prime minister.

Ajit Ranade: This question has not come up yet—financial transparency. We at ADR have tried to get the income and expenditure statements from all political parties and we have had a lot of trouble, faced a lot of stonewalling. They said that a political party is not a public authority, you cannot ask us this question, this is fiducially private information, etc., etc. We had to struggle and finally we did get the information.

Mr Advani, should not all political parties subject themselves to a law which requires them to publish financial information like any company or trust or a hospital or a temple does? Why cannot we have a simple regulation that, every year, parties will publish both income and expenditure statements to the citizens of India? Can you please support this?

L.K. Advani: Broadly, I would be in support of this particular law provided laws relating to black money are also developed in a manner as to curb the growth of black money in the country. There has to be a comprehensive approach to the problem. But I do agree fully that transparency in financial matters in politics has a lot to do with internal democracy within the party. And you require laws for that as well.

SECTION 5
SCIENCE & SOCIETY

1
CIVILIZATION—IN SCIENTIFIC TERMS, JUST A FEW SECONDS OLD!

Nothing, perhaps, is quite as fascinating or quite as humbling as a realization of the vastness of the cosmos. Human beings are notoriously egocentric and small-minded, being obsessed with things that are insignificant in the cosmic context.

A look at our origins is a humbling exercise in itself. As Carl Sagan, the late American cosmic physicist-turned-media superstar, said: 'Significant events in our personal lives are measured in years or less: our lifetimes in decades; our family genealogies in centuries; and all of recorded history in millennia. But we have been preceded by an awesome vista of time, extending for prodigious periods into the past, about which we know little—both because there are no written records and because we have real difficulty in grasping the immensity of the intervals involved.'

Just how immense these intervals are can be gauged by charting a Saganesque cosmic chronology. Imagine the fourteen-billion-year lifetime of our universe (that's how old it is, give or take a billion years) compressed into a single 365-day calendar year. Then, as Sagan argued with delicious logic, every event in the universe—from its Big Bang origin to the formation of the earth's crust to the emergence of our planet's first living organisms to, finally, three million years ago, the birth of man—can be accurately represented on our new cosmic calendar by a specific month, day, date, hour, minute and even second. The following time chart, drawn from Sagan's calculations, puts the 'importance' of the human race in the right cosmic perspective.

According to our cosmic calendar, the Big Bang (which, so to speak, kicked off the cosmos) occurred on 1 January, New Year's Day. According to Sagan's compressed 365-day cosmic calendar, nothing much happened for the next four 'months'. On 1 May, the Milky Way galaxy was born. Our solar system, which is one of the humbler, smaller members of the Milky Way's trillion-strong membership, came into being a good four months later, on 9 September.

The earth itself came along pretty nippily just five days later, on 14 September. And nine days after that, on 25 September, our very first 'living' ancestors, amoebae, made their formal bow. Things dawdled for a while after that: the first rocks formed on earth around 2 October, and the oldest fossils (bacteria and blue-green algae) came into being on 9 October.

Then another lull for a couple of billion years while, presumably, the gods were preoccupied. Finally, on 1 November, an event of true earth-shaking dimensions occurred: the origin of sex by microorganisms. Hereafter, living organisms acquired a gender and the bacterial version of Eve must have blithely raised a cell in celebration.

On 12 November, the oldest fossil photosynthetic plants saw the light of day and three days later, on 15 November, eukaryotes (the first-ever cells with nuclei) made their debut.

Now things get interesting in our 365-day cosmic calendar, compressed from the universe's fourteen-billion year existence. On 1 December, significant quantities of oxygen begin to develop on earth, setting the ground for creation. A fortnight later, the earth's first worms are born and three days later, on 19 November, the first fish begin to inhabit the sea.

Things are beginning to heat up—literally. The sun is shining brightly and the first mammals arrive on land on 21 December, followed two days later by reptiles. The first trees sprout on this day too.

Then, on 24 December, the legendary dinosaur makes his terrestrial debut. Two days later, the first mammals are born and the day after that, the skies are populated with the earth's first birds. By this time, 28 December, the four-'day'-old dinosaur species becomes extinct...and the world's first flowers begin to bloom.

The next two or three days, as the end of the cosmic calendar approaches, see feverish activity. The gods are working overtime. The twenty-ninth day of December sees the emergence of the first primates, the next day marks the evolution of giant mammals (ancestors of today's elephants) and 31 December, the last day of our cosmic calendar, witnesses the gods' creative tour de force, their cosmic pièce de résistance: the birth of human beings.

The last day of December is packed. In its twenty-four hours is compressed every event of the past several million years of human existence. Let's chronicle these action-packed hours in more detail.

By lunchtime, the Ramapithecus (an ape-like fellow who is thought to be our earliest ancestor) is grunting around in what is today known as East Africa (where every race on earth evolved). He develops gradually, shedding hair and acquiring cognitive skills, to evolve by 10.30 p.m. that evening, way past dinnertime, into the first recognizable human being. Yes, the human race occupies precisely 1.5 hours—the last ninety minutes—of the cosmic year.

By 11 p.m. our ancestors have begun to use stone tools and at 11.46 p.m., 'Peking Man' has domesticated fire. The most recent glacial period (the Ice Age) occurs at 11.56 p.m. and, as late as at 11.59 p.m., Europe is still inhabited by shaggy-haired, naked cavemen.

The last sixty seconds of our cosmic year are pacey. At 11.59.20 p.m., agriculture is invented (in more conventional terms that was 6,000 years ago—thus these last few seconds contain the events of several millennia). The first cities and the Neolithic civilization are born at 11.59.35 p.m. And the dynasties of Egypt and Sumeria are founded ten seconds before zero hour (the present). At 11.59.53 p.m., the Trojan war occurs and the Mycenean culture is founded. The next second sees the first Assyrian empire, and the founding of Carthage by Phoenicia.

At 11.59.54 p.m., Emperor Ashoka rules India and the Chin dynasty reigns over China. A second later, Lord Buddha is born. Christ is born at 11.59.56 p.m. and the Roman Empire falls one second later. At 11.59.58 p.m., the Byzantine Empire is founded, Mongol conquests begin and the Crusades are fought in Europe. The penultimate second of creation in our compressed cosmic calendar sees the beginning of the Renaissance period in Europe, the emergence of experimental science and the birth of the Chinese Ming dynasty.

The stroke of midnight represents the discovery of America, the growth and decay of the European colonial empires in Asia, Africa and South America, and the two World Wars.

And the very last split second of the cosmic year represents man's exploration of outer space, nuclear weapons and advanced computer technology.

That's it—the history of our fourteen-billion-year-old universe compressed in a normal twelve-month calendar year. It throws one a bit off balance and shatters some cosy notions to discover that, in such a cosmic year, the Earth does not come into existence till September; that dinosaurs emerge on Christmas Eve; that primitive men and women originate at 10.30 p.m. on New Year's Eve; and that all of our recorded history occupies the last ten seconds of 31 December.

Humbling, isn't it, to realize that we bright, important humans came into being in the last hour of the entire cosmic-compressed year? And that civilization is, in cosmic terms, literally a few seconds old.

What this little exercise also teaches us is that human beings should stop taking themselves too seriously. Life, really, is too short—in more ways than one.

We're now into the opening of the second cosmic year. It might be interesting to discover what will be happening and who will be around next New Year's Eve. In cosmic terms, that's fourteen billion years from now.

2

THE ROLE OF THE SCIENTIST IN THE 'NEW WORLD'

Pico Della Mirandola wrote in the fifteenth century: 'The human race is somewhere at the midway point of creation, capable of rising towards the angels or of descending towards the beasts.'

An apt observation—and one that is especially relevant in today's world where technological advancement and sophistication implies the ability to destroy more people, more quickly; where scientists are increasingly being used as pawns by politicians to serve their own geocentric ends; and where for every scientific discovery used to further human happiness another is employed to destroy it.

Since science cannot exist in a vacuum, it is vulnerable to various external pressures. How these can be resisted, and why they must be, is probably as important as the individual scientific discoveries themselves.

Science today, more than ever before, needs to draw heavily from the arts and philosophy, without which it will, to use a Descartean phrase, 'have head but not a heart'. One without the other is inadequate.

The early decades of the twenty-first century will probably bring seminal changes in the scientific realm. Space travel, superior artificial intelligence and extensive 'robotization' will create a wholly new science-social equation. We are now entering an era where science and technology will move so fast that the social sciences, humanities and other non-scientific disciplines could be left behind. The dangers of this have not yet been fully understood by most, neither scientists nor non-scientists. It is time they are, and corrective measures applied.

Another fifty years of this growing disparity can lead to only one thing: men and women who might be able to travel to outer space or communicate by interstellar radio waves, but who still will not know how to handle the emotional, social, cultural and psychological pressures that these technological times will inevitably bring.

Arthur Koestler echoed much the same sentiment in *The Ghost in the Machine* when he said: 'There is a streak of insanity which runs through the history of our species...man's native equipment, though superior to that of any other living species, nevertheless contains some built-in error or deficiency which predisposes him toward self-destruction.'

Will rapid technological progress catalyse that predilection for self-destruction? The fact that almost every new technology innovated by man since the Second World War has been used by one part of the human species to threaten destruction of the other is hardly reassuring. Niels Bohr and others 'discovered' the atom bomb as a purely scientific endeavour and the result today is a build-up of lethal nuclear arsenals that could, within twelve hours at any given period, destroy every living organism on this planet.

Most other new technologies have been similarly militarized: laser technology for special firearms, computer technology for guided missiles, space technology for spy-and-hit aircraft and bio-genetic technology for germ warfare. The portents are grim.

Koestler, expressing his disgust for the ways of 'advanced' humans, suggested sardonically the development of a new 'civilizing pill' that would subdue man's baser instinct.

No such luck. As civilization advances, civilized behaviour regresses. Remember what Bernard Shaw's famous character Dr Barnabas said: 'If the poverty of our vision leaves us [...] as the only hope, then we must indeed go the way of the mastodon and megatherium [...] and all the other scrapped [human] experiments.'

■

A civilization that lives side by side in uneasy conjunction with nuclear bombs, chemical germ weapons and napalm is no civilization at all.

From this, two viewpoints emerge, both dangerously unsound. Let us state each so that their flaws can be clearly seen and an alternative viewpoint of the role of science and the scientist in the New World can be redefined more precisely.

The first view is of the obscurantist—the anti-science bigot. The words of Wilbur H. Ferry, vice president of the 'Fund for the Republic' (one of those peculiar bodies only Americans could spawn or support) express this school of thought graphically: 'I have great qualms about permitting science and technology to continue their headlong progress unbraked. We should, if necessary, redraft the US constitution to keep research in check—to guarantee that it proceeds at something less than a runaway pace and that its fruits are judiciously applied, with the welfare of the people paramount. The sovereignty of the people must be re-established, rules written and regulations imposed. This must be done by statesmen and philosophers consciously intent on the general welfare, with the engineers and scientific researchers summoned from their caves to help in the doing when they are needed.'

While this sort of thing is what went out of date with the Ku Klux Klan, its puerile semantics merely hide a basically dangerous attitude: that scientists are terrible chaps intent on wreaking havoc on us sensible, honest-to-goodness folks. This is bigotry at its worst.

The opposite viewpoint, held by many laymen, is equally

untenable and naive: that scientists, because of their superior training and knowledge, are the saviours of the world and the guardians of man's destiny.

Everything we have said in this section disputes both these viewpoints. The judicious viewpoint, of course, is a sensible, balanced attitude towards science and scientists.

At their pinnacle, science and religion (not rituals) complement each another. Indeed we can hope that one day science, with its logic and underlying precision, will evolve its own 'religion'—an idea first propounded by Sir Julian Huxley—which would teach that rational thinking and theological philosophy are not necessarily irreconcilable.

Bertrand Russell, one of the finest examples of a mind straddling the worlds of science and philosophy (he was both a brilliant mathematician and a philosopher), once said: 'I think it is the duty of the philosopher to make himself as undistorting a mirror as he can. But it is also his duty to recognize such distortions as are inevitable from our very nature. Of these, the most fundamental is that we view the world from the point of view of the here and now, not with that large impartiality which we attribute to the Deity. To achieve such impartiality is impossible for us, but we can travel a certain distance towards it. To show the lead to this end is the supreme duty of the philosopher.'

To traverse that road is the supreme duty of the scientist.

3
THE INTELLIGENT UNIVERSE

It is the most challenging question in human history: does intelligent life exist elsewhere in the universe? Stephen Hawking, the former Lucasian professor of mathematics at Cambridge University (the chair Sir Isaac Newton once held) and arguably the world's greatest living theoretical physicist, says it probably does. Other scientists like Roger Penrose, the leading mathematical physicist, agree. The philosophical and religious implications of discovering intelligent life on another planet are huge. At this level, science and faith converge.

As an undergraduate reading physics and mathematics, I wrote a three-part cover story weighing the scientific evidence for intelligent life in the universe for *The Illustrated Weekly of India*, then a flagship of The Times of India group. The story, which ran over three issues in March 1976, posed the question: 'Is ours a unique cosmic civilization—a freakish, unfathomable joke of nature? Or are we just a tiny speck of dust in an obscure corner of the cosmos, merely one of several billion advanced civilizations, each one flourishing with its own commerce and culture, politics and philosophy?'

Thirty-eight years later, the question remains tantalizingly unanswered. But evidence is mounting. The weight of scientific opinion now holds that the universe teems with life, some of it technologically and spatially so advanced that it could be unrecognizable were we to encounter it.

Our universe is around 13.70 billion years old. It was created at Time Zero—the point of singularity at which there was nothing: no matter, no space, no time. Within this absolute space-time vacuum (postulated by the Hawking-Penrose singularity theorems based on Einstein's General Theory of Relativity), an event occurred which no leading scientist has yet been able to fully explain. That event, some speculate, probably involved the mutual annihilation of a positron-electron twin pair carrying identical (positive and negative) charges and mass. The result of this vacuum fluctuation was the Big Bang, the widely accepted theory of how our universe began.

Before Time Zero, during the pre-universe nothingness, it is hypothesized that constant and instantaneous mutual annihilation of positron-electron pairs occurred several trillion times every second. These multiple collisions cancelled each other out, leading to a perpetual state of zero mass, zero time and zero space—the perfect vacuum. The mutual annihilation of electrons and positrons, however, occurred in unimaginably small crevices of time—10^{-100} seconds or less. To the observer it would look like nothing was occurring—the event started and ended before it could be observed and, therefore, as far as the observer was concerned, had not occurred at all. From this nothingness, a freak, once-in-a-quadrillion positron-electron pair escaped mutual annihilation 13.70 billion years ago, causing the Big Bang and the creation of our universe as well as a mirror negative universe.

As the universe expanded, stars were formed within huge solar systems with orbiting planets like the earth. Billions of such solar systems made up dense clusters of galaxies with their esoteric black holes, which exert such a powerful gravitational pull that even light bends when it passes near them.

Our nearest solar system is Alpha Centauri. To get there,

travelling at the speed of light, would take 4.3 years. Travelling at the speed of the world's fastest experimental spacecraft, Helios II (1,57,000 mph), it would take over 12,000 years to reach Alpha Centauri. Other solar systems are even further off. Galaxies are, of course, trillions of miles away.

Our galaxy, the Milky Way, contains around 350 billion solar systems—many, as NASA's Kepler space telescope recently confirmed, with orbiting planets like earth with surface water, moderate temperature and life-supporting oxygen. Andromeda, the galaxy closest to the Milky Way, is even more massive with over 1,000 billion solar systems. It is around 2.70 million light years from us. So if electromagnetic radiation originating from a planet in Andromeda began transmitting 2.70 million years ago—the Plio-Pleistocene era on earth—it would have barely reached us this year.

And in these distances lies the answer to the second big question: if it exists, why hasn't intelligent life from extraterrestrial planets, presumably with highly sophisticated communications and transportation technology, made contact with us? Humans, after millions of years of evolution, from Australopethicus hominids to Neanderthals through to 'modern' man, began sending out electromagnetic radiation (in its earliest form as radio transmissions) a mere 122 years ago. Those signals have today scarcely reached the edge of our solar system cluster. Time and distance, both unimaginably vast, offer one explanation of why no contact has been established with us by other intelligent species.

So while we are certainly not alone in the universe, we may not make contact with other planetary life for centuries. But there is little doubt that one day contact will be made. What shape, form and mode that contact takes is uncertain. But when it does happen, it will mark one of the most important events in our recorded history.

All of human intelligence and wisdom, from Aristotle and

Aryabhatta to the Vedas and Einstein, does not have an answer, however, to the third key question that has divided sages and philosophers over the centuries: why does the universe exist at all? As even scientists concede wryly, God alone knows.

4

WHO READS NEWSPAPERS ANYMORE?

In India, still a growing number of people. Globally, a rapidly declining number. The steep fall in newspaper circulation in the United States has set alarm bells ringing in 'old' media companies in the West.

Over the past few years, there has been a precipitous 33 per cent fall in the circulation of American newspapers. Many have closed down, downsized or been acquired. Some, like *The Times*, London, have changed size, style and format into 'compacts'—somewhere between broadsheets and tabloids—to stop readers fleeing to new media.

Rupert Murdoch, owner of News Corp., one of the world's biggest media companies, saw the writing on the wall nearly a decade ago. In April 2005, he delivered a speech to the American Society of Newspaper Editors on 'Digital Natives vs Digital Immigrants'.

The digital immigrants are the millions of (mainly young) people who are deserting newspapers in droves for online news sites. Among those under the age of twenty-five, who have literally grown up with a computer in their lap and the Internet a mouse-click away, growing numbers simply don't read newspapers at all anymore. They get their primary news online, surf the net on community and social networking sites and only occasionally switch on television for entertainment in the evening. For American media companies, the most alarming trend is the fall in TV viewership: the Internet has hit major television networks almost as hard as it has hurt newspapers.

The biggest worry is the flight of classified advertising from newspapers to online sites. As a result, former blue-chip media stocks like News Corp. and Time-Warner are being hammered down on the New York Stock Exchange (NYSE). Their comeback strategy? To go online themselves. Murdoch has been especially aggressive and has over the past few years acquired several websites and placed some of his newspaper sites behind a firewall to boost online ad and subscription revenue.

In India things are, as always, somewhat different. There are still only 160 million (but rising) Internet users in the country and newspaper circulations are continuing to grow in double digits every year. With purchasing power expanding rapidly, the number of those who can afford to buy a daily newspaper is growing. With rising purchasing power, too, comes more cable and non-cable TV homes, delivering an ever-rising television audience.

Even so, newspapers reporters and editors will need to tweak their content and approach for a new generation bred online. No longer are readers willing to be lectured to by editorial writers. They want a conversation, not a monologue. Forceful opinions will still count—especially if they are backed by fact, originality and conviction. But be prepared for a robust, interactive dialogue with your readers. The new breed doesn't want to be talked to but talked with.

■

Nations get the government—and media—they deserve. In a rapidly evolving, two-track India, the media is in a state of flux. Western newspapers, radio and television had decades in which to morph from sombre media purveyors of information to tabloids of infotainment in the freewheeling Internet era.

Indian media meanwhile has leapfrogged an entire generation—in terms of trends and technology—and the result is cacophony. We have over 800 TV channels with nearly 100 more waiting to be launched.

Amidst all this rapid change, India's newspapers have largely retained their quality. In Britain, tabloid newspapers outsell quality broadsheets by an astounding 10:1 margin. In India, the ratio is the reverse.

However, the story changes radically in television. The ferocious competition for TRPs has made Indian television a manic beast. Virtually every TV channel magnifies 'developing' stories as 'breaking news' in a frenetic effort to draw eyeballs. Most Hindi news channels use every ruse they can think of—superstition, ghost sightings, sting operations, astrology, sex—to lure viewers who surf constantly and voyeuristically.

TRP-phobic TV networks live in constant fear of losing marketshare to a rival channel which has a more riveting story. In all this competitive frenzy, the government has discovered an opportunity: if broadcasters can't regulate themselves, the government will.

One of the principal purposes of the media in a democracy is to hold the government to account. Government-mandated regulation seeks to do the exact opposite by allowing proxies of the government to hold the broadcast media to account instead. The idea is unsuited to an evolved democracy and Indian broadcasters have done well to unite vociferously against it.

■

Ultimately, of course, the market will get what it wants. Television, like all other media, is a mirror of society. If Indian viewers thrive on superstition, sex and stings, that is what TV channels will serve to them. Critics wrongly assume that media moulds society. In fact, society moulds media—and this is true in any democracy, Western or Asian.

The most media can and should do is report with accuracy, integrity, responsibility and professionalism. But the content of the reportage—news or entertainment—must be left to the individual judgement of the editor. A TV channel, like a newspaper, will rise or fall on the quality of that judgement. And the government has no role whatsoever to play in this.

■

Press freedom is not a gift from the government: it's guaranteed by the Constitution. The relationship between the first and fourth estates is complex at the best of times. With the media exposing scam after scam, the UPA government, instead of fixing the problem—alleged criminal conduct within the government—is targeting the watchdog.

Instead, the government must give the Press Council more teeth with properly legislated regulatory powers. Today, the Council can only reprimand newspapers which violate accepted codes of journalistic conduct. Just as listed companies are supervised by SEBI and other sectors such as telecom, insurance and banking have their own regulatory bodies with specific jurisdictions, so should a reinvigorated Press Council.

Television needs a separate body to act as regulator. Every major country in the world has made this distinction. In Britain, for example, the Press Complaints Commission (PCC) deals swiftly, transparently and decisively with complaints against newspapers and magazines while Ofcom deals with complaints against television and radio broadcasters. But even Britain's PCC does not have the power to fine the print media—only to name and shame newspapers which break its code of ethics.

The Leveson judicial inquiry set up by the British government following the *News of the World* phone-hacking scandal has recommended tough independent regulation for the UK media. But Justice Leveson's proposals have met with severe opposition from even the treasury benches in the House of Commons.

In the United States, the First Amendment, which guarantees free speech, is the guiding principle in relation to media. Print media is not regulated by the US government at all; the newspaper industry follows its own self-regulatory code of conduct. American television is regulated by the Federal Communications Commission (FCC) but the cable and pay TV industries are largely exempt even from FCC supervision. An open, vibrant, competitive media market, the US government has long believed, is the best regulator. Australia has separate regulators for print and broadcast media but neither has punitive powers.

■

India, of course, is different and requires a different set of regulations. We need to build our own regulatory model. There's no question that Indian media requires a robust supervisory framework. However, a newly empowered Press Council should not have government representation. Britain's Press Complaints Commission is proud of the fact that not one of its seventeen members is from the government or the Opposition. The majority of members are drawn from civil society: professionals, academics, even workers' representatives.

Journalists in India should not fear a stronger, more effective Press Council and a separate empowered broadcasting authority under new legislation which will both protect press freedom and establish higher standards of media accountability. This will end many of the malpractices that have damaged the media's credibility. And credibility is the media's only currency. Lose it, and you have nothing left.

The Internet has meanwhile reset the equation between the producers and consumers of media. Blogs, Twitter, Facebook and other social media networks have become powerful platforms in influencing national debate by allowing traditional consumers of media (readers and viewers) to become producers and opinion-makers themselves. This is mainstream media's civil society moment and it hasn't come a day too soon.

5
TENDULKAR: THE BRADMAN OF OUR ERA?

A little before Sachin Tendulkar was born, a Marylebone Cricket Club (MCC) team visited West Buckland School in Devon to play an annual one-day match. Opening the school's batting, I scored a duck. After our match, over tea, the MCC captain asked me, in jest, when India would produce 'its own Bradman'. The answer, in retrospect: 24 April 1973.

Tendulkar, now an honorary life member of the MCC, is rightly acknowledged as one of the greatest Test cricket batsmen since Sir Donald Bradman. Having made cricket history with his long-awaited 100th international century—albeit against Bangladesh and after a year-long delay which took some of the shine off the achievement—the missing link in Tendulkar's career remains his inability to deliver in crunch situations.

A cricketer with Tendulkar's enormous natural talent and longevity would be expected to have won (or saved) far more Tests for India than he has. It is a lacuna which, along with his failure to get past 37 runs in five Tests at Lord's since 1990, will—like Bradman's failure in the 1932-33 Bodyline series against Douglas Jardine's England—remain a troubling blemish.

Retiring almost exactly twenty-four years to the day he made his Test debut in November 1989, Tendulkar showed he was as good a judge of when to end his career as he was of the line and length of the tens of thousands of deliveries he faced from the world's best bowlers.

How will history judge Tendulkar against Bradman? Comparisons across eras are neither easy nor always fair. But make them we must: Roger Federer vs Rod Laver, Tiger Woods vs Jack Nicklaus, Lionel Messi vs Pelé.

■

According to sports historians, Bradman's Test average of 99.94 puts him at a level above every other cricketer. Let's examine that thesis more closely. Bradman played thirty-seven of his fifty-two Tests on home soil. Of those, ten were against India (in 1948) and South Africa (in 1930-31)—then the Bangladesh and Zimbabwe of Test cricket. Not surprisingly, Bradman averaged 201.50 against South Africa and 178.75 against India. Strip those ten Tests off his record and Bradman's overall average falls to 88.30.

Against high-quality bowling, Bradman faltered by his own standards. Playing the West Indies fast bowlers at home in the 1930s, he averaged 74.70 per inning over five Tests. And in his last series against England in 1948, Bradman averaged even less—72.57, again over five Tests.

Yet Bradman towered over his peers. Of his many talented contemporaries, Sir Jack Hobbs—possibly England's greatest batsman—averaged 56.94. Wally Hammond, another England great in the Bradman era, averaged 58.45. Averages, of course, never tell the full story. Bradman scored twenty-nine centuries in fifty-two tests— roughly a century every 1.8 Tests. Tendulkar has scored a century every 3.9 Tests. Hobbs, by way of comparison, scored a century every 4.1 Tests and Hammond a century every 3.9 Tests. Only West Indian greats George Headley (2.2 centuries per Test), Clyde Walcott (2.9) and Everton Weekes (3.2), South Africa's Graeme Pollock (3.3) and

England's Herbert Sutcliffe (3.4) have a better century-to-Test ratio than Tendulkar.

Among all Bradman's Australian contemporaries, the batsmen with the next highest Test average were Bill Ponsford (48.22) and Stan McCabe (48.21)—both under half of Bradman's. A statistical gap of over 100 per cent between top-level peers is very rare in any international sport. Tendulkar, though, can claim an extraordinary statistic of his own: in addition to more than 25,000 runs in first class matches, he has scored 18,426 runs in 463 one-day internationals at an average of nearly 45. In all, Tendulkar has made more than 34,000 runs in international cricket with 100 centuries. That is a record Bradmanesque in itself and unlikely to ever be bettered.

An extraordinary fact about Tendulkar has escaped comment: he is one of very few international cricketers since 1877, when Test cricket began, whose Test career has straddled four decades—the 1980s, 1990s, 2000s and 2010s. Even the great Bradman could traverse just three decades in Tests—from the 1920s to the 1940s.

Bradman, however, had two advantages. First, he played thirty-seven of his fifty-two Tests against just one opponent—England. Second, he never had to face the world's best bowlers, most of whom were then Australian. Tendulkar has played against nine Test countries and been spared facing only the Indian bowling attack. Bradman also had two disadvantages. Unlike Tendulkar, he played on uncovered, damp, seaming wickets; and he played without a helmet and chest and armguards. The impact of these factors on Tendulkar and Bradman's overall career performance is impossible to assess.

More pertinently, while Bradman's career spanned nearly twenty years with a six-year break during the Second World War (when, in his early thirties, he could have been at his peak but suffered from debilitating fibrositis), he played less international and more domestic cricket than Tendulkar. Bradman scored 28,067 runs in first class cricket at an average of 95.14. But 75 per cent of those runs were made domestically. In sharp contrast, only 35 per cent of

Tendulkar's 25,000-plus first class runs (at an average of over 57) have been made in domestic cricket. Tendulkar has scored the majority of his runs against not only more varied but stronger international bowling attacks.

But beyond numbers lies that elusive quality: class. Ken Barrington had a Test average of 58.67, well above Tendulkar's, but you wouldn't have missed a day in office to watch him bat. With Tendulkar, you would.

To return to our original question: how will history judge Tendulkar against the Bradman benchmark? Very highly. Anyone who watched Tendulkar bat knows that he judged the line and length of a ball a fraction of a second quicker than any other Test batsman. His bat-speed, balance, footwork and hand-eye coordination were a rare gift. The world produces a batsman like him at best once in half a century.

That then is where the argument must rest. Bradman was the rarest of rare talents in the first half of the twentieth century. Since 1948, when he retired at the age of forty, there have been very few batsmen who have come close to him in cricketing genius—till Tendulkar. Sachin's Test average may not tower over his peers' as Bradman's did. But for sheer artistry, appetite for runs in every format of the game, longevity, and a steely determination hidden beneath a gentle smile, Tendulkar has proved himself Bradman's worthiest successor.

6
POLITICS, ECONOMICS, RACISM

Is there racism in international sport? Ask any Indian, Sri Lankan, West Indian or Pakistani cricketer—or any black footballer playing in continental Europe—and the short answer you will get is: yes.

But there is also change in the air.

Till 1963, the acronym 'ICC' stood for Imperial Cricket Conference, with all its colonial connotations. Astonishingly, England and Australia had veto power over every ICC decision. Over the past few years, the situation has changed dramatically. The veto of course is long gone and ICC now stands for International Cricket Council. Its headquarters has shifted from London to Dubai and back to London, and the Indian subcontinent now delivers over 80 per cent of world cricket's revenue.

Racism is intimately connected with economic and political power. Till the early-1800s, when the mighty Ottoman empire straddled Eurasia in a crescent-shaped arc from Yugoslavia and Kazakhstan to the entire Middle East and North Africa, European diplomats were seen as supplicants. Ottoman caliphs rarely granted audience to white intermediaries and European monarchs were treated with polite disdain. The same was true of China of the time. The Confucian Chinese of the late-1700s and early-1800s treated Christian Europeans and their kings and queens with thinly veiled contempt.

Then came colonialism and the Industrial Revolution. The balance of political and economic power shifted rapidly from East to West. China went into isolation and decline. The Ottomans sided with Germany in the First World War and by 1918 their empire was wiped out. White racism flourished worldwide. There was segregation in the US and apartheid in South Africa.

Between the 1920s and 1950s, Europe and America controlled world economic, military and geopolitical power. Then the reversal of fortune began, first with the rise of Japan as an economic superpower in the late-1960s, followed by China and now India.

Americans and Europeans (and Australians), till recently filled with hubris, now queue up for business opportunities in China, India, the UAE and Saudi Arabia (the latter two previously ruled by the Ottomans). Indian and Chinese companies are buying out global corporations. Young Europeans are flocking to work in Indian IT companies. This trend will only accelerate as the economic balance of power shifts back to Asia.

White racism, in its virulent twentieth-century form, is destined to die as this century unfolds. Will Chinese and Indian racism replace it? Unlikely. China and India both have a 5,000-year history of cultural richness. Nouveau economic and political power made Europe and the US arrogant and racist for nearly two centuries. But with strongly embedded cultural traditions of respect and humility, the same ingredients of economic and geopolitical supremacy are unlikely to create a Chinese Ricky Ponting or an Indian Damien Martyn.

■

What follows, in this context, is an abridged version of my article published in the London Times, *just before the Reliance World Cup in 1987, on race, apartheid and cricket.*

When the International Cricket Council meets tomorrow in London, it will have more than cricket on its mind. The World Cup, to be held later this year in India and Pakistan, may be jeopardized by the controversy between the West Indies Cricket Board and the Test and County Cricket Board (TCCB) over the West Indians' determination to raise the issue of South Africa at the meeting.

This is the view, it is believed in India, that the TCCB and its chief executive, Alan Smith, would be quietly happy to promote.

The strategy serves a purpose: to divide the black cricketing nations—the West Indies on the one side, India and Pakistan on the other—by hinting that if the West Indies push their point too hard tomorrow, England (and, as a consequence, Australia and New Zealand) might find themselves unable to take part in the World Cup.

Thus, the TCCB hopes that India and Pakistan will vote against the West Indies board in the interests of a turbulence-free World Cup.

This is the first time the World Cup is being held outside England. There is the feeling in Indian cricketing circles—wholly misplaced, I hope—that the TCCB is not overjoyed at the prospect of losing its monopoly on the event. And if Australia, the West Indies and others insist—as they will—on hosting subsequent cups, England's own turn might not come again for the remainder of this century.

7
How Indian Hockey was Turfed Out

One afternoon, as I watched the late Tiger Pataudi, India's former Test cricket captain, playing a hockey match at Bombay Gymkhana, I realized that few were aware how good a hockey player Tiger was. He had long retired from Test cricket but played a brilliant game for the club that afternoon. Later, chatting casually, he remarked, pointing to the lush green field: 'The tragedy of Indian hockey is that we no longer play on grass like this.' Tiger was appalled that the international game had switched to astroturf, putting Indian players at a disadvantage.

Between 1928 and 1980, India won eight Olympic gold medals in hockey. After 1980, we have not won a single hockey gold. At the 2012 London Olympics, India's hockey team finished last in a field of twelve.

The reasons for this are complex. The principal cause is the betrayal of the country's national sport by those elected to guard it and the ruthless duplicity of European and Australasian hockey authorities.

Till the early-1970s, hockey worldwide was played on grass. Indian players, bred on the fields of Punjab, Kerala and Goa, were unbeatable. Only Pakistan, with a similar lineage, offered competition. All that changed in the mid-1970s. The International Hockey Federation (FIH) altered the rules to make synthetic astroturf the mandatory playing surface for international hockey tournaments.

The 1976 Olympics in Montreal was the first Games in which astroturf was used in hockey. For the first time since it began playing hockey in the 1928 Games in Amsterdam, India did not win even a bronze medal. The Indian Hockey Federation (IHF) should have objected to this change of rules. Whether through collusion or apathy, it did not. All Olympic Games henceforth were played on hard astroturf.

India has few astroturf grounds. They are expensive to lay (costing over Rs 8 crore) and difficult to play on. While grass, on which hockey had been played internationally for nearly a century, allowed skilled Indian and Pakistani players to trap the ball, dribble and pass, astroturf suits the physicality of European and Australian hockey players, shifting the emphasis from technical skill to raw power.

Affluent Western countries like Holland, Germany and Australia have hundreds of astroturf grounds. The disadvantage to India is palpable. Not surprisingly, since 1980, Europe and Australia have dominated world hockey. India and Pakistan have slipped out of the world's top five hockey-playing nations.

Indian sports administrators must share the blame for this. Not only were they complicit in allowing the change in playing surface from grass to synthetic astroturf, they were slow to adapt to it once the rules had been changed. Astroturf grounds were not laid. Local tournaments continued to be played on grass. Thus, when India played abroad, it started with a huge handicap. As Sardara Singh, former India hockey captain, said in a television interview: 'Hockey players in India play on astroturf for the first time at the age of nineteen or twenty and find it hard to adapt.'

■

What is the way forward? While astroturf cannot now be wished away, India can use its growing commercial influence to host a separate annual field hockey tournament. The game would be transformed. Just as tennis is played on different surfaces (grass at Wimbledon, clay at the French Open and hard courts at the US and Australian Opens), there is no reason why hockey can't have two optional surfaces: astroturf and grass. Like tennis players adapt to grass, clay and hard courts within a span of months (between the French Open in May, Wimbledon in July and the US Open in September), so can professional hockey players.

A start can be made with the Hockey India League (HIL) which attracts top global talent. The league is telecast live and has a growing audience. Its franchise ownership is patterned on cricket's IPL. Indian sponsors can play a major role here to promote the use of natural turf.

India's hockey authorities, fractured by internecine rivalries, have little global clout. It is India's corporate sector, with an interest in future Olympic gold medals, which must therefore lead the campaign to restore natural turf as one of two alternative playing surfaces of choice in future international hockey tournaments. Grass is hockey's natural surface. It tests skill, not just strength.

India has begun winning Olympic medals in individual sports since the Beijing Games but none in team sports like hockey. That must change. In India, less than 0.1 per cent of the population (around one million people) has access to the facilities, nutrition and training that athletes from Western and most Asian countries do.

In 'sports access' terms, our population is equivalent to New Zealand's. It is no shame to win fewer medals than smaller, richer countries. But it is a shame not to give our national sport, hockey, a level playing field.

SECTION 6
VINTAGE

1
IT'S TIME FOR US TO BUILD FACTORIES, NOT SHRINES

8 March 1995

Reacting to my column on 15 February, 'Muslims Float to the Top as the Cream of India', Ashok Chowgule of the Hindu Vivek Kendra has sent me a long and chiding letter. His chief accusation: I did not condemn strongly enough the 'harm that the Muslim rulers have done to this country's psyche'. Mr Chowgule quotes Will Durant to drive home his point: 'The Mohammedan conquest of India is probably the bloodiest story in history. It is a discouraging tale, for its evident moral is that civilization is a precarious thing, whose delicate complex of order and liability, culture and peace may at any time be overthrown by barbarians from without or multiplying within.'

Responding to my subsequent column on 1 March, 'Give the Shiv Sena Its Head and Watch It Crack Up', Muslims have accused me of recommending a Shiv Sena-Bharatiya Janata Party government in Maharashtra.

Both accusations, like Cinderella's glass slippers, are based on an illusion. Let us deal with the Hindu Vivek Kendra's comments first. Mr Chowgule begins his letter by saying: 'In the whole article you have completely absolved the Muslim community of any blame for the situation as it exists today. You have mentioned Akbar but you have not mentioned Aurangzeb. It is a sad commentary on Indian "intellectuals" that they have negated the harm that Muslim rulers have done to this country's psyche.'

Two errors here. First, my 15 February column did not absolve the Indian Muslim community of blame 'for the situation as it exists today'. It, in fact, blamed Indian Muslims unequivocally: 'Indian Muslims are among the most backward in the Islamic world... Part of the damage is self-inflicted. Indian Muslims must stand up and say once and for all that they are Indian first and Muslim only second. Without that commitment to India, they cannot expect, nor deserve, Hindu sympathy and support.'

Second, in the very paragraph where I extolled Emperor Akbar's secularism, I said: 'It is true that the early Turko-Afghan invaders were cruel, even barbarous. They murdered by the thousands, pillaged whole villages and forcibly converted Hindus to Islam en masse. These are unequivocal crimes and history rightly records them as such.'

The specific contextual point I made about the Mughal Empire—and it is one that organizations like the Hindu Vivek Kendra must understand once and for all—is this: the Mughal Empire was bad; the British Empire was worse. Many Mughal emperors, including Aurangzeb, were (like their Turko-Afghan predecessors) exceptionally cruel men who desecrated Hindu temples and committed huge atrocities. No words can condemn strongly enough such wanton destruction of a country's religious heritage.

However, the broader point I made which the Hindu Vivek Kendra and organizations like the Vishwa Hindu Parishad consistently miss is that the British, Portuguese and French caused much greater harm to India in the two centuries following the end of the Mughal Empire. Indian historians of a certain persuasion are so obsessed with the 'Muslim' question that they ignore the real enemy: European colonialism.

The Mughals destroyed temples, forcibly converted lower caste Hindus and behaved with great mendacity. But they did not deliberately strangulate India's economy and industrial growth as the British did, nor cause widespread impoverishment and famine. When the British 'left' India in 1947, the average Indian peasant was actually poorer in per capita terms than in 1757, when the British occupation of India began following the Battle of Plassey. During the otherwise abominable Mughal Empire, Indians ate better, lived better and were clothed better than during the reign of the British Empire.

It is right to condemn the Mughals for their barbarity—I do so unconditionally—but it is equally right and necessary to condemn the British for impoverishing an entire subcontinent and dividing it along communal lines. Both were crimes and both must be judged as such by history.

Alas, Hindu organizations with their tunnel vision see only Muslim cruelty in India's past. It is time they broadened their horizon to include European colonialism as an equal, indeed a bigger culprit in the systematic defrauding of India.

∎

Mr Chowgule wonders why my 15 February article chastises both the Congress and the Bharatiya Janata Party for India's communal problems: 'It is most unfair that you blame the BJP, in addition to the Congress.'

I blame the BJP because it established communalism on India's political agenda in the eighties. It made communal politics respectable. Ordinary Muslims and Hindus who had lived together in peace for decades suddenly began to distrust each other. I blame the Congress because it appeased Muslims in the worst possible way to win votes. The Shah Bano case is just one example. More unforgivably, during communal riots when Muslims begged for protection from the government, the Congress betrayed them.

The BJP's role has been more insidious but not less harmful.

The Ram Janmabhoomi agitation in the early nineties underscores all that is wrong with the BJP. A modern political organization should build houses, not temples, factories, not shrines. India needs hospitals and schools, not more places of religious worship. The BJP's argument that the Babri Masjid represents a historical Muslim injustice which can only be corrected by building a Ram temple there is right in principle but wrong in practice. The real problems that confront India are poverty, illiteracy, housing, corruption and urban crime to name a few. These are the issues on which the BJP should be spending all its considerable energy and time. It does not do so because these issues are more complex than breaking and rebuilding religious structures.

The BJP had a wonderful opportunity in 1991, when it won 119 seats in the Lok Sabha, to play the part of a responsible Opposition and keep the Congress on its calloused toes. Instead, it took to easy politics, inflamed communal passions in Ayodhya and as a result deprived itself of political respectability and India of the genuine two-party system every mature democracy needs.

This is particularly unfortunate because the BJP has sound economic ideas and a disciplined cadre. It would, for example, craft a more assertive foreign policy than the Congress, especially on vital issues such as the Non-Proliferation Treaty and world trade. So if it wishes to be a realistic and credible alternative to the Congress at the Centre next year, and build on its successes in Gujarat and Maharashtra, it must put religion on the backburner and concentrate on the issues that really matter.

Mr Chowgule quotes a letter by Professor Bandukwala in *The Times of India* (10 June 1994): 'Muslims are desperate for socio-economic change, for good education and for economic development. The only condition which Muslims impose on a reformer is that he operate within the parameters of Islam.' Mr Chowgule deprecates this conditionality: 'It is necessary that we look at people as individuals and not as a member of a religion or a caste. It is only under these circumstances that we will have true secularism in this country.'

He is, of course, correct. Professor Bandukwala represents a Muslim worldview which is bad for Indian Muslims and bad in principle. Muslims in India must operate within the framework of the constitution, which allows sufficient leeway—in some cases far too much—for their religious sensitivities. You cannot have 12 per cent of India's population governed 'within the parameters of Islam' as Professor Bandukwala suggests and expect to be treated by the majority Hindu community in a secular fashion. You reap what you sow and if Indian Muslims sow the seeds of communalism by insisting on separate laws for themselves, they will reap the ill wind of a communal backlash.

■

Indian Muslims must decide once and for all whether they wish to live in a secular country like India where secular laws supersede Islamic ones or in an Islamic theocracy like Pakistan where Islamic laws supersede even basic civil liberties. If they wish to take the former course, there can be no case for Professor Bandukwala's conditionalities of Muslim development within Islamic parameters. If they prefer the latter alternative, they are living in the wrong country.

Many Muslims are aggrieved at what they perceive as victimization by the police of those accused in the Bombay bomb blast conspiracy (most of whom happen to be Muslim). It is clear that the bomb blasts were aimed at a Hindu civilian population and masterminded by expatriate terrorists in 'revenge' for the anti-Muslim riots of January 1993. No Indian Muslim can have anything but the deepest contempt for those behind the bomb blast conspiracy. Bal Thackeray, whose party I severely indicted in my 1 March column, is right for once when he says that the people behind the bomb blasts are the true enemies of India and should be hunted down and punished.

The Hindu Vivek Kendra quotes from M.J. Akbar's book, *India: The Siege Within:* 'It needs to be pointed out that India remains a secular state, not because one-fifth of the population is Muslim, Sikh or Christian, and therefore obviously has a vested interest in a secular constitution, but because nine out of ten Hindus do not believe in violence against the minorities. If all the Hindus had been zealots, no law-and-order machinery in the world could have prevented the massacre of Muslims who are scattered in villages and towns all across the country.'

But that is precisely the point made in my 15 February column: 'India is a mature country with a long history of religious tolerance and compassion. The strength of India is this secular tradition. While nations struggle with racism and ethnic strife, India has shown that 900 million people can live together in relative peace.'

India is the only country in the world where an 80 per cent majority community allows minorities absolute religious freedom—both by constitutional statute and in actual practice. Even the United States, Britain and France, to take three liberal Western democracies, do not allow quite the constitutional freedom to Muslims in their own countries that 'Hindu' India does. India's stance should be applauded and the gesture reciprocated by Indian Muslims by not insisting stubbornly on Islamic law superseding India's own secular laws.

The Hindu Vivek Kendra's Mr Chowgule ends his long letter with some faint praise: 'We applaud your enlightenened statement, "Indian Muslims must stand up and say that they are Indians first and Muslims second."' I would take that advice a bit further: Reject the leadership of extremist Muslims, recognize India's secular constitution, and live by it.

And I would tell Indian politicians, both Congress and BJP: Stop relying on religion to win political advantage. The British disgraced themselves in doing so—do not repeat the mistake. The British had an island to escape to. Indian politicians will have nowhere to hide.

Note: *As this 1995 column shows, I've been a long-time critic of both the extreme Muslim and Hindu fringes.*

2

THE WEST'S FALSE PROJECTION OF ITSELF

April 1991

An important part of the war in the Gulf is being fought on the front pages of Western newspapers. Persuasive rhetoric, cloaked in velvet prose, tells millions of readers how nasty and brutish a fellow this Saddam is (true) and how altruistic and principled the Western response to his aggression has been (false).

Saddam may deserve all the condemnation he has got, especially for his alleged gruesome role in torturing young children to extract confessions from their parents. But the way the Western media has glossed over the historical crimes perpetrated in the Gulf by the West earlier this century is, in its own way, equally condemnable.

In an article in the *Daily Telegraph*, Robert Harvey writes: 'There is [now] the issue of reparations and punishment. These are non-negotiable for the West, unless the principal sufferers, the Kuwaitis, agree to waive them. It is only with the deepest reluctance that the West would drop its plans to bring Saddam and other principal war criminals to trial.'

Reparations and punishment? If Iraq's Saddam Hussein can be

tried, as Mr Harvey suggests, for 'war crimes' and punished with claims of reparations, half of Asia and Africa could rightfully insist on massive colonial reparations from Britain and France which would run into billions of dollars.

As far as punishment for colonial crimes is concerned, only historical trials may now be feasible for the main culprits are long dead but even these would serve an important purpose and lesson.

Certainly, just as the American government recently awarded compensation to the descendants of innocent Japanese illegally interned in the US during the Second World War, a case could be made for compensation to the descendants of African slaves who worked and died on white-owned plantations.

In a significant development, Nigerian President Ibrahim Babangida, who will host a meeting of the Organization of African Unity (OAU) this June, has announced that a detailed bill for reparations for centuries of slavery will be presented to Western nations at the OAU conference. According to AFP, the French news agency which is the least Westocentric of the world's major wire services, 'The leader of a US delegation, Senator Bill Owens of Massachusetts state legislature, long-time advocate of reparations, told the conference that the Americans owed $65 billion to Africa and to blacks in compensation for five centuries of slavery and colonisation.'

In his speech, General Babangida said: 'We call on all the countries of Europe and the Americas to compensate Africa for the untold hardship and exploitation that the continent had been subjected in the past. Between 10 and 30 million young and virile Africans were taken to the Americas to work on sugar, cotton and tobacco plantations during the slave trade era. We make these demands because the services of our forefathers in the American plantations were unrewarded and unpaid for and because the exploitation of Africa during the period of colonial rule further impoverished us and enhanced the development of the West.'

Similarly, a colonial crimes tribunal could posthumously try British officers who killed thousands of Indians during Britain's occupation of India in the eighteenth century and British administrators in West Bengal whose incompetence and malfeasance caused two million deaths during the Great Bengal Famine of 1943.

A detailed calculation shows that Britain's colonial debt to India is around $500 billion (Rs 900,000 crore) at 1990 prices. There is a strong case for taking the matter to the International Court of Justice at The Hague.

The West's historical record scarcely permits it to adopt a stance of moral superiority on the Iraq-Kuwait conflict. The West, after all:

- Invented large-scale slave trading, causing death and suffering to millions of Africans.
- Illegally occupied through military conquest large tracts of Asia, Africa and Australasia for material profit—again causing misery and deprivation to millions in the occupied countries, as well as crippling development in these countries.
- Slaughtered hundreds of thousands of indigenous 'Red' Indians in North America and Aborigines in Australia and appropriated their land.
- Fought dozens of small, and two very large, wars over the past 300 years, mostly in Europe and America but occasionally exporting their militarism to other continents.

More recently, the leader of the Western alliance, the US, invaded Grenada and bombed Libya, killing Colonel Gaddafi's five-year-old stepdaughter.

■

It must be remembered that Kuwait is historically and geographically as much an integral part of Iraq as Scotland is of the UK. It was illegally and forcibly converted into an independent 'country' in 1961 by the West seeking a pro-Western sheikhdom to protect Western interests—military and commercial—in the Gulf.

If France and Britain hadn't imposed themselves (with considerable military brutality) on West Asia in the early twentieth century, after the Ottoman Empire collapsed, in order to exploit the region for power and profit, many 'Arab' problems, including Palestine, Israel and Iraq, would never have arisen at all.

Saddam is a nasty and brutish dictator but he hardly possesses a monopoly on either quality.

Note: *More on the Gulf War and the West's historical role in West Asia—not always benevolent—follows on subsequent pages.*

3
WHY V.P. SINGH IS NOT A LEADER

December 1988

LEADERSHIP. That, in a word, sums up the V.P. Singh problem. Consider: here we have a man of impeccable moral authority, widely recognized as upright, incorruptible, decent. Why then has his challenge for the alternative leadership of the country, pregnant with promise till a few months ago, dissipated so rapidly? The answer may be less complicated than we think.

There are good leaders and bad leaders. V.P. Singh's problem is that he is, in the purest sense of the word, not a leader at all. A good, moral, upright man—perhaps. But leadership, with all its rigorous nuances, eludes him. Rajiv Gandhi, in contrast, is by now regarded by most people as a bad leader—but the tacit assumption of leadership, good or bad, rests solidly on his beleaguered mantle. It doesn't on V.P. Singh's.

The qualities that define leadership in Indian politics are many, but four stand out. The most important of these, of course, is the power to inspire. Inspirational politics went out of fashion after Independence. During the British occupation of India, political activists motivated followers—and the common people—with a mixture of idealism, passion and a clear vision of the future.

Today, Indian democracy, having passed several litmus tests over the past forty years, needs a fresh dose of inspirational politics. V.P. Singh, with his bland moral righteousness, has not struck the right chord among the electorate for he has missed the crucial point of this political genre: to inspire you must create your own edifice of ideas; merely pulling down another's will not do.

When V.P. Singh was expelled from the Congress (I) last summer, three schools of thought sprang up. The first, rubbing its hands in glee, concluded that Rajiv's days as prime minister were numbered and it was simply a matter of time before the former finance and defence minister replaced Bofors-stricken Rajiv as PM.

The second school of thought, more circumspectly, viewed V.P. Singh's expulsion and his subsequent denunciation of his former boss with grave misgiving. Just when the country needed unity, here was the messy prospect of a Gandhi-V.P. Singh war which could do only the ragtag Opposition any good.

The third line of thinking focused on the likelihood of a collusion of interests emerging between the saner Opposition parties, such as the Janata and V.P. Singh's co-rebels (Arif Mohammad Khan, Arun Nehru, V.C. Shukla and others). This, proponents of the third school of thought argued, would have given the country a genuine Opposition alternative to the Congress (I) at the next general election.

V.P. Singh quickly proved all three schools of thought wrong. He made the fatal error of vacillating between the Left and the Right. This effectively destroyed the quality of idealism and independence that the Indian electorate respects—and expects—in its leaders. Then he reignited the charge of feudalistic thinking that a former Raja must try doubly hard to banish when he failed to condemn the Roop Kanwar sati incident. Politically, this was damaging; morally, it was devastating. People asked themselves: do we want a prime minister who doesn't have the courage of his convictions to openly criticize an act that, stripped off its religious camouflage, amounts to murder? The moral platform of V.P. Singh, in many ways his strongest political raison d'etre, had suddenly sprung a leak.

■

Which brings us to the second vital quality of leadership: the ability to provide vision. Jawaharlal Nehru, to take a common example, was a visionary. He recognized the strengths of his people, built on them, understood their weaknesses, and worked to eliminate or at least minimize them. He had a clear idea of where the country was and should be thirty years hence and a clear idea of what needed to be done to bring that about. Could one say the same of V.P. Singh?

The sad realization soon dawned on people that V.P. Singh had made a fine finance minister because he is essentially an executer, not a leader; a doer, not a thinker; a craftsman, not a visionary. There is, of course, nothing wrong in this except that such men don't make good prime ministers. They simply make good deputies.

The third test of leadership, and the one that Singh most conspicuously failed, is the ability to rise above pettiness. You cannot lead, as Rajiv Gandhi has lately discovered, by assuming that you can solve—or even understand—people's problems by meeting them for a few minutes outside your Range Rover before going back home to your PC and Nakamichi.

The sense of shallowness, caused by the failure to rise above narrow selfish interests, has, however, not escaped V.P. Singh—it engulfs him. It shows in his choice of lieutenants (V.C. Shukla). It comes through in his lack of concrete ideas to build the nation. Where is the V.P. Singh grand design for a better India? Rooting out corruption in public life is the beginning of the solution, not the end, as Singh seems to suggest.

The main issues of industrial productivity, pragmatic economic planning, decentralizing the bureaucracy, inculcating a work ethic and so on are not addressed at all. Foreign policy, defence, law and order—none of these features significantly in V.P. Singh's speeches. Where is the vision we rightfully expect from a leader? What we need from a man who regards himself as a future chief executive of India are clear-cut, statesmanlike policy guidelines on Sri Lanka, Pakistan, the superpowers, the nuclear option and a host of other issues. There is, after all, a limit to how long you can go on and on about Bofors.

Finally, then, comes the fourth prerequisite of leadership—one that, alas, once again eludes the Raja: being a good administrator. A quick caveat here: when he first became prime minister, Rajiv had a corporate manager's or technocrat's approach to things—define objectives, fix targets, monitor implementation, analyse results. Of course it didn't work and of course it couldn't have. So out went the yuppie managers and in came the old-style political fixers. But while Rajiv's experience has proved that you can't run a country by management technique alone, it has proved that certain things do work better and faster with MBO (Management By Objectives) theories.

V.P. Singh's record in this sense is mixed. As chief minister of Uttar Pradesh, he was a capable but not an outstanding administrator. Ironically, people deified him over the dacoit issue. Resignation over a failure to control dacoits proves a high degree of morality but also reveals a low level of administrative competence. In any other country, a resignation that was self-admittedly caused by such a lapse would be regarded as a political failure. But in India's unique feudal-religious-social ethos, it is looked upon as a political triumph.

■

During his two-year tenure as finance minister under Rajiv, V.P. Singh showed himself to be a clear thinker and steadfast follower-up of policy decisions. But his overall administrative competence tended to get diluted because his means so often got mixed up with ideological ends. Thus tax raids became an end in themselves—self-justifying—rather than a means to achieve a broader end: elimination of economic corruption. Liberalization of the economy too became an end when it really should have been regarded as the means to achieve higher productivity and to boost industrialization. When implementation and ideals are inextricably mixed, the result is often confusion.

The reason V.P. Singh became a phenomenon in mid-1987 lay in the deep disillusionment Rajiv had caused among ordinary people. The rapid disintegration of the V.P. Singh phenomenon lies in his failure to understand the needs of the Indian people at the precise moment that they felt betrayed by the trust they had placed in Rajiv Gandhi in 1984. That need was for leadership of the nation, for Rajiv had abandoned his claim to it.

V.P. Singh failed because he was content to belittle Rajiv's vision without offering even a glimpse of his own.

Note: *V.P. Singh, barely a year after this piece was written, would go on to become prime minister for eleven turbulent and divisive months.*

4

THE DUAL MORAL STANDARDS OF THE WEST

26 February 1991

Following the killing—'death by accident' is an unsuitable military euphemism—of over 300 women and children in a Baghdad air shelter by US bombers last fortnight, one would have expected to encounter, at the very least, the civilized sentiment of remorse among the people (if not the political and military establishment) of the West.

However, such sentiments can no longer be taken for granted in Western public opinion.

Consider the results of an opinion poll published by the *The Sunday Times* of London. The survey, conducted *after* the civilian bombing slaughter in Baghdad, revealed that 80 per cent of Britons approve of the continuing multinational bombing of Iraq. This figure, extraordinarily enough, is 6 per cent higher than the figure of a few weeks ago, before the bombing of the civilian raid shelter took place.

The conclusion: the British public regards the killing of Iraqi women and children as a legitimate collateral of war.

Had the situation been reversed, and an Iraqi attack on London killed 300 British women and children, the reaction would have been slightly different.

The Sunday Times, in another report, has quoted senior Pentagon officials as privately admitting that the US air attack on the Baghdad shelter was 'a mistake'. The report said: 'US intelligence identification of the building as a military bunker was based on old information from the '80s which had not been updated.' While publicly defending the attack, Pentagon officials 'privately acknowledge that they were wrong not to check whether the building was being used by civilians. Most of the evidence points to an intelligence blunder'.

The Pentagon source went on to say that a decision had now been taken 'not to target bunkers in order to avoid similar casualties'.

What conclusions do these revelations lead us to?

First, the US military authorities lied when they had said, shortly after the early morning bomb attack on the civilian air raid shelter, that the building was 'definitely a military command and control centre'.

Second, that Western public opinion has two sets of moral standards—one for Western civilians and another for Iraqi civilians.

As one reporter observed: 'Despite the gruesome TV footage of bodies being carried out of the Baghdad air raid shelter bombed by US planes, more than eight in ten people in the UK said the increase in Iraqi civilian casualties had made no difference to their support for the Allied effort.'

If that weren't bad enough, '71 per cent of Britons did not think the Allies should stop bombing military targets in or near Iraq's cities even if civilians were killed or injured.' That is not the end of the perverseness. A Harris opinion poll for the London *Observer* revealed that 20 per cent of Britons actually want the war escalated.

Contrast this with the findings of an American team led by Ramsey Clark, a former Attorney General of the United States, just back from a 2,000-km tour of war-devastated Iraq between 2 and 8 February.

Harish Chandola, *The Indian Express* correspondent writing from Damascus, was the only Indian reporter to file a detailed report on Mr Clark's letter to the UN Secretary General, Javier Perez de Cuellar, outlining his team's observations.

Mr Clark wrote: 'The bombing that has occurred throughout Iraq is the clearest violation of international law and norms of armed conflict, including the Hague and Geneva Conventions and the Nuremberg Charter. It is uncivilized, brutal and racist by any moral standard.' Mr Clark's report is worth reading in full. It is a devastating indictment of the Western military operation on Iraq.

Mr Clark's team, which travelled 1,000 km by road and visited Baghdad, Najaf, Basra, Diwaniya, Hilla and Hasseriya, reported that 'there have been 3,000 infant deaths since November 1990 in excess of the normal rate, attributable solely to the shortage of infant milk formula and medicines on account of the Allied bombing. Only 14 tonnes of baby formula have been received during that period, compared to 2,500 tonnes of monthly consumption in the past'.

Driving 3,000 kilometres over highways, Mr Clark said he saw several hundred vehicles, oil tankers, tractor trailers, lorries, pickup trucks, a public bus, a minibus, a taxicab and many private cars destroyed in aerial bombardment and strafing.

'As with the city streets in residential, industrial and commercial areas, where we witnessed damage, we did not see a single damaged or destroyed military vehicle, tank, armoured car, personnel carrier, and other military equipment, or evidence of any having been removed. We neither heard nor saw any evidence of any military presence in the areas of damage described in this letter.'

A Reuters correspondent, Mamoun Youssef, saw unedited footage from the Worldwide Television News Agency on the Baghdad air raid shelter bombing. There were pictures of bodies of infants 'scorched black by the intense heat'.

Oman Adnan, a seventeen-year-old survivor, lost his three younger sisters, mother and father. He said: 'I was sleeping and suddenly I felt heat and the blanket was burning. Moments later I was suffocating. I turned to try and touch my mother who was next to me but grabbed nothing but a piece of flesh.'

On the side of the building and on top was written in big, bold letters, in English and Arabic: 'Shelter'.

A few days after the American bomb shelter 'blunder' in Baghdad, the Royal Air Force made its own little error. As Group Captain N. Irving said, British war planes dropped three high-explosive bombs on the Iraqi town of Falluja 'by mistake'. One hundred and thirty civilians were killed.

■

It is clear that by invading Kuwait, Saddam Hussein has broken international law. But it is also becoming increasingly clear that by grossly exceeding the mandate of UN Resolution 678, America and its allies have breached international law as well.

It is ironic that America's former attorney general (and senior-most legal officer) is now convinced that 'the killings of civilians and the destruction of residential areas and utilities in Iraq constitute war crimes', a charge (quite properly) made against Saddam Hussein by the Allies.

None of this, unfortunately, has been widely reported by the Indian press. But, as Mr Chandola's excellent report in *The Indian Express* on Ramsey Clark's devastating indictment shows, a good story is always there provided you look hard enough for it.

Note: *The Gulf War which brought CNN to centrestage, was under-reported in the Indian media despite brave individual journalists exposing Western excesses.*

5
IS THERE LIFE IN OUTER SPACE?

28 March 1975

In November 1961, the most august scientific body in the United States convened a meeting at the National Radio Astronomy Observatory in Greenbank, West Virginia. Because of the sensational nature of the question to be discussed, the meeting was held in secret. The subject was 'Intelligent Extraterrestrial Life'. And the participants were astronomers, biologists, physicists and philosophers. One of the participants, Melvin Calvin, was awarded the Nobel Prize for Chemistry while the meeting was in progress.

Why then did such a collection of internationally renowned men insist on secrecy? The answer is simple.

They feared ridicule—not only from the public, but also from their scientific colleagues. Intelligent extraterrestrial life was a revolutionary concept in 1961. Again, their fears were founded on historical precedent.

Those radical minds of the Renaissance who dared suggest that the Earth was not the centre of the cosmos were condemned by society. Men like Giordano Bruno were burned at the stake. Galileo

Galilei was imprisoned. Nicolaus Copernicus suffered social and scientific ostracism.

The situation is slowly changing. The shift in the climate of opinion about extraterrestrial life was reflected by a scientific conference held in 1971, in Byurakan, Soviet Armenia, on the subject. The delegates included several Nobel Laureates. The meeting was sponsored jointly by the Soviet Academy of Sciences and the National Academy of Sciences of the United States.

No longer was secrecy necessary. On the contrary, intense public interest was aroused. Stimulating debate began, people asked themselves searching questions. Are we alone in the universe? Is ours a unique cosmic civilization—a freakish, unfathomable joke of nature? Or are we just a tiny speck of dust in an obscure corner of the cosmos—merely one of several billion advanced civilizations, each one flourishing with its own commerce and culture, politics and philosophy?

At a recent Stanford University symposium, every member of the conference agreed that the discovery of extraterrestrial intelligence was of first-rank scientific importance and that the electromagnetic search for intelligent life is a worthwhile scientific investment.

Recently, Polish, German and American space scientists said at the conclusion of the 24th Hermann Oberth Conference that extraterrestrial life 'somewhere in the universe is not only possible but also probable'.

These conferences were only a few in the series of symposiums being held all over the world to discuss the growing plausibility of the idea that extraterrestrial life *does* exist. Today, scientific and public interest in the subject is enormous.

■

Thousands of pairs of eyes and ears around the world are riveted on gigantic optical and radio telescopes searching, straining, listening for the slightest hint that we are not alone...that the throbbing nerve-centre of the cosmos pulsates with life—and that we are a part of this cosmic community.

But isn't all this in the realm of conjecture? While admittedly speculative, modern astronomy possesses certain tangible scientific data which strongly suggest that the biological evolution of life on earth is not a unique occurrence. We have only just begun to realize the utter insignificance of planet earth in the cosmic context.

Our planet is unspectacularly similar to those in other stellar systems. Our sun is only an average star at the outer rim of the Milky Way galaxy, approaching middle age and about as outstanding as a hippie in Greenwich Village.

We now know that the basic building blocks of life can be synthesized in the laboratory under artificially simulated conditions. Organic compounds, of which all of us are made, have been found in meteorites and in interstellar space. Astronomical spectroscopy is able to determine the chemical compositions of stars billions of light years away. Its findings are unambiguous. The same atoms that exist on earth are found at enormous distances in far-off galaxies. Even more remarkable, these atoms are present everywhere in the universe in roughly the same proportions as on earth.

Why then should intelligent cosmic life be the exclusive prerogative of earth?

Descartes brings out the same point vividly in his famous declaration: 'To believe that the earth alone in the universe has life is to believe that, of a million seeds sown in a cornfield, only one will grow.'

■

Before we can commence our exciting voyage into the extraterrestrial realm, we must answer two questions. First, what are the environmental conditions necessary for organic evolution to begin, be sustained and finally flourish? And second, are such conditions met in other parts of the universe?

It is now believed that most stars have a system of orbiting planets much like our own. We can imagine each star to be surrounded by a spherical zone in which the temperature is equable and conducive to the genesis of elementary life. Such a zone of habitability is called an 'ecosphere'. Of course, the size of an ecosphere depends on the size of the parent star. In our solar system, only one planet lies within the ecosphere: earth.

Dr Carl Sagan, the distinguished Cornell University astrophysicist, and Professor I.S. Shklovsky of the Soviet Academy of Sciences, estimate that two billion stars in our galaxy alone would have inhabitable planets lying within their respective ecospheres.

Another condition of habitability is that lifeforms need a constant source of radiation. A star must, therefore, emit approximately unvarying doses of heat and light over billions of years. The vital importance of this factor can be gauged by imagining the luminosity of our sun to undergo a change of ±2 per cent. This slight variation would turn our balmy planet into either a boiling cauldron of molten metal or a sub-zero deathtrap of solid ice.

By a profound quirk of nature, which we rather ungratefully take for granted, the sun has changed its luminosity by just 0.2 per cent in hundreds of millions of years. And spectroscopic studies show conclusively that the overwhelming majority of stars in our galaxy and in other galaxies are also remarkably constant in their radiation output.

But this is not all. To harbour indigenous life, a planet must have a sufficiently strong gravitational field so that it can 'trap' an atmosphere. One reason why the moon cannot possibly support life is its comparative lightness and, consequently, lower gravity. Molecules of oxygen, nitrogen and hydrogen have long since escaped from the lunar surface. In the absence of atmosphere, an ocean of water—or any other liquid, for that matter—is impossible to maintain. According to Dr Sagan, 'Liquids or dense gases seem required for molecular interaction in the origin and evolution of life.' Dr Sagan concludes: 'Except for the remote possibility of the sub-surface origin and evolution of life, a planet must have an atmosphere to be habitable.'

This should not lead us into a form of oxygen-nitrogen 'chauvinism'. Sometimes the presence of even hydrogen or ammonia is sufficient for the existence of life. Indeed, many organisms (some on earth too) thrive on hydrogen and are poisoned by oxygen. The important thing is the presence of atmosphere—not the type of atmospheric atoms.

The final hurdle an emerging lifeform would have to surmount is that of time. The first unicellular organisms on earth evolved only two billion years after the planet came into existence. It seems certain that organic life will need to have a parent star and orbiting planets with a long lifespan so that the slow process of biological evolution can begin.

■

After having gone through the entire gamut of conditions necessary for the evolution of intelligent life, how many planets remain in the reckoning and how many have fallen by the wayside?

Professor Horst Lob of Giessen University states that, according to his estimates, 'up to 6 per cent of all planets in the universe could be inhabited.'

Dr V.S. Venkatavardan, Fellow in Geophysics at the Tata Institute of Fundamental Research, says, 'Several hundred billion planets in the universe are virtually certain to have life.'

Note: *Nearly thirty-nine years ago, while still at university, I wrote a three-part cover story series for* The Illustrated Weekly of India *on a subject—the cosmos—I return to time and time again. This is only the first part of that series. The search for extraterrestrial life meanwhile continues in scientific institutes around the world and with renewed vigour.*

6

ASIA'S TIME HAS COME

24 April 1988

Prime Minister Rajiv Gandhi's recent two-day visit to Japan is a welcome sign that the Indian government is finally beginning to realize just how important Tokyo—and indeed the whole Pacific Rim—could be to India's economic and geopolitical future.

However, judging by their traditional preoccupation with the United States, the Soviet Union and Western Europe, Indian opinion-makers seem oblivious to the most important shift in the balance of world power since the fifteenth century: the emergence of East Asia as the world's economic and technological powerhouse. The year 2000 CE will mark the beginning of what economists and politicians around the world are already beginning to dub the 'Century of Asia'.

An American newsmagazine, not known for its pro-Asia bias, wrote: 'As the twentieth century draws to a close, the world is in the midst of a profound geopolitical shift. Everything points to rapidly growing Asian political influence and economic affluence: East Asia alone today produces a third of the world's total economic output, slightly more than the whole of Europe and about the same as North America. Led by Japan, and energetically supported by

South Korea, Taiwan, China, Singapore, Hong Kong, Malaysia and Thailand, the Pacific Rim countries are going to change the balance of world economic and military power more fundamentally than at any time since the fifteenth century when European colonization and overseas settlements began 500 years of Western global dominance.'

Where does India fit into this coming age of Asian supremacy? By virtue of its population, technological self-reliance, skilled manpower and well-developed industrial infrastructure, India could have a powerful, even pivotal role to play in the Century of Asia. Indeed, it must, by all rights be one of the three nations—along with Japan and China—that will give Asian power both credibility and stability.

India too has the advantage of being, unlike Japan and China and most of the 'little dragons' of the Pacific, English-speaking. In a world still governed by American economic, political and cultural ideas, India's proficiency in English, especially in science, technology and international business, offers the country an invaluable edge.

Just one example will illustrate this: Japan, despite its enormous international supremacy in computers, is lagging way behind the rest of the word in software development. The reason? A lack of English-speaking Japanese software programmers and developers. Overseas markets, on which the Japanese industry thrives, simply don't want Japanese-language software. (Of course the English-speaking advantage will start evaporating in around twenty years, when computers become programmable with neutral, non-'language' commands.) For the moment, however, India has a tremendous advantage over its Asian neighbours in five key areas: language, manpower, markets, size and military power. But it has a crucial disadvantage too: a sluggish, un-Asian economy.

India's 1987 GNP of Rs 3,10,000 crore ($240 billion) stacks up pretty poorly against Japan's 1987 GNP of $2,000 billion. In short, Japan with one-eighth of India's population produces eight times as many goods and services. Each Japanese is therefore, sixty-four times as productive as each Indian.

China is a slightly more equal comparison. Its GNP is $350 billion or around 50 per cent higher than India's—not too bad, considering its population, too, is 25 per cent larger. In contrast, though the per capita incomes of other Asian Pacific countries are many multiples of India and China's, their tiny populations will give them little permanent economic clout.

■

Japan, while economically strong, is vulnerable in many other areas. It has not forgotten the trauma of the Second World War and the national shame of defeat: it is, after all, the only country in the world to have suffered a nuclear attack. Though it now spends more on defence ($45 billion a year) than any country apart from the USSR and the US, Japan's military establishment is its Achilles' heel; its army is undertrained, its air force underequipped and its navy undermanned.

Here again, with the acquisition of a nuclear submarine and its growing nuclear missile capability, India can play a powerful role in Asia. China has 3.2 million men under arms, Taiwan 4,24,000 and Japan only 2,26,000. India, with 1.2 million men under arms, thus has Asia's second largest army.

Japan's other handicap is that, like all successful countries, it is the target of envy and dislike among its neighbours. South Koreans haven't forgotten the Japanese colonization of their country earlier this century; Burmese and other East Asians haven't forgiven the brutality of the conquering Japanese armies in the Second World War. Add to that the natural jealousy economic success always attracts and you have a recipe for the Ugly Japanese Syndrome, surely one title the Americans will be happy to bequeath to their Japanese successors as Pax Nipponica replaces Pax Americana.

The future world role of Asia and its three major powers—Japan, China and India—will, of course, depend on the interrelationship between these three countries and the bilateral ones each can strike up with the Soviet Union. Remember, Russia's southeastern jowl hangs ominously over East Asia. Vladivostok, as Mikhail Gorbachev once said, is Russia's 'window on the East'. Indeed Gorbachev publicly conceded in July 1986 that 'the Soviet Union is also an Asian Pacific country'.

■

Given all this, it is clearly bad strategy to focus all our attention on the West. But that, of course, is exactly what we all do: Indian businessmen still visit New York, London and Frankfurt more frequently than Tokyo, Seoul and Beijing. Our senior military schools such as the National Defence College in Delhi still send their best officers to North America and Western Europe for study visits rather than to China or South Korea. Our politicians and diplomats still take their cues from London and Washington rather than from Tokyo and Beijing.

Part of the reason, of course, is habit (a bad one which must be broken quickly). The other part is a crucial misjudgement by India's political, diplomatic and business establishment of the speed with which the epicentre of economic and military power is shifting from West to East.

To prosper and play its rightful role in the twenty-first century, a century that will be dominated by Asian—not Western—economic and military might, India must not only work on its strengths (defence, technology, industry and manpower) and eliminate its weaknesses (slow economic growth) but also start getting to know its fellow-Asians a little better. For historical and cultural reasons, our business, political and academic elite is closer to America and Europe than to East Asia. It is time to change that before it is too late and East Asia shuts its door on the subcontinent.

By the turn of the century, Indians and Chinese will account for 2.2 billion of the world's 6 billion people—nearly half of all humanity. The two countries' armies (nearly 5 million strong) will, by 2000 CE, be twice as large as the combined armies of the USSR and the US.

Rajiv Gandhi, back from Tokyo last week, has the opportunity in the remaining twenty months of his term to forge closer economic and political ties with the Pacific Rim. If he succeeds in doing so, it will be remembered long after his departure from office as his major contribution towards securing for India a world role in the next century.

Note: *Writing this twenty-five years ago, the Asian Century was already visible on the horizon—through China rather than Japan has subsequently taken the lead.*

7

VOTERS RAISE A FIST IN THE FACE OF A ROTTEN SYSTEM

14 December 1994

The slap in the face the Congress received in Karnataka and Andhra Pradesh last week has not perceptibly reddened many ministerial cheeks. The conventional wisdom is that state election results are not an accurate political barometer for the Lok Sabha polls, due only by June 1996. And yet, the real message of Andhra, Karnataka and Sikkim is addressed to politicians of all parties: do not take voters for granted. Bad government will be punished at the polls, good government will be rewarded.

The defeat of the Bharatiya Janata Party in Uttar Pradesh last year and the decimation of the Congress in the South this year are warning signals of public disaffection that politicians can ignore at their peril. The criminalization of the political system is now all-pervasive. And nowhere is the rot so evident as in our criminal justice system. It is a national disgrace that thousands of undertrials languish for years in jail while politicians with criminal records live lives of luxury and known Indian terrorists operate with impunity from Dubai and Karachi.

Sanjay Dutt's case is not that of a typical undertrial but nonetheless cuts to the bone of what is rotten about criminal justice and politics in India. Dutt has now been in a Bombay jail for nearly five months. His crime: possession of an AK-56 semi-automatic assault rifle. It is blindingly clear, especially after the arrest of Yakub Memon, that the Bombay serial bomb blasts in March 1993 were orchestrated from Dubai and Karachi by Dawood Ibrahim and his Inter-Services Intelligence 'associates' as revenge for the anti-Muslim riots in Bombay in January 1993. All the major breakthroughs in the bomb blasts case so far have come from the Central Bureau of Intelligence (CBI) and other investigating agencies at the Centre.

The Bombay police have been relatively unsuccessful in their investigations into the bomb blasts case and have rounded up dozens of fifth-rung criminals: loaders, minor smugglers, cargo handlers, drivers and coolies. The two main suspects, Dawood Ibrahim and Tiger Memon, remain free despite the CBI and the Bombay police having a fairly clear idea of where they are and how they masterminded the March 1993 blasts, the single worst act of terrorism in Bombay since 1947. Right from the beginning of the investigation, the Bombay police have been under enormous pressure to show that they are not completely out of their depth.

■

The Justice Srikrishna Commission, investigating the Hindu-Muslim riots of January 1993, is doing a fine job of compiling and hearing evidence. But what will come of its findings when the long, tortuous process ends? The relatives of the people who died in the Bombay riots nearly two years ago still seek justice; the murderers are still mostly free and, despite the awaited conclusions of the Srikrishna Commission, will probably remain free even after that.

It took an article on the front page of *The Times of India* last month for the Bombay High Court to take cognizance of the plight of undertrials, many thousands of whom have already spent more time in jail than they would have even if they had been convicted for their crimes.

In another path-breaking development last week, the division bench of the Bombay High Court converted a report in the *The Times of India* by Milind Ballal (5 December 1994) into a suo moto writ petition. The article told the story of seventy-four-year-old freedom fighter Nathubhai Mehta, against whom (and thirty-one others) a police case was filed ten years ago but which has still not come up even for hearing.

Our judicial system is so slow that it often defeats the purpose of natural justice. This in turn encourages the use of extrajudicial methods to settle disputes: assault, extortion, intimidation, even murder. Thus the law, by its own infirmity, creates lawlessness.

The blame for all this belongs clearly at the top of the pyramid: the political executive. And, as the South has shown last week, as the North showed last year and the entire country showed in 1977, politicians should not take the Indian masses for granted.

India is a tolerant, forgiving society. We tolerated the invading Turk-Mughals and the British. We (some of us at least) even forgave them. But the injustices being today heaped upon the ordinary people of India by those in authority is an abuse of the trust and power vested in them. It cannot go on forever.

If politicians do not clean up the system, the system will one day flush them out.

Note: *The criminalization of India politics, now virulent, began over twenty years ago. This 1994 piece shows how urgently we need police and judicial reform and how overdue the Supreme Court's July 2013 order barring MPs and MLAs convicted by a trial court was.*

8
WHAT SHOULD THE PROPRIETOR-EDITOR RELATIONSHIP BE?

29 January 1991

Kuldip Nayar, who has plunged pack into the hurly burly of Indian journalism from the frosty detachment of international diplomacy, wrote in a recent newspaper article: 'The other thing that worries me about journalism today is the entrance of business houses into publishing. What is happening is that newspapers are being run by businessmen who earn money by selling certain things—be it textiles, cement or steel. The money they earn from these fields are being delivered into publishing, to avoid paying tax. And while they are doing so, they also begin to influence and control the news gathering process. These industrialists are not really interested in running a newspaper. What they are interested in is using the publication to achieve their business purposes. That is what is so frightening. I am not against businessmen wanting to get into publishing. But if they are genuinely interested, why don't they give their money to a trust which runs a newspaper? Why are they part of the same set-up?'

Why not, indeed. But Mr Nayar misses the real point: who is, and who should be, the real boss in a newspaper—the editor or the proprietor?

Clearly, in India, and almost everywhere else, it is the proprietor. Most good newspapers, of course, cling to the pretence that the editor's right is paramount, that it even supersedes the proprietor's, and in any editorial dispute the editor's view must prevail.

In practice that never happens.

Ramnath Goenka of *The Indian Express* is as redoubtable a proprietor as any editor could hope to have. Yet he has fired editors—including the toughest one of them all, Arun Shourie—the moment they crossed a certain predetermined line.

In the UK, the proprietor of *The Observer*, 'Tiny' Rowland, nearly sacked his editor, Donald Trelford, over an article on southern Africa four years ago. (Yes, the same Trelford of Pamella Bordes fame.)

Rupert Murdoch has sacked countless editors in his media empire across three continents and so has Robert Maxwell.

Given such occupational hazards, can editors and proprietors still work out a civilized code of conduct that demarcates areas of responsibility and minimizes those of conflict?

They can, they must and, in many cases, they have already begun to.

In November 1988, to mark its 150th anniversary, *The Times of India* hosted a symposium on media, where several international editors (including Andreas Whittam Smith, founder-editor of *The Independent*, and Peregrine Worsthorne, the recently knighted editor of the *Sunday Telegraph*), were present.

In a paper to be read at the symposium, I was asked to dwell on the relationship between editors and owners. Having been both—simultaneously—at Sterling Newspapers for over ten years, it was thought I understood the contradictory needs of each.

I did not—and still do not—but ventured to say this which I reckon summarizes the problem if not the solution:

'The government has often said that the Indian press is not really free because it is owned by monopoly business houses who, through the newspapers they own, promote vested interests and causes. This is plainly false. Newspapers and magazines everywhere in the world are owned by big business houses and this does not necessarily compromise their independence. Some are multidimensional publishing companies—like Time Inc., where even the forests it owns are meant for supplying raw material to the newsprint mills it owns—while some, like Lonrho Plc, which publishes the London *Observer*, have dozens of non-publishing business activities. Clearly, publishing, while not quite as brazenly commercial an activity as, say, making textiles or sugar, has to be a commercially viable enterprise or it will not survive.

'The solution, therefore, is not to delink publishing from big business or to have a national fund for newspapers to draw from, as one union minister unrealistically suggested recently, but to ensure that journalists have the integrity and sense of responsibility—and therefore the authority—to run their papers without interference from their proprietors.

'An editor must be the executive head of a publishing company and, in all editorial and some non-editorial areas too, his opinion must matter as much if not more than that of the proprietor or chairman.

'That is the way to run a truly responsible and visionary publishing company: free from government interference and proprietorial diktat.'

■

The reason why otherwise upright newspaper (and magazine) publishers bend with the political wind is that so many of them are vulnerable to the economic pressure the government can bring to bear upon them. Despite the constraints, however, the role of the press in a democracy must be to report facts, investigate them and present them to readers with fairness and dispassion.

The press is responsible to only one constituency—and it's the same one the government (or the Opposition) is accountable to: the people. Thus the confrontational tenor the press-government equation often takes is spurious and irrational. There should be—and can be—no confrontation, simply because the government and the press are on the same side—the country's.

Or are they?

Let us first ponder some examples of the press-government equation in other democracies. In Britain (the country whose model we have often—erroneously—followed) the independent press is sharply divided by political ideology. The conservatives have their *Telegraph* and *Spectator,* the liberals their *Guardian,* the moderates their *Times,* the labourites their *Daily Mirror* and the leftists their *Star* and *New Statesman*. While these papers and magazines traditionally support the parties they 'endorse', they are independent enough to be those same parties' sternest critics (well, sometimes).

But this is one of those bad British habits that tends to get left behind in the old colonies; in India this sort of (essentially wrong) model has taken root. Thus we have the 'establishment' *Hindustan Times,* the 'opposition' *The Indian Express* and the 'moderate' *The Hindu.*

Among magazines the party distinctions are thankfully less defined and a certain degree of genuine independence exists in, for example, *India Today, Sunday, The Week* and others. This is partly because the magazines, being newer, have adopted (unconsciously) the American rather than the British concept of press-government relations.

The British concept arose because history demanded that the press play a large political role in eighteenth- and nineteenth-century Britain and the tradition of 'party' papers was thus firmly established. America does have its Republican and Democrat cheerleaders (*The New Republic* and *The Boston Globe* respectively) but the bigger fish

(The New York Times, The Washington Post and the *Los Angeles Times)* have managed to avoid a party tag. So have most of the mainline magazines, though the sympathies of *Time* clearly lie with the GOP and those of *Newsweek* with the Democrats.

The press-government relationship is a tricky one and too much closeness is as bad as too much distance. The press has a job to do, and so does the government. In the discharge of their respective duties some conflict of interest is inevitable, particularly in the hurly-burly of democracy. But then democracy also accommodates (or should) a great deal of give and take. This is where a mature press and a mature government ought to paper over their differences and unite in a common cause: nation-building.

It is important to bear in mind that when the independent press criticizes the government, it does not criticize the government *per se*, but the actions (and the results wrought by those actions) of the government. It is thus an impersonal exercise. It is time politicians of all shades realized that the independent press is not anti-Congress or pro-Opposition. It is pro-India.

Note: *This was published a month before Indira Gandhi's assassination, when the relationship between the government and the media was as fraught as it is nearly thirty years later.*

9
SYCOPHANCY IN PUBLIC LIFE

March 1984

The signs are everywhere. Sycophancy is now so endemic in Indian public life that half of New Delhi seems to be paying obeisance to the other half. Everyone seems to be doing it: Industrialists who are mini-emperors in their home territories of Bombay. Calcutta and Madras sit for hours gnawing their nails outside the offices of joint secretaries in the Finance Ministry. Bureaucrats, in turn, bend halfway forward in front of their ministers. And ministers, normally so full of bombast, are reduced to gibbering children in front of the prime minister.

What is everyone so scared of? The apprehensions of tremulous, favour-seeking industrialists are understandable; faint-hearted bureaucrats, too, can be forgiven their obsequiousness. But what of the ministers, those public personages who hold responsible public office at the behest of the electorate? The sycophancy, the spinelessness, the intellectual mediocrity they display should make the electorate harbour grave doubts about the wisdom of permitting them to run the nation's affairs.

When Mrs Indira Gandhi was in Bombay recently, state

Congress (I) party workers excelled themselves in vying for the title of the PM's most loyal servant. Banners littered Mrs Gandhi's and Rajiv's route from the airport to the city with messages of varying degrees of servility and inanity. 'Welcome our great leader' was all right as things went—albeit strong on sycophancy, weak on grammar. 'We are the humble servants of Smt Indira Gandhi' was sillier (though doubtless quite accurate) and showcased the value attached to slogan sycophancy. 'India is Indira' was not only inaccurate but also grossly unfair to both Mrs Gandhi and to India.

People holding public office have a duty, first to the public and only second to their party leaders. Thus when a Congress (I) minister said recently that he was 'Indira's loyal soldier', he was insulting both Mrs Gandhi and the people of India. What he should have said was: 'My leader, Prime Minister Indira Gandhi, and I are both loyal soldiers of the people of India whom we have been elected to serve.'

■

Three points arise from all this. First, sycophancy is not, as it might appear, harmless vacuity on the part of a backward but overenthusiastic section of Congressmen. This makes the dangerous assumption that the prime minister is more important than causes, and more important than the people she is elected by and duty-bound to serve. (The word 'minister', in fact, derives from Latin and means servant. 'Prime Minister' therefore, literally, means the primary servant of the people. In India, the meaning is taken as quite the opposite—the primary master of the people.)

Second, the kind of men and women who behave in the way many of our MPs and ministers seem to do are not the kind in whom the nation's trust can be reposed. What sort of quality of public servant can we expect when most 'career' politicians are men with no backbone and little self-respect, men who crawl when asked to walk?

Third, the disease cuts across party lines. The BJP, Janata, Lok Dal and all their various aggregate party permutations are populated by men cut from the same shabby cloth.

Amidst all this rot, public life in India has acquired a stench so palpable that men of merit shy away from entering it. The loser? India.

The curious thing in all of this, of course, is why Mrs Gandhi allows such unbridled sycophancy to fester around her. There is little doubt that she detests its petty outward manifestations. She (and Rajiv) display periodic bouts of ill temper with their loyal servants. At Bombay airport, she once scolded a Congress (I) high-up for wasting flowers on garlanding her. Couldn't the money spent have been put together and used for public good? she asked.

Rajiv was equally cross when a whole retinue of Congress (I) workers came to see him off at Bombay airport, wasting not only public money but also public time. Mrs Gandhi has time and again lectured her party men like schoolboys (which, mentally, many are) for wasting time and money on routine, ceremonial functions. Yet, they never seem to get the message.

Question: Why don't Mrs Gandhi and Rajiv (both sensible and intelligent people) get tougher on their partymen's more obvious acts of sycophancy and servility? Answer: Both are also shrewd politicians. Mrs Gandhi knows perfectly well the hidden advantages of overt sycophancy. The 'Indira is India' syndrome might embarrass her privately, and intellectually, but in the hinterland it does wonderful things for her image and is a terrific vote-puller.

Similarly, the 'loyalty' bordering on servility shown by her partymen might be privately repugnant to her: yet she does not (and will not) discourage it too seriously for it, too, burnishes her image in the eyes of her party minions.

Mrs Gandhi is a shrewd politician first and a sensible private person second. To stay the undisputed leader of her party she has to ensure two things. First, that her 'loyal soldiers' project her as the saviour of India to the masses (hence her tepid objection to the 'India is Indira' catchline). Second, that no credible opposition to her emerges from within the party (sons are allowed).

To achieve this, there's no better way than to surround yourself with mediocre drum-beaters who'll sing your praises to the masses and bend or crawl whenever you grant them an audience. But sometimes such loyal servants turn out to be liabilities (such as Mr A.R. Antulay) and sometimes rebellious (Mr Siddhartha Shankar Ray). In either case they have to be politically exorcised.

In the end, the political arithmetic is simple. You want to run a country of 700 million people. Why complicate a tough job by having bright people around you who'll tell you where you're going wrong?

Note: *This March 1984 piece could well have been written today: sycophancy is as endemic as it was in Indira Gandhi's time. Only the names of the mother and son have changed.*

10

CLEAR THE STABLES AT BCCI

2 July 2007

A cricket tour of the British Isles should be a player's—and fan's—delight. Cool, crisp summer weather, manicured grounds, challenging batting conditions, green, pleasant county games. But India's current tour of England and Ireland has an underbelly that hides a laundry list of problems.

We have a well-meaning coach, Chandu Borde, who is completely unsuitable for the job. We have a clutch of senior players—Tendulkar, Ganguly, Dravid, Kumble, Yuvraj—who have arm-twisted the BCCI into restoring their Rs 50 lakh 'A' grade annual contracts. And we have, worst of all, the BCCI, which must be the second most regressive cricket board in the world (after the Pakistan Cricket Board whose infamy even the BCCI could not match, however hard it tried).

What is wrong with the BCCI?

The challenge is to revamp the board so that Indian cricket is liberated from the incompetence, greed, opacity and politics that have imprisoned it for decades. It is time to find the key and free the sport from its long confinement.

Start at the top. Sharad Pawar might do a better job as agriculture minister if he devoted as much time to his ministry as he does to the BCCI's Byzantine politicking. Rule number one at the 'new' BCCI must be simple but uncompromising: no politician may hold any office on the board.

The BCCI's president must be elected from professional ex-cricketers who have played Test or first class cricket. The same unyielding rule must apply to the BCCI's secretary, treasurer and board committee members. There is a rich vein of ex-cricketing talent in the country (from G.R. Vishwanath and Bishen Singh Bedi to Mohinder Amarnath and Dilip Vengsarkar) that can be mined. A BCCI board comprising men of such outstanding calibre, integrity and professionalism would transform the way Indian cricket is administered.

Second, the ex-cricketer-run BCCI must recruit a professional chief executive to manage the organization on a day-to-day basis, who will introduce transparency and be accountable to the BCCI board.

Third, the BCCI must set up a five-member internal committee to negotiate television and other media advertising rights—again with complete transparency in the bidding/auction process. It should also set up its own legal and media relations cell to ensure public accountability and prompt dissemination of information.

Fourth, the richest cricket board in the world, with several thousand crore rupees in TV rights accruing to it every year, must have a transparent and professional mechanism to select Test and ODI teams, grade players, fix remunerations, establish guidelines for brand endorsements and allocate funds to develop training academies nationwide and to modernize grounds, stadia and pitches. The money earned by marketing Indian cricket is today frittered away—no one except the notoriously opaque BCCI knows exactly where this money goes. A reconstructed BCCI would make money efficiently and spend it transparently.

■

Finally, coaching. The shenanigans over Graham Ford and John Emburey and the stopgap arrangement of appointing Chandu Borde for the ongoing England and Ireland tour would never have occurred had the BCCI been controlled and managed by men like Vishwanath, Amarnath, et al.

The BCCI has converted our cricketers into mercenaries, who are more concerned with elongating their careers artificially so that they can stay on the BCCI's gravy train for as long as possible. As a result, a whole generation of talented cricketers find their paths blocked.

Virtually every major cricketing nation outside the subcontinent has a cricket board run by well-paid professionals who are subject to the strictest public scrutiny. As India gets ready to take on England in the ODI and Test series, it is time the BCCI's politician-stuffed board is emptied to make way for professional ex-cricketers and a full-time CEO. And if a Public Interest Litigation (PIL) is needed to achieve that end, so be it.

Note: *As this 2007 column shows, I've long argued for a revamped BCCI—well before the IPL made it the world's most powerful, and unaccountable, sports body.*

11
AMERICA HAS NEITHER MONEY NOR GUNS TO CONTROL THE WORLD

11 January 1995

How rich is rich? According to the 1995 World Bank Atlas released on 29 December, India is still one of the poorest nations on earth. Per capita income is $290, placing India somewhere between Rwanda and China.

But wait. Figures can lie. If purchasing power parity (PPP) is factored into the equation, India's per capita income quadruples to $1,250. The World Bank and the International Monetary Fund now include PPP-based per capita income figures for all countries in their annual surveys. The PPP formula neutralizes the cost of goods and services you can buy in local currency against the currency's dollar exchange rate. For example, the rupee buys roughly four times the value of goods and services in India than the dollar equivalent buys in America. Ergo, PPP places the 'real' value of the dollar (in purchasing power terms) at roughly Rs 8 and not the official rate of Rs 31.37 in 1995.

PPP is obviously a fairer indication of per capita income because it links income to purchasing power. When measured by PPP, the World Bank is now saying, India is less poor than most people think. All this alarms rather than pleases India's finance ministry. The donor countries of the International Development Association (IDA) are shortly to decide the 11th replenishment criteria for allocation of assistance to developing countries.

The current cut-off point for IDA assistance eligibility is a per capita income of $800. If PPP norms are used by the IDA (which at present they are not), India will no longer be eligible for international funding since it will no longer be a truly poor country by PPP definition.

According to that definition, an average Indian is today 'only' twenty times poorer than the average American, ten times poorer than the average Greek and twice as poor as the average Chinese. But he is still several times richer than the average Rwandan, Somali and Vietnamese and, to put things in perspective, just about as wealthy as the average Bangladeshi.

Since the size of a country's economy determines its influence in the world, the PPP ratings augur well for India. Hidden in the World Bank statistics is this nugget: at $1,250 per capita income, India's Gross National Product by PPP is a hefty $1.1 trillion, nearly four times its GNP in dollar terms. This puts the size of India's economy in the same league as Europe's big four: Germany, France, Italy and Britain. Add to this Manmohan Singh's forecast that India's GNP will grow by 6 per cent a year from 2000 onwards and you have a $2 trillion economy in ten years. Only three countries would then have larger economies in PPP terms than India: the United States (around $12 trillion), China ($5 trillion) and Japan ($4.5 trillion).

■

All this has a major bearing on the new world order the West is trying to sculpt. The old world order was authored for most of this century by four countries: the United States, Britain, the Soviet Union and France. During the forty-year Cold War, an uneasy but effective 'balance of nuclear deterrence' between the three Western powers and the Soviet Union ensured relative peace and stability in Europe. The break-up of the Soviet Union and the reunification of Germany, however, unleashed powerful geopolitical forces.

As it had been for nearly 1,000 years, Europe is now once again riven by war. The rebellion in Chechnya, the savage conflict in Bosnia and the growing instability in the Soviet Union's former republics are a daily reminder of Europe's tribal, warlike past when Angles, Jutes, Saxons, Vikings and Goths battled for land, fief and money.

The prosperity and tranquility of Western Europe are under real threat from the sectarian fissures in Central and Eastern Europe. With the recent induction of Sweden, Finland and Austria into the European Union, the world's richest and largest trading bloc now has a common border with Russia for the first time. And Russia's conflicts, including the violent revolt in Chechnya, horrify West European leaders.

The West has two major problems. The first is simply geographical. With an unstable Russia lurking at the European community's borders and Bosnia simmering within sniffing distance of Italy and Germany, the cherished dream of a peaceful Europe is turning into a nightmare. The North Atlantic Treaty Organization (NATO), the bedrock of Western security for forty-five years, has proved militarily unable and psychologically unwilling to cope with the crisis in the former Yugoslavia. Its air strikes, under United Nations mandate, have so far failed to break Serb resolve and put a large question mark over NATO's effectiveness in a multi-polar world.

The second problem for the West is commerce. Instability is bad for business. Western Europe has sunk a lot of money into the former communist economies of Eastern Europe. Apart from Poland, Hungary and Romania, that investment seems to be going down the drain. Russia, the dismembered fragments of the former

Yugoslavia and many ex-Soviet republics are reneging on debts and contracts and causing West European businessmen sleepless nights.

All this threatens Western Europe's nascent economic recovery after a four-year-long recession. Recent figures from the Organisation of Economic Cooperation and Development show that growth in the industrialized economies will average 2.5 per cent in 1995 but slip to below 2 per cent in 1996. This is less than half the growth rate expected this year and the next in Asia and Latin America.

The new world order, after the demise of the Soviet Union, was not supposed to read like this. Instead of making the world a more peaceful and prosperous place, the end of the Cold War has ignited little bush fires all over the globe.

In an effort to recapture the initiative of peace and prosperity, *The Economist* offers Western leaders a solution in its special year-end issue. Its solution is democracy-by-intervention and goes something like this: the West should intervene militarily in countries where the people seek democracy but are burdened by a cruel dictator (Haiti, Somalia, Cuba). The rule of thumb for such an intervention is that, one, the oppressed people should clearly seek it, and two, the West's interests should be furthered by the intervention.

This is silly stuff even by the *The Economist's* engaging standards. Who decides when a helpless country needs Western intervention to save it from a local dictator? The United Nations? NATO? President Clinton? All three are highly unreliable judges of whom to invade, when and why: the United Nations because four-fifths of the Security Council's permanent membership is dominated by veto-carrying countries from Europe and North America; NATO because it protects the strategic interests of the Western alliance, not the rest of the world; and President Clinton because America's policy of foreign intervention has, on balance, done more harm than good over the last forty years.

■

The West withheld democracy from Asia, Africa and Latin America for as long as it possibly could. It used military force to impose colonial dictatorships, at times with brutal force, as in French-occupied Algeria, US-occupied Philippines and British-occupied Malaya. Now it talks benevolently of delivering democracy to countries that have local dictatorships and whose politics are really none of its business. Why?

Because for the first time since the eighteenth century the West no longer controls the ebb and flow of world events. It has neither the money nor the guns to do so. It can only regain a semblance of control by using the democracy-by-intervention argument as a camouflage for good old-fashioned gunboat diplomacy.

But this is not imperialism, *The Economist* protests innocently: 'The outsider's only legitimate business is to ask, Do you want to govern yourselves—and, if the answer is Yes, to be prepared to step in and remove the obstruction. The West has, in democracy, something that most other people want to share. If it does not help them to win a share of it, the West will feel bad, and the anti-democrats of the twenty-first century will grow stronger. If the West does help, it will gain both in self-confidence and in the new friends it creates for itself around the globe. These are solid reasons why that non-imperialist project, the spreading of the empire of democracy, will remain on the Western agenda.'

What extraordinary piffle.

The West is bedevilled by chronic low growth, saturated markets and the looming spectre in Western Europe of de-sovereignization: the Deutsche Mark and the French franc may cease to exist when a single European currency is introduced in 1999 and decision-making on even foreign and defence policy will devolve to Brussels.

Ordinary Britons, French and Germans are appalled by the prospect of thus subordinating their proud national identities. But history is a great leveller. Europe was a seething mass of warring tribes 1,500 years ago when great hordes of Angles, Saxons and Jutes roared across the plains of Germany to settle England. Asia was then the centre of learning, culture and trade. Europe had its moment in the sun—nearly 500 years long—following the 'discovery' and colonization of Asia, Africa and North America.

Now it is reduced to defending its corner by citing the gift of democracy as a reason to intervene militarily in other nations' affairs when all it really wants to do is to protect its own geopolitical and commercial interests. That is why it requisitioned a forty-nation invasion force to push Iraq out of 'democratic' Kuwait. And that is why it will not, out of enlightened self-interest, save 1.2 billion Chinese from the harsh rigours of a communist dictatorship though Beijing fulfils all but one of *The Economist*'s criteria ('the cost, in money and soldiers' lives') for gallant Western military intervention.

■

For its part, India's foreign policy agenda for the last half decade of this century should rest on two fulcrums. First, we must press uncompromisingly for a restructuring of the UN Security Council so that it reflects the geopolitics of 1995, not 1945. In the new Council, permanent members France and Britain must go; India and Japan should take their place. This will lead to a fairer creation and dissemination of international policy.

France and Britain will naturally argue that any change in the permanent membership of the Council will lead to delayed and confused decision-making. That is a red herring. No world governing body can have a moral mandate if it represents the will of less than 40 per cent of the world's population. Take China away from that equation and the other four white permanent members—the United States, Russia, Britain and France—represent a mere 11 per cent of the world's population. A restructured UN Security Council, with India and Japan replacing France and Britain as veto-carrying permanent members of the Council, would be a fair and effective global policeman.

The second key part of India's foreign policy agenda is to work increasingly closely with China and Japan on economic and security issues. Europe rose to pre-eminence and prosperity in the last fifty years because it unified after centuries of bitter warfare. In a similar manner, India, China and Japan should now close ranks.

In the end, the West understands and respects power: economic and military. It has used both, often illegitimately but usually to good effect, for three centuries. Asia, and particularly India, must now do the same but with a less cynical agenda of self-interest. Unlike the nouveau riche of the international community, who made most of their money in the last 200 years, India has a past to live up to, not live down.

Note: The decline of the West, predicted here some twenty years ago, and the rise of Asia is an increasing reality though China's recent assertiveness in the South China Sea and aggression on India's borders, often in collusion with Pakistan, could jeopardize the Asian solidarity I advocated in this article in 1995 and in several others subsequently.

12

THE INDIAN PRESS AND INDIRA GANDHI

August 1984

It is difficult to think of a sensible, impartial Indian political commentator today (apart, perhaps, from Mr Inder Malhotra) who has a good word to say about Mrs Indira Gandhi. There is, on the other hand, a surfeit of political writers and editors who criticize her incessantly—and often unfairly—on every conceivable policy issue.

Why this obsessive antipathy?

The reasons are complex: some are perfectly valid and based on fact. Others are spurious, founded on emotion.

First, the good reasons.

Journalists feel, rightly, that Mrs Gandhi is autocratic. She treats her partymen like a personal retinue of servitors (which, of course, many are) and her country as a personal fiefdom (which it thankfully isn't and cannot be unless the Constitution is torn up).

According to popular journalistic theory, Mrs Gandhi is, by nature, undemocratic. She would, were it possible, hold elections infrequently, if at all. Indeed, she regards elections as a necessary evil. This theory, though a bit ragged at the edges, holds a kernel of truth. The Emergency lost Mrs Gandhi the heart of most Indian journalists: whatever soul was left evaporated in the presence of her subsequent combative attitude towards the media. The result: the press and the prime minister smile politely at each other in public and make rude noises about each other in private.

Journalists regard Mrs Gandhi as bearing a grudge against them, a leftover of the Emergency experience. This, of course, is not true. Mrs Gandhi is not anti-journalists, only anti-inconvenient journalists.

■

Independent-minded journalists object in principle to Mrs Gandhi's politics of divide-and-rule. Kashmir, Andhra, Karnataka—everywhere an Opposition party comes to power, a process of destabilization is begun by the Congress. This can mean one of two things: either Mrs Gandhi genuinely believes that her party is the only one capable of giving India good government, or she dislikes having only a part of the cake, and would go to extreme lengths to get all of it, irrespective of whether her party deserves it or not. Either reason is a bad one: the first suggests arrogance, the second, avarice.

Several journalists contend that the Congress (I)'s *modus operandi* breeds corruption, inefficiency, favouritism and so on. For instance, the concentration of decision-making power in a few Cambridge-educated hands smacks of amateurism. You don't run countries that way. At the other extreme is the responsibility given to incompetent people (even at the ministerial level) simply because they can bring an extra clutch of caste/tribal/minority votes at the next elections. Good politics, bad statesmanship.

Corruption, inefficiency and favouritism, of course, are not Congress (I) birthrights: the Opposition is well-versed in those fine arts too. In fact, the appalling Janata Government of 1977-79 made a bigger mess of the country, despite the short time at its disposal, than the Congress had done in the previous three decades.

But every government must be judged by absolute standards,

not its predecessors'. By most yardsticks, the Congress (I) fails the test. It might be more efficient and less corrupt than any Opposition alternative would be today. But it is less efficient and more corrupt than it should be. As the leader of the ruling party and of the government, the blame for that must rest with Mrs Gandhi.

Good government, stripped of its political component, is basically good management. Management of people, management of resources, management of ideas. And intrinsic to all this is the development of talent, of individuals who can take over the reins when called upon to do so.

Mrs Gandhi is a good politician but a bad manager, which is why the Congress (I) is excellent at getting itself elected but hopeless at providing good government to its nation. That's the irony. Good managers can govern well, but rarely have the specific skills needed to get elected in order to have a chance of governing at all. And good politicians are too busy politicking to worry about governing.

The antagonism between Mrs Gandhi and the Indian press, however, is not entirely the prime minister's fault. There are at least three erroneous reasons for the press's anti-Mrs Gandhi-ism.

Familiarity breeds contempt, and politicians and journalists, rubbing shoulders as they do all the time, develop a finely honed disdain for one another. Hence journalists tend to pounce on the slightest instance of a politician's peccadilloes—personal or political. Politicians thus often get a raw deal at the hands of the media and Mrs Gandhi, being the most visible symbol of the country's body politic, bears the brunt of the flak.

The second reason why journalists criticize Mrs Gandhi so avidly is that it makes heroes of them. Investigative journalism is *de rigueur* these days, and brave, stinging pieces against the government in general and Mrs Gandhi in particular are one way of proving one's journalistic credentials. Ergo, the plethora of Indira-baiters. The PM is perfect target practice: she can't (or won't) fire back.

The third reason why journalists dislike Mrs Gandhi is because she ignores them. That rankles. Journalists are a notoriously prickly lot. Hate them, criticize them—but don't ignore them. Mrs Gandhi does just that. Worse, she lionizes the foreign press. Belittled, Indian journalists react with hostility.

Of course, being anti-Mrs Gandhi—or anti-anyone else for that matter—is not a journalist's job; reporting and interpreting facts is. It is perhaps time that Indian journalists and Mrs Gandhi stopped being so concerned about one another and started paying more attention to their respective constituents: readers and voters.

Note: *This piece, written at the peak of Indira Gandhi's power, examines why the Indian media was hostile to the senior Mrs Gandhi during her prime ministership.*

13
AT LAST, NARASIMHA RAO SAYS SOMETHING AND DECIDES SOMETHING

28 December 1994

Prime Minister Narasimha Rao's legendary ability to say nothing, do nothing and decide nothing took a knock last Thursday when he engineered the resignations of Kalpnath Rai, B. Shankaranand and Rameshwar Thakur. This move, alas, will not be enough to rescue his vanishing reputation.

Shankaranand and Thakur should have gone last year when the Joint Parliamentary Committee implicated them in the securities scandal; Rai should have been sacked a month ago when the sugar scandal unravelled.

The resignation of Human Resources Development Minister Arjun Singh of course falls into an entirely different category: it is the signal for party dissidents to begin the final stage of their two-year campaign to undermine, weaken and finally replace Rao. If the Congress does badly in the February 1995 assembly polls, Singh will be ideally positioned to make a leadership bid.

All this bodes ill for the prime minister and his chances of leading the Congress to victory in the next general election. Rao's deafening silence on Babri Masjid, Mandal, Harshad Mehta, organizational elections and, till now, the sugar scandal has won him few friends. The economic reforms programme, his singular if unfinished achievement, is in imminent danger of being mugged by anti-reformists within and outside the Congress. If the Congress loses Maharashtra and Gujarat next February, it will be wiped out of state-level government virtually throughout the country for the next five years.

That may in itself not be a harbinger for the 1996 Lok Sabha poll. But restless and increasingly apprehensive Congressmen will not be easily appeased: they sense an ill wind in 1996. According to one intelligence report, the Congress may win less than 200 seats in the next Lok Sabha. The Bharatiya Janata Party, faced with the waning appeal of Hindutva, is unlikely to win more than 140, and the combined Janata Dal-led 'Third Force' may at most muster 80 seats. That means small regional parties will again hold the key to forming the next government. This time they will be less receptive to Congress overtures than they were in June 1991.

■

The prime minister still has a few arrows in his quiver. The first is the shambolic Opposition. The Janata Dal, despite its victory in Karnataka, is a spent force nationwide. Ramakrishna Hegde, N.T. Rama Rao and others will try to fashion a secular front by next year but, with V.P. Singh in a deep sulk, it may have limited electoral potency. Paradoxically, the stronger such a secular front is, the better the BJP will do.

The BJP fortunately has its own satchelful of problems. The pull of Hindu revivalism is weakening. Even the Northern cowbelt, where the BJP's saffron politics caused such havoc in 1990 and 1991, has realized how destructively medieval L.K. Advani's party can be.

Three-and-a-half years of economic reform, greater access to satellite television and rising disposable incomes have made even the rural poor realize that salvation does not lie in building temples but in building factories, schools, colleges and hospitals.

The BJP will be in serious danger of being regarded as an embarrassment in a rapidly globalizing economic and cultural ethos if it bases its entire national electoral campaign on emotive issues like the Ram temple. Unfortunately, it has few alternatives. On the economy, its thunder has been stolen by Manmohan Singh. The BJP's top brass has been reduced to quibbling over multinational-led liberalization.

The BJP will have to walk a tightrope for most of 1995. On the one hand, it will continue to flog its anti-Muslim line in the hope that there are enough communal bigots who will take up the bait. On the other hand, the BJP will project itself as the natural party of 'middle India': minding the nation's economy with a swadeshi (anti-MNC) liberalization programme, however absurd that may in practice be.

The hallmark of a mature democracy is the existence of two strong parties, one slightly left of centre, the other slightly right of centre. If the BJP can fulfil the role of such a right-of-centre party without having to stoop to disruptive tactics as it has done for most of this decade, its emergence as a national political force should be welcomed.

■

Consider now the Union Cabinet. We have had a food minister, Kalpnath Rai, deeply embroiled in a scandal, who resisted resigning till he was virtually carried out of his office kicking and screaming. We have a petroleum minister, Satish Sharma, whose brother faces serious money laundering allegations. We have an external affairs minister, Dinesh Singh, whose paralytic stroke last year has gravely affected his ability to discharge his official duties. We had till last week a health minister, B. Shankaranand, and a rural development minister, Rameshwar Thakur, who clung on to their jobs for nearly two years after being indicted for their role in the stock scam by the Joint Parliamentary Committee.

Meanwhile, the two most efficient ministers in the first Rao cabinet of 1991-92, P. Chidambaram and Madhavrao Scindia, sit on the sidelines, reduced respectively to writing columns for business magazines and managing the affairs of Indian cricket.

As commerce minister, Chidambaram was, along with Manmohan Singh, the early architect of economic reform. He resigned in August 1992 for what would by the standards of the sugar scandal be regarded as a minor transgression: investing Rs 100,000 in the shares of Fairgrowth Financial Services Ltd through his lawyer-wife. The company was later notified in the stock scam but when Chidambaram invested in it, by cheque and with complete transparency, it was one of India's most admired finance companies.

The BJP can put together a decent cabinet if it wins the next general election (which, mercifully, it will not), especially if it casts its net wider than the Congress has done outside politics. In the United States, cabinet ministers do not have to win elections. The president chooses the best candidates from business, academics and the professions. Unfortunately, we have chosen to follow the Westminster system under which all cabinet ministers have to become a member of either the Lok Sabha or Rajya Sabha within six months of their induction into the cabinet.

This means that there is no differentiation between professional competence and the ability to win elections, which are often mutually exclusive, unlike in Britain where average constituency sizes are tiny (less than 50,000) and politicians are mostly middle-class professionals. In India this is simply not so. Constituencies usually have more than 500,000 voters and many candidates are chosen for their criminal rather than their professional records.

The back door through which unelectable technocrats are ushered in is the Rajya Sabha. This artifice can surely be taken a step forward. Around ten seats in the Rajya Sabha can be reserved specifically for non-political cabinet appointees without the attendant charade of registering the candidate's 'usual place of residence' in some remote corner of the country (Assam, in Manmohan Singh's by-now famous case).

■

Clearly the next few months will be dominated by politics rather than economics. Rao needs to grasp the nettle and from now onwards campaign on a reformist platform. Indians are a mature electorate. If Rao and his ministers can tell the story of economic liberalization convincingly and show Indian citizens how the next stage will bring tangible benefits to the rural poor, the Congress may surprise itself and gloomy poll forecasters by actually winning the critical February 1995 assembly elections. This would give the party the momentum and confidence it needs in the final run-up to the 1996 general election. It would also nip Arjun Singh's ambitions in the bud.

But for that the Congress leadership must take its case to the country. People want to know how economic reform will help them. Ministers do not say how it will. They want to know how privatization and foreign investment in infrastructure can actually make life better for them. Again, ministers and MPs have not bothered to explain it. They want to know why prices of food and other essential commodities continue to rise even when the official rate of inflation has halved in the last three years. The MPs have no answers. Economic reform has been allowed to become a weakness out of sheer Congress ineptitude when, properly explained, it could have been an enormous strength.

Despite that, the prime minister has been singularly lucky in three ways. He has had four successive good monsoons since June 1991. He has had India's finest finance minister since C.D. Deshmukh joined Jawaharlal Nehru's first Cabinet forty-six years ago. (Manmohan Singh has taken India from being an inefficient socialist economy to a nearly free market economy in less than four years and without the hyper-inflationary trauma faced by other countries—for example, Russia—which began their reform programmes at roughly the same time.) And he has had T.N. Seshan who, despite his at times annoying bombast, has shown that elections in this vast, complicated land can be miraculously free of violence and rigging.

By achieving this strictly within the ambit of his constitutional powers, Seshan has also shown that the Indian Constitution is one of the world's most brilliantly conceived and written documents. If it is applied properly to issues ranging from the conduct of elections to the conduct of Parliament, the Constitution can be the steel frame that supports our democracy. That, in the end, is more important than which party wins the next general election, and certainly more important than who, Rao or Singh, is the next prime minister.

Note: An early prediction in December 1994 of the emergence of a regional 'Third Front' in Indian politics, the BJP's foibles and the rise of Manmohan Singh.

14

THE NO ALTERNATIVE FACTOR

10 June 1995

Schizophrenia is not an illness you would normally associate with political parties. But this is precisely what the Bharatiya Janata Party seems to suffer from. Two senior BJP leaders issued statements last week following a meeting of the party's national executive in Panaji. One made a great deal of sense; the other did not.

Atal Behari Vajpayee, leader of the Opposition in the Lok Sabha, stated flatly that a BJP-run India would make a nuclear bomb. He went on to add that while the BJP favoured nuclear disarmament, 'it had to begin with those who possessed the weapons.'

Full marks to Mr Vajpayee and the BJP for an unambiguous statement of intent that is based on a clear-headed perception of India's national interest. Moments later, however, the BJP shot itself in the foot. Its former president, Murli Manohar Joshi, came out of the national executive meeting and declared that all cases of foreign investment in Indian consumer industries 'will be reviewed by a future BJP government'.

Let us deal with Mr Vajpayee's remarks first. These were reflected in an official resolution passed by the party's national executive: 'The

BJP is in favour of a nuclear weapons-free world, but not of a world in which a few countries possess nuclear weapons and all the rest are subject to their hegemony.'

That is roughly the Congress position but with one important difference. The Congress has over the past one year been gradually succumbing to American pressure to slow down the Prithvi and Agni missile development programmes. Prithvi, according to gleeful United States officials, though now militarily operational, has 'not been serially produced' and Agni 'is in hibernation'.

The BJP rightly feels that such equivocation on the nuclear issue—and on missile development—will compromise India's future security. On this issue the BJP's stand, and the forthright way it has articulated it, cannot be faulted. It is right in saying that India must develop nuclear weapons immediately. It is also right in saying that this policy should not be clandestine (like Israel's) but should be declared openly without fearing a Pakistani nuclear weapons programme backlash. And it is especially right when it says that the Congress government's recent backtracking on Agni and Prithvi under United States pressure must be immediately reversed.

India is not a signatory to the Non-Proliferation Treaty. It will not be a signatory in the near or distant future unless the NPT is radically altered to make it a fairer agreement. And if India is not an NPT signatory there is no reason to be merely a 'nuclear-capable' power; it is time to become a declared nuclear power.

■

To its credit, the BJP has always been consistent in its nuclear policy; the Congress has in contrast shown sloppy thinking and been outmanoeuvered by the Americans. The NPT Renewal and Extension Conference is scheduled to begin in New York next Monday. India will not be represented at the conference but it should use quiet diplomacy to convince nervous fence-sitters like Egyptian President Hosni Mubarak to have nothing whatsoever to do with a treaty that

President Bill Clinton last Wednesday called 'the most important agreement in the world'. The NPT is the most outrageously iniquitous agreement in the world. The BJP has said this more clearly than the Congress and that speaks well for its consistency, clarity and self-confidence.

However, just when the BJP had begun talking sensibly about issues that actually matter (nuclear policy) rather than those that do not (Ram Janmabhoomi), it produced a ludicrous comment on foreign investment policy which casts a large shadow of doubt over its economic competence.

Speaking at the BJP's national executive meeting just after Mr Vajpayee had delivered his statement on the party's nuclear policy, Murli Manohar Joshi declared that all (not some; all) cases of 'foreign investment in consumer industries will be reviewed by a future BJP government.' This is in stark contrast to the BJP's forward-looking nuclear policy.

According to a school of thought, and it has numerous students drawn from all political parties, India does not need foreign investment in consumer industries. The logic goes like this: since Indian businessmen can make consumer goods with domestic technology, why allow foreign companies to bring in and operate the same 'low' technology?

This is Mr Joshi's argument too and it has three large holes. The first is that all foreign investment—high-tech or low-tech, consumer or heavy industry—provides employment to Indian workers, creates wealth for Indian shareholders and spins off new business opportunities for Indian retailers and ancillary units. Whether foreign investors manufacture computers or cornflakes in India, they will still have to build factories in India with foreign money.

Take the US cereal giant Kelloggs. It spent Rs 1 billion last year to build a 5,700-metric tonne plant in Taloja, Maharashtra. It has since employed thousands of local workers, given new business to a multitude of street corner grocery shops, provided large contracts to the paper and packaging industries and plans to go public next year when Indian shareholders will be added to the list of people to benefit from Kellogs's investment in India.

The same holds true for Coca Cola, Pepsi, Panasonic and a host of other foreign companies that have invested hard currency dollars to give Indians First World quality products at Third World prices. If you sent these consumer companies packing just because they are consumer companies, you would be punishing the Indian consumer, retailer and factory labourer, not the foreign company which would promptly relocate to Mexico or Sri Lanka.

But don't such companies cater only to the consumption needs of the miniscule elite? They don't. For every rich, irrelevant Indian teenager who buys Coke for Rs 5, there are scores of ordinary, often poor, Indians who benefit directly and indirectly from the jobs and increased economic activity such investments engender. Of course, Indians can make (and do make) cereals and colas but if foreigners want to spend millions of dollars in India to compete with them on a level playing field, there can be only one ultimate winner: the Indian consumer.

That brings us to the second big hole in the BJP's argument against foreign investment in consumer industries. Competition raises quality and lowers prices. Why should Indians—upper, lower or middle class—be denied international quality products at reasonable prices? If domestic producers—for example, TV set manufacturers— were protected by banning Panasonic and Sony, they would have continued giving us second-rate TV sets at deluxe prices. Remember, too, that even the most rudimentary consumer product requires high-technology production facilities and modern factories.

The third big hole in the BJP argument is that foreign investment in the Indian consumer industry gives foreign investors huge profits. It does not. None of the major foreign consumer companies have made much money from their operations in India. Many have incurred huge losses because of the expensive high-technology plants they have set up in India and the lavish marketing they have had to do though the Indian media. Pepsi is awash in losses; Coke is in the red as well; Kelloggs, according to its managing director for India, Ms Damindar Dias, will take ten years to break even in India. Clearly the fear that foreign consumer companies are making a fortune fleecing poor Indian consumers is a myth. If anything, it is domestic producers who have been fleecing the Indian consumer for decades with shoddy, overpriced goods.

It is ironic that on two critical issues—nuclear weapons and foreign investment—the BJP has a sensible policy on the first and the Congress a sensible policy on the second. It is in India's national interest that we become a fully declared nuclear weapons state. And it is equally in India's interest that we make foreign investors compete with one another, and with domestic industry, to give Indian consumers high-quality products at reasonable prices in every sector, bar those which are closed to them due to security reasons.

■

The lack of clear-headedness about what really constitutes our national interest has lowered the quality of debate in Parliament and outside. The number of politicians who can be relied upon to act in the public interest—indeed even recognize it—are few. An outstanding exception is Commerce Minister P. Chidambaram, who has provided strong and visionary leadership to his ministry.

The sweeping new liberalizations announced by him in the Exim policy on 31 March are the best economic news India has had since the 1992 and 1993 budgets. The Chidambaram reforms will give great impetus to India's integration with the global economy. Since trade is a critical issue in India's relationship with the West, Mr Chidambaram's reforms can only strengthen the hands of Indian nuclear diplomacy.

In the few short months that he has been back in the Union Cabinet, Mr Chidambaram has shown what innovative economic leadership can achieve.

Meanwhile, the rest of the ruling party continues to flounder in a sea of meaningless rhetoric. At the recent preliminary Congress Working Committee (CWC) meeting, 127 Congress leaders spent nine hours giving Prime Minister P.V. Narasimha Rao, also the Congress president, the mandate to 'take any step he deemed fit to rejuvenate the party, especially in view of the recent poll reverses'. The party leadership attributed these poll reverses to Arjun Singh's and N.D. Tewari's perfidy, the misuse of TADA, communal riots, corruption, local bossism, rebel candidates and virtually every other plausible excuse.

The CWC meeting demonstrates all that is wrong with the Congress: the party is calcified, corrupt, slothful, parasitical and probably deserves to be defeated at the 1996 general election.

The problem is the TINA (there is no alternative) factor. The BJP has between eight and twelve months to defeat TINA and give Indian voters a genuine democratic choice between at least two electable parties. But unless Professor Murli Manohar Joshi takes a few lessons from Dr Manmohan Singh and Mr Chidambaram on foreign investment, that choice will remain severely limited.

Note: Three years before the Vajpayee-led NDA-1 government took office in 1998 and ordered Pokhran-II, I strongly advocated India exercising its nuclear option by testing a nuclear device.

15

AMERICA WAS NOT MOVED BY BENAZIR'S SWEET TALK

19 April 1995

Set against today's crop of foot-shuffling, platitudinous world leaders, Pakistan's forty-one-year-old prime minister, Benazir Bhutto, stands out. She is the first, and only, woman leader of an Islamic state. She was educated at Oxford and Harvard. She is articulate, charming and knowledgeable. She is patriotic. All this should make her an outstanding prime minister. It does not.

As a leader, Ms Bhutto is fatally flawed. Last week she charmed American lawmakers on Capitol Hill, had lunch with President Clinton, appeared on three major TV talk shows and met the editorial boards of four newspapers. Her ten-day coast-to-coast tour of the United States was a media success but a political failure. She accomplished none of the objectives she had set for herself.

The most critical of these was to persuade Washington to waive the Pressler Amendment. Under the Pressler law, no American administration can sell weapons to Pakistan without first certifying that Islamabad does not have a nuclear device. President George Bush could not produce such a certificate; nor so far has President

Bill Clinton. The Pressler Amendment is the only law in the United States specific to a country—a dubious distinction for Pakistan.

Benazir has made a waiver of the Pressler Amendment the cornerstone of Islamabad's foreign policy. But all she got in Washington last week was a vague promise from Mr Clinton that he would 'review' the amendment. With a presidential election year around the corner, that is a promise Mr Clinton is not going to be able to keep.

The amendment's author, Larry Pressler, underlined this when he warned President Clinton last week not to waive the restrictions imposed on Pakistan under the act; he asserted that during a recent CIA briefing he had received credible information that Pakistan has already built five nuclear devices.

Islamabad ordered twenty-eight F-16 fighter jets from the United States five years ago. Without a waiver of the Pressler Law it will not get them. To add insult to injury, President Clinton did not commit himself during his talks with Ms Bhutto to even returning the $1.4 billion that Islamabad paid Washington for the F-16s and related military hardware in 1990.

Further disappointment followed. Benazir repeated her longstanding request that America mediate in Pakistan's dispute with India over Kashmir. Mr Clinton declined politely but firmly. He also refused to press the United Nations to mediate in a dispute which Pakistan has been trying—unsuccessfully—for a decade to internationalize.

■

But it was during the three major TV talk shows she appeared on (ABC's *Good Morning America*, *MacNeil-Lehrer* and *Larry King Live*) that Benazir exposed the growing isolation of her government and the feebleness of her own leadership in failing to stop Pakistan's rapid descent into civil anarchy.

Let us take a look at the *Larry King Live* interview since it was seen widely in Asia. Mr King is a veteran television anchorman. Unfortunately, like most other American TV anchors, he knows little about Asia and next to nothing about India and Pakistan. The questions he put to Benazir would have made most professional broadcasters outside the United States squirm with embarrassment.

'I believe,' Mr King began earnestly, 'that you are meeting President Clinton at a state dinner tomorrow.'

'Oh no!' said a startled Benazir. 'The President is only giving me lunch. Vice President Al Gore is hosting the dinner.'

Here was one of America's most highly rated TV personalities interviewing the prime minister of an American ally and he did not even know that there was no official presidential dinner scheduled for Ms Bhutto. (It is, in fact, widely known that the Clinton presidency has virtually stopped the practice of hosting state dinners for visiting dignitaries. Even British Prime Minister John Major and Egyptian President Hosni Mubarak who preceded Benazir to Washington made do with a White House working lunch.)

More seriously, Mr King—earnestness giving way now to self-righteousness—asked the Pakistani prime minister why India and Pakistan were producing nuclear weapons at all. 'You know what it's called?' he asked, leaning forward as if dispensing a particularly rare pearl of wisdom. 'It's called MAD—Mutually Assured Destruction. Don't you think it's irrational for India and Pakistan to build nuclear devices?'

In reply, Benazir did not point out that America and its allies between them possess enough nuclear warheads to blow up the planet several times over; that the United States is the only country in the world which has actually used a nuclear bomb on a civilian population (Hiroshima and Nagasaki); and that if India and Pakistan's tiny nuclear programmes were indeed MAD, how would Mr King describe America's multibillion dollar nuclear weapons programme? Instead, the Pakistani prime minister replied lamely: 'Yes, Larry, human beings are sometimes irrational.'

The interview got even more bizarre when Mr King, keen now to keep middle American viewers interested in the proceedings, asked the prime minister what she had discussed with Hillary Clinton in Islamabad a few weeks ago. Even Benazir was exasperated by that. 'Why,' she exclaimed crossly, 'does everyone in America ask me what Hillary and I talked about?'

'Because,' said Mr King in complete seriousness, 'she is our First Lady.'

On every level, the Bhutto-King interview was a disaster. Not once did Mr King ask Ms Bhutto why Pakistan was helping terrorists in the Kashmir Valley. Washington came within a whisker in 1993 of declaring Pakistan a terrorist state, on par with Sudan and Iraq. Mr King clearly had not done his homework or he would have used that information in his interview. Nor did he ask about the intra-Muslim violence in Karachi which has claimed 1,300 lives in the past one year. It was left to a better-briefed telephone caller (the programme takes phone calls from viewers towards the end of the show) to ask the Pakistani prime minister that question.

■

Ms Bhutto's main concern in America, of course, was not impressing Larry King but President Clinton, and this she singularly failed to do. The odds were always stacked heavily against her. Pakistan is a near-fundamentalist Islamic state and the United States is not particularly well-disposed towards fundamentalist Islamic states at the moment. Pakistan's usefulness to America in the seventies was based on it being a secret diplomatic conduit to China. Washington's top officials visited China clandestinely through Pakistan in 1971 to open the way for a path-breaking Sino-American approachment.

Dr Henry Kissinger, one of the principal actors in the 1971 drama, has acknowledged Pakistan's contribution in this aspect on several occasions including during his recent Indian lecture tour. In the eighties, Pakistan's usefulness to Washington lay in Afghanistan, where Islamabad proved a reliable ally for over a decade in the fight to stop the expansion of Soviet influence in the region. In the nineties there is a role void. The Soviet threat is gone, conduits to China are not needed anymore. Being an American ally is largely a thankless job for Pakistan these days. There is now, in fact, a further complication: the Non-Proliferation Treaty that Washington wants Pakistan to sign—because that is the only way it can persuade India to even discuss the outrageously one-sided treaty.

Unfortunately, Pakistan cannot afford to throw away its nuclear bomb-beneath-the-pillow option for fear of India becoming a fully declared nuclear state.

Inevitably, Benazir's ten-day American sojourn ended without any tangible benefit for Pakistan. The epitaph was written by Jesse Helms, the chairman of the Foreign Relations Committee, who introduced her as the prime minister of India before other senators gently corrected him.

•

As for Larry King, he could not wait to get Benazir off the show and bring on a 'guy you all have been waiting to see here'. That turned out to be a gentleman called Gerry Spence who has just written a book called *How To Argue and Win Every Time*. Mr King spent more time interviewing him than he did Benazir.

If American television, reeling under the weight of popular culture, has trivialized politics, the print media has managed to keep a sense of perspective. While the magisterial *The New York Times* ignored Ms Bhutto's entire visit, other American newspapers analysed Indo-Pakistani relations with something close to accuracy.

That, alas, spelt more bad news for Ms Bhutto. One American newspaper pointed out that she had lied when she claimed publicly: 'Pakistan does not possess a nuclear device. The American establishment has also said Pakistan does not have a nuclear device.'

Why is that a lie? Because American Defence Secretary William

Perry told the Foreign Policy Association in New York the exact opposite three months ago: 'We believe Pakistan does possess a nuclear device.' And William Perry is the most authoritative defence spokesman for the American establishment.

It is this politics of distortion that has terminally weakened Pakistan's case on Capitol Hill and in the White House. The CIA knows that Islamabad has succeeded in converting highly enriched uranium into 275 pounds of bomb-grade heavy metal. A Pakistani nuclear bomb can probably be assembled within forty-eight hours, possibly within twelve. Given that fact, President Clinton cannot waive the Pressler Amendment, cannot deliver the contracted F-16s and cannot resume military aid. That is the message Ms Bhutto carried home with her along with Mr King's homilies.

Note: *Three years later, in 1998, Pakistan became a declared nuclear-weapons power following India's own nuclear test.*

16

CALCUTTA, POVERTY AND JOFFE

19 March 1991

To those of us who do not live in Calcutta—and that's a good 840 million of us—the media slugfest over the filming of *City of Joy* might seem puzzling. It should not.

The death of an *Aajkaal* reporter (already terminally ill with cancer) following an alleged assault by a film crew member, the court injunction against the filming, the crew's violation of the court order, the CPM-sponsored agitation to stop the film being shot in Calcutta—all these add up to an intriguing media story.

But outside West Bengal, few newspapers and magazines have taken the story seriously, treating it as just another of Calcutta's periodic cultural eruptions. Given time, the din would die down. But the din will not die down and, in any case, the wrong sort of noises are being made and heard. The core issue is: should a foreign film unit be allowed to make a movie in India with reasonable fetters? The answer, in any democracy, has to be yes—as long as the fetters are reasonable. The only obvious caveat is that national security not be compromised and the conduct of the foreign crew be governed by local professional norms.

Most Calcuttans have over the years developed an allergy to films by foreigners glorifying Calcutta's poverty. There are good emotional grounds for this attitude but not many good rational ones.

Film-makers can deal with poverty in three ways: glorify it, exploit it, or explain it. The glorification of poverty is the conscience-bitten Westerner's way of coming to terms with human suffering on a scale he does not experience at home. Such spiritualization of suffering can deteriorate fairly quickly into self-deception, but if a film-maker wants to deceive himself and his audience, that is surely his business.

Exploiting poverty is another matter altogether. Western film-makers, however, are mostly a sensible lot (true bigots don't have the talent to make films) and very few would deliberately use poverty cinematically to mock the destitute. That would cripple their reputations internationally.

The many films shot in India since 1947—from *The River* by Jean Renoir in 1949 to *The Deceivers* by Nicholas Meyer in 1987—have all largely treated Indian poverty sympathetically, if not particularly originally.

Even Louis Malle's *Calcutta* and *Phantom India* were not insensitive to the extraordinary courage and fortitude of the country's poor.

The real problem, unfortunately, is not the filming of poverty but poverty itself. Films like *Phantom India* can be banned; poverty can't.

Which brings us to the third—and only sensible—way to deal cinematically with themes of poverty and human suffering: be honest, open and constructive.

When foreigners—or Indians like Satyajit Ray—make films on social themes, realism demands that poverty be shown. It is a fact of Indian life and dusting it beneath the Persian rug at the Oberoi Grand when a foreign film or TV crew arrives in Calcutta does not serve anyone, least of all the poor.

On the contrary, a sympathetic, understanding portrayal of

deprivation and destitution can lead to greater consciousness, among Indians and foreigners, of what can be done. Mother Teresa's Missionaries of Charity, Dr Jack Preger's roadside clinics, the AshaDaan drug rehabilitation centre in Bombay—all have benefited greatly in funds and manpower through international media exposure of their good work.

■

But shouldn't foreign film-makers also take their cameras to the nuclear power reactor in Trombay, the rocket launching site in Sriharikota, the gleaming petrochemical plants at Patalganga and the Tata Institute of Fundamental Research in Bombay?

Isn't India more than just slums and festering human sores? Is it not a significant (and growing) scientific, technological and industrial power?

Why do foreign film-makers show only beggars on the streets of Calcutta and Bombay?

These are the questions critics of films like *City of Joy* ask. The answer is simple and a little sad: pathos sells movies, research labs don't. A steel-and-chrome, nuclear-powered India racing into the twenty-first century would make a good documentary (if the right director, Indian or foreign, got the funding together) but it would not make a film ordinary people in Paris or Frankfurt would go out to see. That is the unfortunate reality and we have to learn to live with it.

But the response of our own film-makers should also be more assertive. Let the Ronald Joffés and Iain Smiths shoot Calcutta to their hearts' content. Meanwhile, send an Indian crew to film the 50,000 homeless men and women who freeze every night in cardboard boxes on the streets of London; the savage racism of Brixton and Birmingham, where white thugs defecate at the doorstep of Sikh homes; the football hooliganism that erupts on a Saturday afternoon when thousands of drunken young Englishmen paint their faces and torsos and knife each other. Travel further afield to the southern United States. To Alabama and Louisiana, where blacks still live in fear of the Ku Klux Klan. Or parts of Miami and New York where drug lords from Colombia, Jamaica and Cuba machine-gun one another in orgies of premeditated violence. What themes lie in wait for the enterprising Indian film-maker!

If India has material poverty, the West has deprivations of other kinds crying out for a non-Western cinematic point of view—and no one in Europe or America will ask an Indian film director to show them the script before shooting.

In the final analysis, a bad film condemns the maker more than the subject, just as a good one does the reverse.

City of Joy may make some Calcuttans angry, but in the end a city that has endured so much and survived it all is above such make-believe heat and dust.

Note: *Our sensitivity to foreign film-makers showing poverty persists with Slumdog Millionaire and others—but it really shouldn't. We should instead make films on racism in the West, gun control and the breakdown in families as indeed some western film-makers, both in popular culture and in arthouse films, often do.*

17

REFLECTIONS IN A GIMLET EYE

15 March 1991

Captivity can make the creative adrenalin flow. Two years and a month in hiding have resulted in Salman Rushdie producing two new books: *Haroun and the Sea of Stories*, a children's fantasy novel which also explores by metaphor the theme of censorship, appeared to mild acclaim last year and, later this month, Granta/Penguin India will publish a collection of Rushdie's journalism spanning the last ten years.

Imaginary Homelands: Essays and Criticism (1981-1990) represents a side of Rushdie little known to most people outside the regular readership of quality British and American newspapers.

Most of Rushdie's journalistic writing over the past ten years has been done for *The Guardian*, *The Independent on Sunday*, the *London Review of Books*, *The Times* and *The Times Literary Supplement* in Britain and *The New York Times* and *The Washington Post* in America. But so far, and rightly too, it has been Rushdie's literature rather than his journalism that has made his reputation.

In the six novels he has written so far—five fiction, one non-fiction—Rushdie has tackled themes of alienation, Islam, political deceit and racism.

Grimus, his first novel, was a flop. His second, *Midnight's Children*, published when Rushdie was thirty-four, won the Booker Prize and quantum-jumped the Kashmiri-descended, Bombay-born author from advertising copywriting to serious journalism and literature.

Shame, a parody on Zia ul-Haq's Pakistan, got mixed reviews as did *The Jaguar Smile*, a non-fiction and slightly off-key foray into the contemporary politics of Central America.

His fifth book, *The Satanic Verses*, earned him worldwide fame and a death sentence. *Haroun and the Sea of Stories*, Rushdie's sixth book, was a tribute to his thirteen-year-old son Zafar, who lives with the author's estranged American wife, Marianne Wiggins.

At forty-three, Rushdie is now at the crossroads of his literary career. If he emerges unharmed from his current ordeal, his best work may still be in the future.

■

Imaginary Homelands: Essays and Criticism (1981-1990) is a punctuation mark in Rushdie's life, a taking-stock. It is a collection of seventy essays, reviews, articles and speeches written by Rushdie over a ten-year period between 1981, when he published *Midnight's Children*, and 1990, when he wrote *Haroun and the Sea of Stories*.

Rushdie's fiction is often difficult to ingest. His essays are precisely the opposite: cogent, witty, sensitive, intense.

The idiosyncrasies of Rushdie's fictional characters have led many to think of Rushdie as an esoteric writer, removed from reality.

This collection destroys that myth. Rushdie comes across as a cold-eyed, acute observer of men and matters in a racially hostile society, an unremitting critic of Western pretension and an unyielding believer of free speech and thought.

Above all, Rushdie writes strikingly well. His prose is clever, funny, erudite, coherent, self-deprecating, ironic and discursive.

He has the equipment, both literary and intellectual, to sup with the very best in contemporary literature. Because this is the first time Rushdie's journalism has been put together under one cover, it is worthwhile quoting his views at some length on the variety of subjects that engage him. 'Imaginary Homelands', the title of this book, was the name of a paper Rushdie presented at a seminar on Indian writing at the Festival of India in London in 1982.

It encapsulates Rushdie's sense of 'unbelonging', a sense that threads its insidious way through much of his prose and thought: 'A few years ago I revisited Bombay, which is my lost city, after an absence of something like half my life. Shortly after arriving, acting on an impulse, I opened the telephone directory and looked for my father's name. And, amazingly, there it was; his name, our old address, the unchanged telephone number, as if we had never gone away to the unmentionable country across the border. It was an eerie discovery. I felt as if I were being claimed, or informed that the facts of my faraway life were illusions, and that this continuity was the reality.'

Rushdie is not particularly strong on Indian politics. You cannot really be, can you, sitting in Islington (as pre-fatwa Rushdie used to) and commenting on the politics of Moradabad. This naïveté shines through brightly in his political essays on the subcontinent: 'The Riddle of Midnight: India, August 1987'; 'Censorship'; 'The Assassination of Indira Gandhi'; 'Dynasty'; 'Zia ul-Haq, 17 August 1988'; and 'Daughter of the East'.

As he writes solemnly in 'The Assassination of Indira Gandhi': 'Two cliches about India [...] in these first hours since the news of the assassination broke, reared their wizened old heads. Firstly, the probability of a military coup in India to establish a parallel dictatorship to that of Zia is [...] so slight that it can be discounted, if only because the entire history of India demonstrates the impossibility of conquering the place by military force. Secondly, the bullets that killed Mrs Gandhi did not "prove" the unsuitability of democracy for India [...] The idea of a united democratic, secular India can survive this terrible day.'

Fine sentiments and, in the latter part, worth highlighting to a Western audience innocent of the resilient ways of Indian democracy. But the part on military rule, giving credence by denial, reveals a rusty political stethoscope.

■

Rushdie is surer of foot on British politics. He is scathingly right about Margaret Thatcher and racism and brilliantly right about the 'new empire within Britain'. He writes: '[...] British thought, British society, has never been cleansed of the filth of imperialism. [...] One of the key concepts of imperialism was that military superiority implied cultural superiority, and this enabled the British to condescend to the repressed cultures far older than their own; and it still does.'

On race, Rushdie is equally contemptuous of British attitudes. Speaking of the stereotype of black people being a 'problem' for the British, Rushdie is brutally frank: 'British racism, is not our problem. It's yours. We simply suffer from the effects of your problem.' Rushdie concludes with an anecdote on Mahatma Gandhi who, when asked what he thought about Western civilization, replied: 'I think it would be a good idea.'

■

Commonwealth literature, that strange and unpleasant literary beast, an agglomeration of literature by former subjects of the British Empire, does not escape Rushdie's scalpel. He cuts it distastefully into several little pieces: '"Commonwealth literature" [...] is that body of writing created, I think, in the English language, by persons who are not themselves white Britons, or Irish, or citizens of the United States of America.' Indeed the term 'Commonwealth literature' has narrowed the body of literature on segregationist lines, creating a ghetto that Rushdie is contemptuous of.

Rushdie was one of the sharpest critics of Richard Attenborough's film, *Gandhi*. In a 1983 article, he said *Gandhi* was a bad film, an inaccurate film and, in some ways, a dishonest film. In particular, he criticized the Amritsar massacre sequence in the film, where Dyer is portrayed as an overzealous murderer and where his actions were condemned in court by the British. Both were patently untrue. Dyer returned to England a hero and was granted a generous benefit fund.

A large part of *Imaginary Homelands* revolves around Rushdie's opinion of his contemporaries' works: V.S. Naipaul, Nadine Gordimer, John le Carré, Günter Grass, Gabriel Garcia Marquez, Raymond Carver, Philip Roth, Saul Bellow.

In 1989, shortly after he went into hiding, Rushdie wrote about le Carré's *The Russia House*, a hopelessly dated West vs the Soviet Union novel published just as Mikhail Gorbachev was dismantling the Cold War edifice.

Rushdie did not conceal his disdain for le Carré's literary abilities. In his criticism of *The Russia House*, he wrote that it had poor characterization and naïve prose. He called the book 'plain fare'.

Le Carré was so furious with Rushdie for this review that he attacked him publicly on another issue: the desirability of the British government spending thousands of pounds per day protecting a man who regularly and publicly scorns Britain.

It was a poor attack, made poorer by le Carré's 'naïve and pretentious prose' and it evoked a contemptuous silence from Rushdie.

■

That Rushdie is himself a prose writer of very considerable skill is not self-evident from his novels, circumscribed as they are by the needs of their plots and characters.

But the skill emerges very clearly in Rushdie's journalism and that is the true value of this collection.

There are some disappointments, however. 'In Good Faith' offers a convoluted, unconvincing and post-dated apology for *The Satanic Verses*, where Rushdie juxtaposes the harem and the brothel to show the ultimate elimination of the impure through the pure.

The same—though less specific—tone of repentance—pervades 'Is Nothing Sacred?', the Herbert Read Memorial Lecture of 1990 delivered on Rushdie's behalf by the playwright Harold Pinter at the Institute of Contemporary Arts, London.

The book ends, prophetically and sadly, with Rushdie's public 'return' to Islam. 'Why I Have Embraced Islam' is a short, poignant, touching but unconvincing statement that no writer should have needed to make.

That, then, is the final, crushing irony: a brown Muslim Indian, who has spent two-thirds of his life in England and made a career out of (rightly) exposing, through literature and journalism, little British stupidities, now needs to seek shelter in the religion he has always scorned, and the protection of a police force he has always held in disdain.

■

Rushdie's is a rare talent, of language and mind. Unlike other 'Indian' writers such as Nirad C. Chaudhari and V.S. Naipaul, Rushdie has dealt with the West on his, not its terms. He has not subverted his thinking to suit short-term ends as so many before him have done and he has proved himself to be a more gifted, more original writer than any contemporary native Englishman.

The fatwa cannot be allowed to interfere with the development of such a formidable and useful talent.

Note: *This is a longish essay in praise of Salman Rushdie's journalism— lesser known than his fiction—some years after my media firm, Sterling Newspapers, hosted one of Rushdie's first post-Booker Prize visits to India in February 1984.*

A year later, in April 1992, I reviewed his next book, Haroun and the Sea of Stories:

A thin despair pervades this book, Salman Rushdie's first since his confinement. Despite the attempt at fantasy, blitheness and magical humour, *Haroun and the Sea of Stories* is a curiously morbid epitaph on the human condition and especially Rushdie's own.

Most of the characters are funny-sad caricatures—Rashid Khalifa, the storyteller (or the Shah of Blah), Blabbermouth, Water Genie, Snooty Buttoo, the Walrus and Khattam-Shud.

Ostensibly written for children, *Haroun* is a modern-day fable for grown-ups in a language that Rushdie has, since *Grimus*, his first novel, made all his own.

Allegories and imagery, dressed up in fantastical, magical settings, permeate the book, but while the style is childlike and innocent, the message is grim and adult. Evil, Rushdie warns, lurks behind every corner and the forces of good must be ever-vigilant if they are to triumph in the end.

The plot, like the undercurrent of sadness that runs through it, is thin. Haroun, a bright, energetic lad, lives with his parents in Alifbay, 'a sad city, the saddest of cities, a city so ruinously sad that it had forgotten its name'. His father, Rashid Khalifa, a likeable but naïve man, tells stories for a living. His mother, Soraya, sings and is a doting wife. The family seems happy and content. But trouble is brewing beneath the calm surface. One fine day, for no apparent reason at all, Soraya runs off with her neighbour, a 'sticky-thin, whiny-voiced' clerk called Sengupta.

As this sad, funny, fantasy tale unfolds, it is clear that Rushdie is dallying with autobiography. His real-life wife, novelist Marianne Wiggins, left him soon after Ayatollah Khomeini's fatwa banished him to a life in hiding. His eleven-year-old son Zafar, whom he hadn't seen for eighteen months and misses desperately, is the same age as Haroun. But Haroun doesn't desert Khalifa in this modern fairy-tale version of Rushdie's life. When his mother, Soraya, runs away with Sengupta, it is a terrible blow to Haroun. The episode humiliates the father he loves—Sengupta had always belittled Khalifa's stories: 'What are all these stories, life is not a storybook or joke shop. All this fun will come to no good. What's the use of stories that aren't even true?'

Haroun and his father journey to the Valley of K (Kashmir, naturally) where Rashid, who meanwhile, burdened with sadness after Soraya's departure, has lost his storytelling voice, can recoup. In the Valley, which some miscreants (Pakistani-trained militants, naturally) call Kosh-mar, more adventures befall the father-son duo.

Characters like Buttoo and places like Dull Lake jostle for attention, as Rushdie reverts to the literary technique of his third novel, *Shame*, by mingling fiction with history.

■

It is important to realize that Rushdie does this time and again in order to drive home his religious and political points without the attendant problem of defamation proceedings. Unfortunately, when he tried the same technique in *The Satanic Verses*, Khomeini issued a death sentence rather than a libel writ and, in many ways, *Haroun* is Rushdie's atonement—if not quite a full gesture of repentance.

Rushdie is too proud a man to apologize to anyone, least of all to obscurantists who have sentenced him to death, but in *Haroun*, using the literary guise of a children's fable, he obliquely sets out his reason for writing *The Satanic Verses*. And the crux of his argument is that being silenced by bigots is a greater sin than any other, more than mocking fundamentalism through literature as *The Satanic Verses* did.

Consider this passage from *Haroun*, for in it is encapsulated Rushdie's central argument against religious censorship: 'Khattam-Shud,' Rashid said slowly, 'is the Arch-Enemy of all Stories, even of Language itself. He is the Prince of Silence and the Foe of Speech.

And because everything ends because dreams end, stories end, life ends, at the finish of everything we use his name. "It's finished," we tell one another, "it's over. Khattam-Shud: The End."

Haroun is an inventive, magical tale by a writer who has created his own idiom. The colour, originality and strength of Rushdie's prose stands out in stark contrast to the sterility of authors like William Golding and Kingsley Amis.

Haroun and Rashid, with the help of Water Genie, travel to Gup City to meet the Walrus in Kahani, the earth's invisible 'second moon'. Princess Batcheat of the Land of Gup has meanwhile been captured by the evil Khattam-Shud (Khomeini?) of Chup City. The forces of Gup and Chup (good and evil) now fight their climactic battle. Though the Guppees are outnumbered, they rout the Chupwallahs.

The whole point of Rushdie's 211-page book is that silence and secretiveness (i.e. censorship) are debilitating. Openness and freedom (i.e. dissent) are enriching. *Haroun* is unlikely to be read, and therefore banned, in Tehran. It is likely, because of its author's fame, to be widely read by children who will be baffled by its adult double entendres. And, of course, it will be read by the literary cognoscenti in the West who will once again wonder at the magic of Rushdie's prose and the sadness of his plight.

18

THE FIRST REFUGE OF SCOUNDRELS?

September 1985

'It was my observation fifteen years ago,' said Auberon Waugh, 'that all the brightest and the best went into journalism, and the second best into diplomatic service and academic life. What went into industry was pretty good rubbish, just a whisker ahead of the absolute rubbish which went into politics.'

Perceptions have not changed since Waugh made that observation. Politics is still 'the refuge of scoundrels' and, judging by the rush for parliamentary tickets every time an election is imminent, there are an awful lot of aspiring scoundrels around.

Two reasons can be advanced for the decline in political standards from the lofty ones set by Pandit Nehru, Sardar Patel and Rajagopalachari. First, since the politicians of the '30s and '40s were spawned by the freedom struggle, which entailed considerable personal and professional sacrifice, only men of mettle, who could make those sacrifices, were prepared to enter public life. Today, politicians are spawned not by such noble causes as evicting the British but by several ignoble ones, usually connected with money, power and the desire to serve that most important constituent—oneself.

Second, the more tawdry parts of our populace are attracted to politics because neither does it involve very hard work (except during election time) nor does it require very high qualifications (214 of our MPs do not possess a university degree).

Few professions, then, offer unemployed job-seekers the kind of financial opportunity and relaxed work-style that politics does; and almost none accords them the fringe benefits that politics bestows. Ask Mr Antulay and Mr Gundu Rao.

When a profession makes such few demands on its incumbents, it is only natural that it will attract large numbers of applicants. Here, too, politics scores over diplomacy, journalism, law and academics. Each of these need the passing of an entrance examination and a rigorous selection interview. In politics, the only entrance examination is taken by the voters, and they are not always the strictest or ablest of examiners.

■

What of the other professions that Waugh attempts to rate? Diplomacy has been reduced by a droll combination of technology and terrorism to an activity whose ineffectiveness is a source of considerable embarrassment to its practitioners. In the good old days, when satellite communications were non-existent, diplomats wielded enormous clout. In the 1980s, with messages traversing from Moscow to Washington in a matter of seconds, even such 'decisions' as whether or not the American ambassador should send a Christmas card to the Russian deputy foreign minister are taken by a third secretary in Washington. The US ambassador has been reduced to a glorified postman, carrying messages of goodwill (and occasionally ill will) from President Reagan to Party Chairman Andropov.

Where Waugh's observations go awry, particularly in the Indian context, is in the respect he assumes the fourth estate commands.

Like politics, journalism is populated by people who knew very little about the profession they were entering before they entered it but make up for it, as politicians do, by assuming that their ignorance is matched only by that of their readers. Journalism, like politics and unlike diplomacy and law, requires no specific qualification and no previous experience.

Since journalists are essentially communicators and not practitioners of a technical craft (like engineering, medicine or law, where specialized knowledge is essential), it might be reasonably argued that being a jack of all trades is more useful than being the master of one.

Professions are like countries. They constantly move up and down the rungs of prestige and power, their relative movements being governed by a dynamic state of equilibrium between historical imperatives, social conditions and financial opportunity. Journalism, currently, appears to be in the ascendancy. While, as yet, not quite 'the brightest and the best' go into it as Waugh would like to believe, the fourth estate is growing in influence and respect, fuelled at least partly by the fact that everyone else needs journalists more than ever before.

Politicians, in these days of television and newspapers and growing literacy, need journalists to project their image; diplomats need them to leak sensitive information to (about the only interesting things diplomats are left with to do these days); lawyers need them as clients (with libel suits becoming big business, lawyers regard journalists as prime clientele).

Note: *Unlike Auberon Waugh, some would argue that politics in India today, nearly thirty years after this piece was written, is no longer the last, but the first, refuge of scoundrels judging by the number of parliamentarians and legislators facing serious criminal charges.*

ACKNOWLEDGEMENTS

Over the years—and they've melted into decades—I've been fortunate to have a family and colleagues who've stood by me through ups and downs, and there have been a few of both.

Professionally, I'd like to acknowledge the several great editors I've worked with: Sham Lal and Girilal Jain in *The Times of India*, when I was a young reporter, and Aroon Purie when I was with *India Today*.

And then, at twenty-five, in the recklessness of youth, when I started my own publishing company, I was fortunate to have the most talented group of journalists of our generation join me: David Davidar, Anurag Mathur, Maneck Davar, Harish Mehta, Anjali Mathur and many, many others.

Together we created India's fastest growing media firm, Sterling Newspapers Pvt. Ltd, launched six pioneering magazines in less than ten years and had some of the most gifted contributing editors work with us in India and globally.

Shashi Tharoor, for example, was our contributing editor, foreign affairs, for a decade, writing his monthly column 'Worldview', uninterrupted from, first, Singapore and then Geneva. Dom Moraes, Henry Kissinger, I.K. Gujral and L.K. Advani were other columnists who made *Gentleman*, our political and literary monthly, one of India's most stimulating and widely read magazines.

Our television, computer and technology magazines (*TV and Video World*, *Business Computer* and *Technocrat*) too were pioneers in their fields. When the Indian Express group of newspapers acquired our company, along with our six magazines and other properties, I continued to serve for another five years on the board of directors with chairman Vivek Goenka and his cousin Manoj Sonthalia, Ramnath Goenka's other grandson, who is now chairman of The New Indian Express group. My gratitude to both for their sage advice.

A special word for my late business partner in Sterling Newspapers, Khushrooh Byramjee. He was a pillar of strength and one of the finest men anyone could hope to have as a friend and colleague.

My gratitude too to M.J. Akbar for whose newspapers—*The Telegraph* and *The Asian Age*—I wrote regular columns. And to Vinod Mehta whose younger brother Harish Mehta was the national affairs editor of *Gentleman* for several years, during which Vinod kept a solicitous eye on him.

In more contemporary terms, I'd like to especially thank *The Times of India*'s editorial director, Jaideep Bose, and his team of talented editors led by Arindam Sengupta, Swagato Ganguly and several others too numerous to mention. I learn from them every time I write for them.

At *The Economic Times*, T.K. Arun and Saubik Chakrobarty have created one of the finest editorial pages in India in terms of both content and design. It is a pleasure to write for this fine paper as well. A special word of acknowledgement to the team at Times Internet headed by Rajesh Kalra, Vinay Pandey and Anshu Tandon who encouraged me to blog and have been among the most professional editors I've worked with.

My grateful thanks to my business partner Bakul Patel, the former Sheriff of Mumbai, for her wise counsel through the past eighteen years at our media firm. We are fortunate to have had shareholders of the quality and sagacity of Rakesh Jhunjhunwala,

Dr Cyrus Poonawalla and the Small Industries Development Bank of India (SIDBI). Their guidance and knowledge have been invaluable.

As a publisher, editor, author and columnist, I've worn four hats simultaneously for most of the past thirty-four years. That's often needed forty-eight-hour work days and impossible deadlines. It hasn't always been easy on the family. And yet, through it all, my wife Kahini and children, Suhail and Tehzeeb, have borne it with stoic good humour. A special word of thanks to my late mother-in-law Nirmala Arte and my father-in-law Admiral Ramesh Arte for their kindness.

My late father was generous and liberal in encouraging me to become a journalist even though it meant forsaking, as the only son, the family's industrial enterprise.

And finally my mother, for encouraging my journalism since I was a teenager. Without her this book could not have been written.

I am indebted to David Davidar of Aleph Book Company for his deep insight which has given thematic shape to this book and to Ritu Vajpeyi-Mohan and her editorial team at Rupa Publications, and especially Suzanne Hughe, for the meticulous and professional execution of this project.

I thank my staff and colleagues at Merchant Media Ltd, in particular Rukshana Kumar, who keyed in the manuscript for this volume.

My thanks, above all, to those readers who have through the years sustained my writing. This book is dedicated to them.

Bibliography

Adams, James T., *The British Empire: 1784-1939*, (Dorset Press, 1991).
Advani, L.K., *My Country, My Life*, (Rupa & Co, 2008).
Akbar, M.J., *The Shade of Swords: Jihad and the Conflict between Islam and Christianity*, (Roli Books, 2002).
Akbar, M.J., *Tinder Box: The Past and Future of Pakistan*, (Harper Collins, 2011).
Balzac, Honoré de, *Cousin Bette*, (Knopf, 1991).
Balzac, Honoré de, *Old Goriot*, (Knopf, 1991).
Basham, A.L. (ed.), *A Cultural History of India*, (Oxford University Press, 1997).
Bass, Gary, *The Blood Telegram: Nixon, Kissinger and a Forgotten Genocide*, (Knopf, 2013).
Bose, Sugata, *His Majesty's Opponent: Subhas Chandra Bose and India's Struggle Against Empire*, (Penguin, 2011).
Cernan, Eugene and Don Davis, *The Last Man on the Moon: Astronaut Eugene Cernan and America's Race in Space*, (St Martin's Press, 1999).
Clinton, Bill, *My Life*, (Hutchinson, 2004).
Dasgupta, C., *War and Diplomacy in Kashmir: 1947-48*, (Sage, 2002).
Dealy Jr., Francis X., *The Power and the Money: Inside the Wall Street Journal*, (Birch Lane Press, 1993).
Dunn, Charles J., *Everyday Life in Imperial Japan*, (Dorset Press, 1989).
Evans, Richard, *Deng Xiaoping and the Making of Modern China*, (Hamish Hamilton, 1993).
Ferguson, Niall, *Civilization: The West and the Rest*, (Penguin, 2011).
French, Patrick, *India: An Intimate Biography of 1.2 Billion People*, (Penguin, 2011).

French, Patrick, *The World Is What It Is: The Authorized Biography of V. S. Naipaul*, (Picador, 2009).
Friedman, Thomas L., *Hot, Flat, and Crowded: Why the World Needs a Green Revolution—and How We Can Renew Our Global Future*, (Penguin, 2008).
Fukuyama, Francis, *The Origins of Political Order*, (Farrar, Straus and Giroux, 2011).
Fuller, Graham E., *A World without Islam*, (Little, Brown and Company, 2010).
Gandhi, Rajmohan, *Mohandas: A True Story of a Man, His People and an Empire*, (Penguin 2007).
Gibbon, Edward, *The Decline and Fall of the Roman Empire*, vols 1-3, (Modern Library, 1965).
Gilbert, Martin, *Winston Churchill: Road to Victory, 1941-1945*, (Houghton Mifflin Harcourt Company, 1986).
Gilbert, Martin, *Winston Churchill: Never Despair, 1945-1965*, (Houghton Mifflin Harcourt Company, 1988).
Guha, Ramachandra, *Gandhi Before India*, (Penguin, 2013).
Guha, Ramachandra, *India After Gandhi*, (Picador, 2007).
Guha, Ramachandra, *Makers of Modern India*, (Penguin, 2010).
Gupte, Pranay, *Vengeance: India After the Assassination of Indira Gandhi*, (W.W. Norton, 1985).
Hart, Alan, *Arafat: Terrrorist or Peacemaker?*, (Sidgwick and Jackson, 1984).
Hayek, Friedrich Von, *The Road to Serfdom*, (Routledge Classics, 2001).
Hiro, Dilip, *Black British, White British: A History of Race Relations in Britain*, (Paladin, 1992).
Holland, Tom (tr.), *Herodotus: The Histories*, (Penguin Classics, 2013).
Huntington, Samuel P., *The Clash of Civilizations and the Remaking of World Order*, (Simon & Schuster, 1996).
Ikeda, Daisaku, *The New Human Revolution*, vols 1-19, (Eternal Ganges Press, 1995-2008).
Jacobson, Howard, *Whatever It Is, I Don't Like It*, (Bloomsbury, 2011).
Johnson, Paul, *A History of the Jews*, (Phoenix Press, 2001).
Kalam, APJ Abdul with Y.S. Rajan, *India 2020: A Vision for the New Millennium*, (Penguin, 1998).
Kissinger, Henry, *Diplomacy*, (Simon & Schuster, 1994).

Kissinger, Henry, *Years of Renewal*, (Simon & Schuster, 1998).
Koestler, Arthur, *The Ghost in the Machine*, (Penguin, 1990)
Lapping, Brian, *End of Empire*, (St Martin's Press, 1985).
Levine, Allan, *The Scattered Among the Peoples: The Jewish Diaspora in Twelve Portraits*, (Overlook Duckworth, 2003).
Majumdar, R.C. (general ed.), *The History and Culture of the Indian People*, vols 1-11, (Bharatiya Vidya Bhavan, 1951-1977)
Manchester, William, *The Caged Lion: Winston Spencer Churchill, 1932-1940*, (Michael Joseph, 1988)
Mason, Philip, *The Men Who Ruled India*, (Rupa & Co, 1992).
Mehta, Harish C., *Cambodia Silenced: The Press under Six Regimes*, (White Lotus, 1997).
Mehta, Vinod, *Lucknow Boy: A Memoir*, (Penguin, 2011).
Menon, Meena, *Riots and After in Mumbai*, (Sage, 2011).
Moraes, Dom, *Mrs Gandhi*, (Vikas Publishing House, 1980).
Mukerjee, Madhusree, *Churchill's Secret War: The British Empire and the Ravaging of India during World War II*, (Tranquebar, 2010).
Naipaul, V.S., *The Masque of Africa: Glimpses of African Belief*, (Picador, 2010).
Pandey, B.N., *Nehru*, (Rupa & Co, 2003)
Ponkshe, Satyawrat, *Rajiv Gandhi: The Pragmatic Prime Minister of India*, (Bhate & Ponkshe Publications, 1986).
Proust, Marcel, *In Search of Lost Time*, vols 1-6, (Chatto & Windus, 1992).
Radhakrishnan, S., *The Principal Upanishads*, (HarperCollins, 1953).
Rohm, Wendy G., *The Microsoft File: The Secret Case against Bill Gates*, (Times Business, 1998)
Roy, Tirthankar, *The Economic History of India 1857-1947*, (Oxford University Press, 2000).
Rushdie, Salman, *Fury*, (Random House, 2001).
Rushdie, Salman, *Haroun and the Sea of Stories*, (Penguin, 1991)
Rushdie, Salman, *Imaginary Homelands: Essays and Criticism, 1981-1991*, (Penguin, 1992)
Rushdie, Salman, *The Enchantress of Florence*, (Random House, 2008).
Rushdie, Salman, *The Ground Beneath Her Feet*, (Random House, 1999).

Sanyal, Sanjeev, *The Indian Renaissance: India's Rise After a Thousand Years of Decline*, (Penguin, 2008).
Sen, Amartya, *The Idea of Justice*, (Penguin, 2009).
Sharma, Ruchir, *Breakout Nations: In Pursuit of the Next Economic Miracles*, (Penguin, 2012).
Shourie, Arun, *A Secular Agenda: For Saving Our Country, for Welding It*, (ASA Publications, 1993).
Simpson, Jacqueline, *Everyday Life in the Viking Age*, (Dorset, 1967).
Singh, Jaswant, *Jinnah: India-Partition-Independence*, (Rupa & Co, 2009).
Taseer, Aatish, *Stranger to History*, (Picador, 2009).
Talageri, Shrikant G., *The Aryan Invasion Theory: A Reappraisal*, (Aditya Prakashan, 1993).
Tharoor, Shashi, *The Great Indian Novel*, (Penguin, 2000).
Thatcher, Margaret, *Margaret Thatcher: The Path to Power*, (HarperCollins, 1995).
Thomas, Hugh, *The Slave Trade: The Story of the Atlantic Slave Trade, 1440-1870*, (Simon & Schuster, 1997).
Todd, Malcolm, *Everyday Life of the Barbarians: Goths, Franks and Vandals*, (Dorset, 1972).
Toye, Richard, (*Churchill's Empire: The World That Made Him and the World He Made*, (Henry Holt and Co., 2010)
Vidal, Gore, *Lincoln*, (The Franklin Library, 1984).
Watson, Peter, *A Terrible Beauty: The People and Ideas That Shaped the Modern Mind—A History*, (Weidenfeld & Nicolson, 2000)
Wells, Spencer, *The Journey of Man: A Genetic Odyssey*, (Penguin, 2002).
Woodward, Bob, *Obama's Wars*, (Simon & Schuster, 2010).

Made in the USA
Monee, IL
03 May 2026

49438685R00194